"This book is the most helpful thing I have been given!" YS

"Your book helped me to get work, even with my criminal record." MA

"This type of careers and resettlement advice is extremely important." PS

"This book has given me the ability to provide for myself and my family." TU

"I recommend this book and the processes to everyone with a criminal record." GK

"The manual you have written is a solid help, refreshing and it covers everything." SL

"This is a unique resource - vital for all those people who has been in trouble with the law or struggled to find employment." RD

"This book has made the entire process of preparing for employment easy; I would have really struggled without this guidance." AM

"I appreciate all the pointers that this book has given me. I have now worked through everything and I can't wait to push my CV out!" LS

"By working my way through this instruction manual, I now have a professional CV and Disclosure which everyone makes the effort to read." EK

"I have never had a CV but now my documents explain who I am and what I am capable of. I have opportunities that I couldn't access before!" GB

"I have started applying for jobs whilst still in prison, saving me time on release and beginning the good new chapter that Phil talks about." IS

"Without this book I wouldn't have known how to make myself so saleable. When I read my documents now, even I want to give myself a job!" XD

"I could not have landed my job without this! I was able to address the prospective employer directly with regards to any concerns they may have." RY

"All of the employers have been interested in me and in the professional documents I provided as a result of this book. Having choices is a new feeling for me, a good one." JC

"Now that I am working, I can support my family and stay away from crime. I feel better about myself and I can hold my head up. It has been a long journey and I never want to go back to square one again." IG

"I have followed the instructions and created my very first CV. I am very pleased with how professional it looks. I am now applying for jobs confidently and I just had my first interview which I think went well, fingers crossed." MR

"This book worked for me. The 'CV Builder' helped me to understand my strengths and gave me a structure. The 'Disclosure Builder' turned disclosure from a negative to a positive and the hundreds of pre-written templates made it easy." LW

"Now I have much more confidence and a more positive attitude towards myself and getting work in the future. In fact, I have already been offered work which would not have happened without Phil Martin's book 'How to get a great job when you have a criminal record'. I definitely recommend it." AN

"My friend and I both had old offences to disclose so we helped each other through this book. We took it in turns to talk through our background stories whilst the other wrote them down. We now have excellent disclosure statements. Doing this brought closure and hope for the future. I will keep you informed of our progress!" SG

ISBN Number 978-1-6961-0020-5

British Library Cataloguing in Publication Data. A catalogue record for this book is available from the British Library.

Contact:

Feedback, comments and questions are welcomed. The author and his representatives can be contacted through the website www.philmartin.co.uk (email info@philmartin.co.uk). His recruitment network can be contacted through the website www.Ex-seed.co.uk (email info@ex-seed.co.uk). Letters and documents can be posted to Philip Martin t/as Ex-seed™ 5 Crabtree Drive, Northampton. NN3 5DR

Prior Notices

This work is sold subject to the following licence, background disclosure, good faith declaration, and legal information:

Licence:

This book, templates and system, are licensed for individual use only, including any library where books are loaned to individuals.

Using any part of this book in a group, class, institution, business or commercial setting without prior written permission is a breach of the licence.

Careers and resettlement departments may purchase USB or CD-ROM software packages containing the proprietary 'CV Builder', 'Disclosure Builder', 'Application Builder' and 'Grant Builder', including all the templates in MS-Word format.

Volume purchases of this book will attract quantity discounts and sponsorship opportunities are also available by prior discussion.

The content to operate licensed workshops based on this book is available for separate purchase with a licence for single or multiple uses, for individual organisations and institutions. The author and his trained associates are also available to facilitate workshops within custodial settings, job centres and organisations if preferred.

Thank you for respecting the author's intellectual property rights.

Background Disclosure:

The author of this work, Philip Martin, has a criminal record. On 24th May 2016, he was convicted of offences of fraud and fraudulent trading and at the time of publication, he is, and remains, the subject of a Company Director's Disqualification Order.

Good Faith Declaration:

The author has empathy and understanding for all victims of crime and nothing in this book is written to encourage, justify or minimise the effects of crime.

The author feels strongly that the most respectful, worthwhile and meaningful thing that he (and the wider justice system) can do for victims of crime is to reduce the risk of ex-offenders committing more crime. This work has been produced with the sincere desire to reduce re-offending, create fewer victims of crime and improve outcomes for society by:

- Supporting the reintegration of ex-offenders into society.

- Practically helping ex-offenders to secure legitimate and stable employment.

- Encouraging organisations to employ ex-offenders and adopt a 'clean-slate' policy in most cases where employment provides an evidentially reduced risk to the public.

Legal Information:

The author recommends full compliance with all licence conditions and court orders. Of particular relevance and importance is the requirement for those ex-offenders who are on licence, to inform their probation officer and ask for their approval, before undertaking paid or unpaid work. Employment is proven to reduce re-offending, so it is likely that a lot of support and practical help will be offered.

The author insists that all representations made to employers are honest. No liability can be accepted for any inaccuracies put forward to third parties by readers of this book. Readers are reminded that all information submitted to third parties must accurately reflect their experiences, skills, qualifications and offences. The pre-written templates are for guidance only, and as effective examples.

The inclusion of quotations by named individuals or organisations, does not suggest endorsement of this work, or of the author, by those individuals or organisations. The majority of stories, testimonials and quotations have been anonymised and identifying information has been removed or varied. The author has attempted to acknowledge known sources and apologises for any that have been missed. Where no source is quoted it should be treated as the author's own opinion.

The author has used his best endeavours as a layperson to ensure that all information is correct and current in the UK at the time of printing. Laws, rules and processes may be different in Scotland.

This book is for general guidance only, the content should not be relied upon in isolation and nothing within the book constitutes legal, financial or medical advice. Personal advice should be sought from qualified third parties. No liability is accepted at law for the outcome of any decisions made whilst relying on the content of this book.

Dedication

To those who believe in a clean slate:

Thank you to everyone who helps and supports prisoners and ex-offenders to live more meaningful and positive lives through employment.

Giving someone a job when they need it, trusting someone who other people do not trust, investing in a person when no one else will and believing in those people that others do not believe in, really does take a leap of faith.

Research shows us that this leap of faith is rewarded with appreciative, hardworking, loyal and determined workers.

It gives me great pleasure to dedicate this book to:

Sir Richard Branson, Tariq Usmani MBE and James Timpson OBE

Thank you sincerely for everything you have done and are doing to help ex-offenders into employment.

Employment is the most important thing that ex-offenders need to build structure and stability in their lives, to regain their self-respect and to reduce re-offending.

It is not just that you employ and help them; these are brilliant and massive achievements in themselves, but on top of this, you also encourage other companies and organisations to do the same.

The public awareness work that you do around the employment of people with criminal records and the resettlement of ex-offenders really does re-educate people away from false assumptions and it is truly admirable.

I would welcome the opportunity to shake your hands and thank you in person, but in the meantime, on behalf of every ex-offender who is seeking legitimate employment, I wish you the very best of success in all your endeavours.

Thank you,

Phil Martin

Contents

"I did exactly what it said (page by page) in this guide. I emailed my application letter, CV and personal disclosure statement to a specialist construction firm who advertised a job I wanted. They telephoned me and said the following:

"We have received your email with CV attached.

I have never had a CV like that before; it was so complete - everything was absolutely perfect!

I have read your disclosure letter as well and understand that too.

I would like to offer you the job on a three-month trial basis.

When can you come in and see us to finalise everything?"

So, the documents worked, and the system worked. I didn't even need to have a formal interview. I am starting my new job next week, it is ideal for me, something I will really enjoy and be able to get stuck into. I just want to say thank you." FS

Preface

I have often wondered how I would cope if I was sent to prison. To be honest I have dreaded to think about it. Like so many of my friends and colleagues, I really admire those who, when in prison or following release, try to pick up the pieces and to do a job and make an honest penny (or, better still, an honest fortune). We certainly don't admire whatever landed them in prison in the first place - on the contrary - but, for us, that's all over. We do admire them for engaging in the struggle (for that is undoubtedly what it is) to re-take their place in the vast, decent, law-abiding section of our community on these islands. And so very many of us want to help them.

You don't have to be religious to believe in redemption.

I think that it is a remarkable achievement for Phil Martin to have written this book. I haven't read every word - thank God, I don't need that degree of detailed advice - but I have read enough to realise what an extraordinarily broad amount of information and wise advice he has managed to contain between two covers. So when, out of the blue, he sent the proofs to me here at the court, I decided to support him by writing this Preface.

I confess that I turned first, and again last, to Chapter 3, "Disclosing a Criminal Record". Surely few of us can claim that everything we have said to everybody has always been honest. But, beyond occasional lapses in our personal lives, most of us have always been honest in other respects; and almost all of us have managed never to be violent. Look, I so wish to endorse everything Phil has said about being upfront about your conviction and imprisonment. If we, on the outside, are allowed by you to know about that, and can see how you present it to us, as in Phil's brilliant examples of Personal Disclosure Statements, it makes us really want to help you.

Oh, and by the way, in my job we have to wear leather shoes. When recently I learned that Timpson's have such an active policy of recruiting ex-prisoners, I resolved always to go to them to get my shoes re-soled.

Good Luck!

8 July 2019   Nicholas Wilson

A Justice of the UK Supreme Court

Support from Tariq Usmani MBE

29th July 2019

Dear Phil,

I hope you are well.

Thank you for giving me an opportunity to review your book prior to its release.

I think it will be a huge asset to those that are taking that very difficult step to move away from a life of crime, which becomes an addictive and powerful vortex.

In terms of a quote, I can give you something I have said many times to many people:

**"We are created as imperfect beings, if someone asks
for a second chance allow them at least a second chance."**

Best of luck Phil

Tariq Usmani MBE
Chief Executive Officer - Henley Homes Group

The Sunday Times Virgin Atlantic Fast Track 100: ranked 38 in the top 100 fastest growing companies in the UK.

"Employers need to be aware of the positives of taking on people who have been in prison. Our experience shows that people from prison, if properly selected, will prove to be just as reliable as recruits who come from elsewhere. It is their personality that matters most."

Sir Richard Branson, CEO Virgin group of companies

"Employment is a key factor in helping people to live crime free lives. It has been proven that if people have somewhere to live, a support network and a full-time job their chance of re-offending are greatly reduced."

James Timpson OBE, Chief executive Timpson and
Chair of the Employers' Forum for Reducing Reoffending

Introduction

Whilst serving a prison sentence for business related offences, I achieved my goal of helping a thousand people in prison through personal mentoring and practical help around the areas of sentence progression, restoring relationships, personal and career development and future life planning.

Funding was withdrawn (without any media attention) from the National Careers Service (NCS) in prisons in 2018 and they were forced to close their service nationwide, ending an important route for people in prison to get back into work.

Predictably, in a resettlement prison (where people are in the final stages of their prison sentences), requests for careers advice became constant and the need to produce detailed CVs and Personal Disclosure Statements increased. After informally meeting this need for several months, whilst still serving my own sentence and with support from Prison Governors, I established my own careers department.

81% of prisoners look for employment upon release.
(Source: Prisoners' Work & Training Frances H Simon)

With funding support from Prisoners' Education Trust (PET) I gained a qualification in Information, Advice and Guidance and drawing on my experience as an employer, I provided careers advice and practical employment support. I sat down alongside each person for two hours (with the templates in this book, it happily now only takes 45 minutes) and we created a high-quality CV and Personal Disclosure Statement together; at later dates we would apply to companies, respond to advertised jobs, prepare business plans and submit grant applications to charities.

The process of creating professional employment documents makes a dramatic difference to self-esteem; people realise that they deserve more and that their families deserve a better life too. These sessions and the ongoing support helped people to imagine and set goals for a crime-free future.

Most people in prison have never gone through the process of talking about their good points and achievements before. They tend to dwell on the bad, on their failings and life problems and rarely look past these negative thoughts and feelings.

A person who believes in them and who has expectations of them is absolutely a catalyst for change. Caring enough to work with someone and give them time and attention is very healing. This level of personal support and clear guidance also helps people in distress to come to terms with their past, to deal with pressing issues and move forwards.

Many years earlier, in 2005, I spoke at a parole hearing and assisted to secure the release of an indeterminate sentenced prisoner, based on the contribution that employment would make to his resettlement. In almost 15 years, 'MJ' has been highly successful and never re-offended. From 2005 to 2012, I employed a number of ex-offenders, including those on Home Detention Curfew (HDC), primarily in property refurbishment and development.

I understand the unique complexities of employing ex-offenders and it is by documenting the substantial experience I gained alongside hundreds of serving prisoners and their employers that I can present this comprehensive guide.

97% of offenders say they want to stop re-offending and 68% say the biggest factor in helping them to do so would be having a job. (Source: Making Prisons Work: skills for rehabilitation MOJ)

The UK currently has 800,000 unfilled job vacancies; paradoxically we have an estimated 500,000 people who are unemployed, despite wanting to work, because of the stigma of their criminal records.

Companies that employ ex-offenders have found them to be loyal, hardworking and dependable; it is logical therefore for employers to consider ex-offenders when recruiting and to implement inclusive recruitment policies.

The system in this book makes a big impact on potential employers and has been proven to successfully help ex-offenders gain employment, resulting in fewer victims of crime.

You will read many case studies of people who have overcome the barrier of a criminal record and successfully entered or re-entered the workplace.

This easy-to-follow system provides a structured framework of help and guidance for families, employment coaches and offender managers.

Whoever you are, I wish you every possible success in this new chapter of your life. Please decide to make the most of the abundant opportunities available and let me know if I can help you in any way.

"The biggest distance you will ever have to travel is to turn around and face a different direction." PM

Thank you to everyone who has been involved in supporting this initiative.

Phil Martin

PS: This book contains numerous quotations and statements; in order to differentiate my opinions and quotes from those of other contributors, I include the initials 'PM' after mine.

"Once I had a professional CV and disclosure letter, I sent them to my probation officer who was very pleased to receive them. For the first time, all in one place, she was able to read my work experience, the qualifications I had gained, that I understood what had triggered my crime and the ways I have changed for the better - what I was proudest of. She was able to clearly see beyond 'H' the criminal, to 'H' the potential employee and productive member of society. My probation officer supported my parole and went one step beyond by asking if she could pass my details to an employer. She arranged an interview for me, and I got the job. I believe that working through the process of creating my CV and disclosure statement made all the difference when it came to me getting released and staying released with a stable job." HS

Chapter 1 -
Stability Through Employment

"Finding stable employment is widely recognised as a contributing factor to the successful rehabilitation of ex-offenders. Industry must step up and accept their role in the process. We can't simply exclude 17% of the UK population from the recruitment process on the basis that they have a criminal record."

Karen Morley, Human Resources Director - Styles and Wood Group (Architects)

The Difference That Work Makes

Permanent employment provides fulfilment and pride and it improves self-esteem. You are setting a positive example for your family and for others around you.

Working people contribute to society and do not have to keep looking over their shoulders. You cannot put a price on peace of mind.

Employment brings numerous benefits to prisoners and society, it provides:

- Stability, structure and routine.
- Dramatic reductions in problematic drug use.
- Improvement to self-esteem and a sense of purpose.
- Demonstrable reductions in reoffending and the creation of victims.
- Legitimate and regular income which allows people to budget and plan.
- Crime free support network and a feeling of acceptance and belonging.
- For employers, a sizeable workforce of hardworking and appreciative people.

"Getting a job is a massive means of helping someone stay out of prison and of cutting re-offending." Former Justice Minister, Andrew Selous MP

On the surface, some crime can appear to bring in more money, but when you take into account Proceeds of Crime Act (POCA) seizures and the years spent unable to earn more than £9 - £12 per week whilst in prison, it becomes obvious which one is the tortoise and which one is the hare; which path is sustainable and which is not.

You may as well make the decision now. It is the right time for you. As one prisoner said to me recently *"Crime is dead to me now."*

"Nowadays, virtually all criminals will get caught, without question. It is just a matter of time. Not if, but when. *Forensic Footprints* and *Digital DNA* are everywhere." PM

Being able to enjoy time with family and loved ones in an unhurried and relaxed environment is very different indeed from visits over a prison table.

If you follow the framework in this guide, you will be empowered to really change your future through getting and keeping a job.

"Utilising the skills that I learnt in prison I was offered a permanent job running a children's restaurant at a tourist attraction. I now enjoy preparing and serving up to 150 meals a day and have renewed confidence in the future." SA

Role Models

Spend time with people who have stable and happy lives. Tell yourself and remind yourself that you deserve this too. Take advice from people who are where you want to be in life. Avoid associating with people who deliberately do not work, who are involved in crime or are planning to commit crime again when they leave prison.

Other former prisoners have found fulfilment in employment - and you can too:

Examples of Successful Ex-offenders	Clare Barstow is now a journalist.
	Jim Smith is now a social worker.
	Maish Bibérovic is now an IT specialist.
	Mark Haines is now a probation officer.
	Frank Cook is now an author and artist.
	Stephen Fry is now an actor and author.
	Terry Mortimer is now a Pentecostal minister.
	Michael Frazer is now a successful entrepreneur.
	Robyn Travis is now an author and public speaker.
	Bob Cummins is now housing association manager.
	Anita O'Connell is now a charity worker for M.I.N.D.
	Laureal Lawrence is now a video production manager.
	Mark Leech is now a client liaison officer in a Law Firm.
	Paul Slater is now a director of a major design solutions company.
	Krista Brown is now recruitment director for a large staffing provider.
	Levi Roots is a successful Caribbean food entrepreneur and musician.
	Tariq Usmani is a property developer and major employer of ex-offenders.
	Derek Jones developed communications technology and systems and is the director of a social enterprise.
	Ian Perkins now owns and operates "Inside Out Ventures" providing laundry services to prisons, training courses and other enterprises.

The re-offending rate is high at 46% within one year of release from prison (Source: MOJ 2016) and this does increase further in subsequent years.

"As ex-offenders, we can either: <u>be</u> the statistics or <u>beat</u> the statistics and build a better life." PM

How to Use This Proven System to Secure Employment for Yourself

This book calls on ex-offenders to leave the past in the past. It also calls on employers to give this large group of people the chance that they so rightly deserve and that they will, in almost all cases, prove worthy of.

This book should be treated as a working manual; it explains the best methods to use to secure employment and how to create the 3 documents which you will need:

- ✓ Personal Disclosure Statement (PDS) (chapter 3).

- ✓ Curriculum Vitae (CV) (chapter 4).

- ✓ Application/ cover letter (AL) (chapter 5).

You will learn the importance of improving your personal skills and employability as well as how to build a long-term stable career.

A fulfilling job can often become the cornerstone of a positive future for you and those you care about.

Imagine that you are assembling a complicated piece of flat pack furniture or a model; **the instructions should be**:

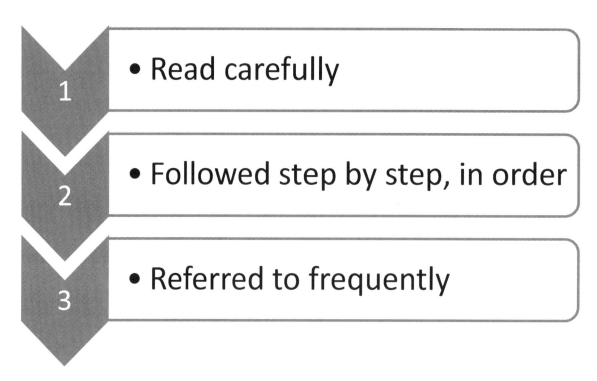

1
- Read carefully

2
- Followed step by step, in order

3
- Referred to frequently

"I treated the instructions and templates like building an Airfix model aeroplane. I am happy with my CV and Disclosure/ Cover Letter. Thank you." MM

I would recommend that you follow these 10 steps:

1	Have a quick skim read through, to familiarise yourself with the layout.
2	After this first skim read, work through each section carefully and thoroughly.
3	Ask for help; you will be amazed by how many people are on your side when you try to gain employment.
4	Use a highlighter pen for important points, make notes in the margins and use post-It notes to track your progress.
5	Use the resources, such as the employment goals sheet, the record of applications made to employers, the to-do list and the cashflow forecast.
6	Progressively work through the guide, one page at a time. You will feel a sense of achievement as you create each document and your confidence and determination will grow.
7	This manual contains hundreds of pre-worded templates. You can copy these if they apply to you or you can edit them as much as necessary. Read everything thoroughly to make sure that your documents are personal to you and accurate.
8	Set aside enough time to create each document. If you are working independently, without help, you will need 2 hours to create a brilliant CV using the *'CV Builder'* and a similar amount of time for your Personal Disclosure Statement using the *'Disclosure Builder'*.
9	Refer to the guide regularly.
10	Set goals for yourself including: • The number of companies that you will apply to. • The date by which you will have created your CV. • When you will have written your Personal Disclosure Statement. You must aim for something to have a chance of hitting it. If you do not have a goal, it is like a darts player throwing a dart whilst wearing a blindfold and not caring what they hit. They do not do this of course; it would be ridiculous! Instead a booming voice tells them what number they need to score, and they aim for that score. **Goal setting does work;** it focuses the mind and helps to keep us on track. Review your progress regularly and hold yourself accountable. This book can only help you if you follow the guidance. Do not give up and say, "I tried that, and it did not work", take responsibility and persevere towards your goals. You can use the "Employment Goals Sheet" on the next page as a template for writing your goals down.

"This guide has really helped me to complete my CV and Personal Disclosure Statement, I am proud of them. I could never have done them otherwise. I know that these will help me to get a job and contribute to life in a positive way." AO

Example Employment Goals Sheet

Employment Goal	Estimated Time Needed	Target Date	Progress Review Date	Date Achieved
Complete my Personal Disclosure Statement PDS).	2hrs	15th September 2020	6th Sept	12th September
Complete my CV.	4hrs	15th October 2020	8th October 2020	9th October 2020
Complete my Application Letter (AL).	30mins	18th October 2020	10th October	20th October
Research which grant providers I meet the criteria for.	2hrs	1st November 2020	22nd Oct	2nd Nov
Create my Personal Grant Statement (PGS).	15mins	7th November 2020	1/11/2020	6th Nov
Research details of 20 companies that hire people with my skills.	3hrs	1st November 2020	Find one each day	Got 20 now on-going
Send the first 10 applications.	1hr 30mins	8th November 2020	5th NOV	7th November 2020
Prepare for interviews by researching the companies I have applied to.	4hrs	15th November 2020	On-going research	Done 3/11

Your Employment Goals Sheet

Employment Goal	Estimated Time Needed	Target Date	Progress Review Date	Date Achieved
Complete my Personal Disclosure Statement (PDS).				
Complete my CV.				
Complete my Application Letter (AL).				
Research which grant providers I meet the criteria for.				
Create my Personal Grant Statement (PGS).				
Research details of 20 companies that hire people with my skills.				
Send the first 10 applications.				
Prepare for interviews by reading "Daily Diplomacy" or a similar book.				

Quotes - What Having a Stable Job Means To Me

The following quotes were given by people with a criminal record who are seeking or have recently gained permanent employment.

"Self-respect." GS

"A fresh start." HM

"Staying positive." SF

"The world to me." RY

"Something to lose." CH

"I will not re-offend." AY

"Earning legal money." TJ

"I can help my family." SC

"Keeping out of trouble." AG

"I will stay out of prison." PD

"I can support my family." BG

"I can hold my head high." MG

"My daughter will rest easy." JI

"I can give myself stability." DC

"Not coming back to prison." ML

"Security and peace of mind." LS

"Having a purpose in my life." FE

"Getting my confidence back." GA

"A second chance at normality." SY

"Changing my life for the better." RS

"I will not be reliant on benefits." JM

"That I am wanted and accepted." PB

"I can fully participate in society." RN

"I'm able to look after my family." GR

"I am highly unlikely to re-offend." AJ

"A legal way to support my family." BP

"A good life for me and my family." SH

"Being accepted and feeling useful." AC

"Everything else will fall into place." DS

"I will not re-offend; it is that simple!" RY

"I will get a chance to change my life." JT

"I can put a life of mistakes behind me." DP

"I have stability in my life upon release." TL

"It will give me a chance to prove myself." LB

"Having purpose, self-worth and dignity." WH

"I can live a meaningful and productive life." VS

"Building a future for myself and my family." **AC**

"I can provide legally for my family in future." WR

"I can resettle back into life without difficulty." BB

"A chance to build stability for my family again." IK

"I can move forward with my life the right way." WJ

"Providing for my family and living a happier life." RA

"Stability and being able to provide for my family." JB

"I am more secure and can make a positive impact." LS

"I can provide for my family and not commit crime." PL

"I can support my family and live a crime-free life." VW

"I can get my life back on track and be a dad again." SM

"I could improve my life and gain my independence." FF

"So much, I can support myself and pay my own bills." MI

"I can continue down the right path and earn legally." MG

"Purpose and structure to my life, feeling productive." LT

"I will not return to prison and I can plan for the future." II

"Independence and a chance to change my life around." FS

"Engaging my mind and achieving something every day." JM

"I can work and provide for myself and beloved family." OU

"I can be settled and provide for my wife and daughter." KH

"Stable housing and the ability to continue my studies." RW

"Supporting my family who have suffered in my absence." EB

"It gives me a chance to re-enter society more smoothly." LS

"I will know that I can leave my criminal past behind me." DS

"Having an income and no reason to come back to crime." PB

"I can support my son and start to rebuild our lives again." AC

"A very structured, independent lifestyle, within the law." NW

"The world to me because I can provide for my kids legally." LL

"A lot; it enables me to start my life again and feel normal." CJ

"Not being unemployed and all the problems that go with it." JO

"That I can support myself, my partner and my step-daughter." AS

"I will get back to living a happy life and supporting my family." AB

"I can put a life of crime behind me and start to build a future." KA

"Everything, it is vital to the ongoing process of rehabilitation." TU

"Getting on my own two feet and standing on my own two feet." CS

"I can have pride in myself and regain a sense of independence." JM

"I can help myself and my family plus remain out of any trouble." DD

"A second chance to prove that things are behind me in the past." NC

"I can integrate back to the community and contribute to society." RR

"Supporting my family in future the way they have supported me." PI

"Providing not just for myself but for my son and get my life back." LB

"I can start to provide for my family and be a responsible person." GM

"Staying out of prison and being a good role model to my children." JP

"I can contribute to both life and my community in a positive way." AO

"Turning my life around and being a productive member of society." SL

"This is exactly what I wanted; with a job I can build my life again." VA

"I will have achieved my goal and will be ready to progress further." MS

"I can better myself and get back to living a normal life with family." ER

"I can provide for my family, stay out of prison and be with my sons." RM

"I would not re-offend, and I would have a chance to put things right." AR

"Proving that I have learnt from my mistakes and that I can be trusted." JC

"I can provide for my family and greatly reduce my risk of re-offending." KA

"I will financially support myself and my family and live a crime-free life." KR

"Enjoying the simple things in life and not have to look over my shoulder." GS

"Being able to buy things for my baby son and being there as he grows up." SR

"I will be able to provide for my family and set a good example for my kids." IL

"I can construct a good solid base on which to start my future work career." CS

"I have a chance of a normal life and to be an accepted member of society." GN

"I can better myself and prove to myself and my family that I have changed." RB

"I can stay away from crime and provide and be there for my family in future." GS

"Staying busy and having a purpose which makes me feel better about myself." DT

"I will have structure to my life and not re-offend. I can hit the ground running." CM

"Proving to someone that I deserve a bit of trust and that I won't let them down." GE

"I will have the best chance at a decent and happy future and personal satisfaction." IN

"Having a good routine and knowing what my next step is so that I can continue to improve." CA

"A new positive direction in my life; an organisation I can commit to and build a future with." KT

"Not hanging around with people who are going nowhere, wasting time and wasting their life." CR

"That I haven't wasted my time and that my new skills and qualifications valued by employers." NA

"Being a respectable person, doing things right and having stability in my life for the first time." SH

"I can think of no better way to show that I have changed than showing up to work each day, following instructions and working hard. I just want that chance." JU

"Everyone deserves to be given a second chance, as not all paths in life would be taken given another chance. I do believe deeply that everyone should have options moving forward and be able to (not forget) but to learn from their past in a positive way and progress through life."
Steve Brands, Director - Heat Connection

Chapter 2 -
Improving Employability

"This book explained exactly what employers look for in employees and clearly showed me what I need to improve about myself." NM

The Staircase of Job Progression

I recommend that you follow the **A B C D** staircase of job progression:

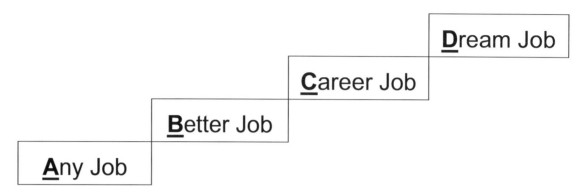

It is best to:

- Get a job.

- Get in the habit of work.

- Gain skills and experience.

- Gain a good financial footing, get financially stable.

- Get referees (people who will give you a reference).

And only then reach up to the next job.

Employers react more favourably to applicants who are currently employed.

Do not be reluctant or embarrassed to complete a period of *transitional employment*. There is nothing wrong with proving your worth to an employer and if that employer does not recognise, appreciate and reward your worth you can always go 'job shopping' again. At least you will be in a stronger position without time or money pressures because you will be in employment of some sort.

You can also use the time that you spend in a less than ideal job to develop more skills and experience and in so doing increase your value to employers. This automatically increases the salary that you attract.

As an oversimplification, there are two primary categories of jobs:

General (unskilled) and **Specialist** (skilled).

There is an overlap between the two categories of jobs with many falling in the middle as 'semi-skilled'.

These categories are compared in the following table.

Comparing General (unskilled) and Specialist (skilled) Jobs

	General (unskilled)	Specialist (skilled)
How Advertised	Almost always advertised.	Recruitment agencies used and existing employees are promoted. Jobs are created for most suitable applicants.
Skills Required	Mostly unskilled, other than general, Transferable Skills (e.g. reliable, hardworking, good attitude, organised and communication skills).	Skilled in specialist area such as Telecoms Engineering, Quantity Surveying or Hospital Consultant.
Qualifications Required	Few qualifications required other than Maths, English and IT, training usually provided.	Industry qualifications expected and a commitment to Continuous Professional Development (CPD) whilst in post.
Recruitment Process	Easy to get the job, simple and short recruitment process.	Requires persistent effort to secure the job; usually involves multiple interviews and a longer recruitment process.
Travel	Opportunities are usually local.	May need to commute.
Wages	Lower than average: typically, minimum wage or living wage.	Higher than average.
Progression	Few opportunities for progression.	Many opportunities for progression with existing employer and with other firms in the same industry.
Ex-offenders Considered?	Company policy usually adhered to with little flexibility. Many companies actively employ ex-offenders (See page 240).	Completely flexible approach dependant on applicant.

The 5 Primary 'Elements of Employability'

Employability means <u>how appealing you are to potential employers</u>.

It is helpful to view potential employers as if they are customers who are buying a service from you.

The service that you are selling is that you will:

- Perform work at the expected standard (or better).

- Within the expected timescale (or even more efficiently).

- In accordance with the employer's rules and procedures.

If you improve your level of appeal to potential employers, you will be paid more and you will have many more job offers to choose from.

I believe that there are 5 primary elements of employability which I explain using the coincidental acronym

Q.U.E.S.T.

Qualifications, Understanding, Experience, Specialist Skills, Transferable Skills

I elaborate on each of the 5 elements of employability as follows:

Q = Qualifications

Qualifications are proof that you know how to perform the job role and that you were able to do it at a certain point in time.

It is important that you gain qualifications because all the recognition that you receive helps your self-esteem and confidence (which are essential requirements when job hunting or progressing in your career).

Qualifications also demonstrate four important things to an employer:

1) That you care about your career.

2) That you have the self-discipline to work over and above merely performing a job role.

3) That you are committed to self-development, that you are willing to learn and undertake further training.

4) They differentiate you from other candidates by showing specific knowledge and skills which are relevant to certain job roles.

U = Understanding

Understanding and knowledge of the basic theory of how perform the job role.

Throughout our working life, we gain substantial amounts of knowledge and understanding on a huge range of tasks.

This does not need to be formally recognised knowledge but may include such examples as the knowledge of how to cook, understanding how to deal with people who are grieving, knowing how to raise positive happy children or understanding how to use a certain software package.

E = Experience

Having previously performed the job role or a similar role.

The most experienced people become confident in their ability to perform the job role well and time efficiently.

Experience means that people can be trusted to work independently and can also show others where necessary.

S = Specialist Skills

Having the physical ability, skill and motivation to perform the job role to a standard that is acceptable in the market place.

Specialist Skills are those skills which are relevant to certain jobs (such as surveying or fork lift truck driving); they are also known as Vocational Skills.

In many ways these are easier to learn and teach than Transferable Skills because we can be shown what to do and then guided and corrected until we gain the skill(s).

Work is the place to gain specialist skills, but we also pick up some skills in our everyday lives. As you will discover from page 150, prison jobs do provide meaningful work experience and people can gain a wide range of specialist skills whilst incarcerated.

Every single person has some specialist skills and every role you perform whether at home or in work place, paid or unpaid, develops skills and abilities.

It is recommended that you constantly build on your specialist skills; this is known in some sectors as Continuous Professional Development (CPD).

If you are more skilled you will attract a higher salary and be more in demand from employers than a less skilled person.

**More than 50% of employers struggle
to fill vacancies due to skills shortages.**
(Source: Chartered Institute of Personnel and Development 2018)

T = Transferable Skills

Transferable Skills are those skills which are important or beneficial in every workplace (as well as in life generally).

Transferable Skills are like a never-ending bank balance that can't be taken away from you and the more you use it, the bigger the balance grows.

These skills are a type of personal equity which you grow and develop throughout your career.

There are 7 primary Transferable Skills which are always valuable:

1. **Functional Skills** (Maths and English).

2. **IT Skills** (Familiar with hardware and common software packages, online competence).

**More than 750,000 people in the UK speak English
so poorly that they will find it difficult to get work.**
(Source: The Times 2017 quoting the Office of National Statistics)

None of us have a genuine excuse not to improve our Maths, English and IT because these courses are available in prison and are fully funded if you are not working or on a low income in the community.

3. **Organisational Skills** (Time management, task planning, reliability, record keeping).

4. **Work Ethic** (commitment, extra mile, rises to challenges, self-discipline, team player).

5. **Problem Solving Skills** (objective approach, creativity, ability to research, use initiative, decision making).

6. **Communication Skills** - Skill with People (friendly, listening, patient, talking clearly, positive body language, good manners).

7. **Mind-set Management** (positive attitude, enthusiastic, resilient, adaptable, inspiring and motivating self and others, leads where appropriate and holds self to high standards).

Skills 3 - 7 are known as "soft skills" because they are difficult to provide evidence of, but they actually have a huge impact to your employability and how you affect people you work with.

Transferable Skills develop the fastest when you are in a professional work environment and when you are intentionally aware that you are working to improve them.

Contrary to some people's opinions, **we can learn** all these skills. We can read books and watch other people who appear to make these things look easy. Try your best to improve a little every day in all these five areas.

We have evolved to be constantly learning whether we are doing so deliberately or not. We should all consciously improve our Transferable Skills at every opportunity.

The most progressive attitude to have is to treat **every day as a school day.**

Identifying Where You Are Most Employable

You will have encountered numerous people who have one or two out of the five elements of employability (Qualifications, Understanding, Experience, Specialist Skills and Transferable Skills) but people who have all five of them in a certain field are rare indeed.

People who only have one or two elements usually receive the lowest reward (minimum wage). People who have all five receive the highest rewards and are in great demand from employers because they are called **specialists**.

The following exercise assumes that your **Transferable Skills** are adequate or that you are working to improve them.

Consider the overlapping areas in the following diagram.

Take 10 minutes to carry out a self-analysis. Sketch out these circles on a sheet of paper and then write your qualifications, understanding, experience and specialist skills in each of the relevant circles.

This simple exercise works clearly highlights those areas where you could most effectively focus in your career and further personal development.

Where 2 or 3 circles (elements of employability) overlap is the field/ industry where you are best advised to focus most of your attention whilst also trying to further improve your employability.

Where 3 or 4 circles overlap is the field where you will be snapped up by employers because you will be highly appealing to them. This is also the field in which you will attract the best salary package.

I have good (and improving) Transferable Skills, as well as the following qualifications, understanding, experience and specialist skills:

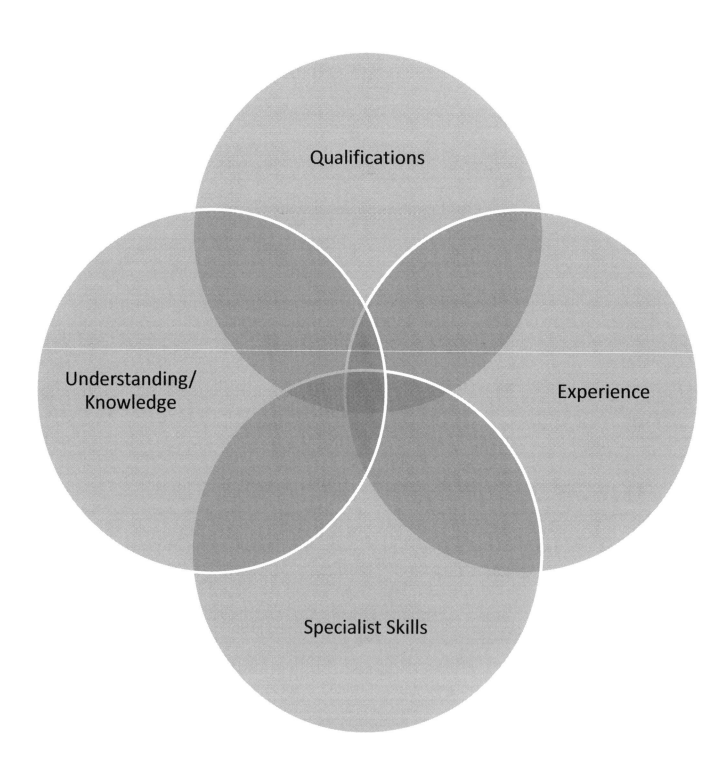

The fields or industries where your skills, knowledge, experience and/or qualifications OVERLAP are where you are most WANTED and most VALUABLE in the eyes of employers.

A simpler way for you may to list your fields or industries on a chart similar to the following examples.

Here is an example of John's assessment

Field/ Industry	Specialist Skills	Understanding/ Knowledge	Experience	Qualifications	Number of YES
Art	NO	YES	YES	NO	2
Customer Service	NO	YES	NO	NO	1
Care work	NO	NO	NO	NO	1
Catering	YES	YES	YES	YES	**4**
IT Coding	YES	YES	YES	NO	**3**

John will be in great demand as a specialist **catering worker/ chef** (4) and will be snapped up by an employer in that field.

Long term, he really wants to formalise his **IT coding** (3) skills, gain qualifications and move into a highly paid career.

Below is an example of Sarah's assessment

Field/ Industry	Specialist Skills	Understanding/ Knowledge	Experience	Qualifications	Number of YES
Hospitality	NO	YES	NO	YES	2
Bricklaying	NO	YES	NO	YES	2
Sales and Marketing	YES	YES	YES	YES	**4**
Financial Services	YES	YES	NO	NO	2
Social Work	NO	YES	NO	YES	2
Ceramics Manufacture	YES	YES	YES	NO	**3**

Sarah is strongest in the area of **sales and marketing** (4) and will be snapped up by an employer in that field.

Long term, her real passion is in **ceramics manufacture** (3) so whilst working in sales, she will study part-time to gain qualifications and improve her employability.

Eventually she intends to relocate to Staffordshire where she expects to accept her dream job overseeing manufacturing in a specialist porcelain factory.

Now complete your own assessment

Field/ Industry	Specialist Skills	Understanding/ Knowledge	Experience	Qualifications	Number of YES

Include everything, all the jobs you have done and all your hobbies and interests. This will allow you to see the sectors in which you will attract the most job offers and where you are most likely to be able to improve your employability.

It is vitally important to always be working on your Transferable Skills.

These will increase your earning potential (and your quality of life) in all areas.

As a reminder, these are IT Skills, Functional Skills (numeracy and literacy), Work Ethic, Organisation, Interpersonal Skills, Problem Solving and Mind-set Management (outlook and attitude).

The way you communicate and interact with other people, people-skills, sometimes referred to as interpersonal skills, are the most important of all.

"I completed my CV and PDS and I can now see a crime-free future where I am actually in stable work." RW

Daily Diplomacy™

The most important employability skills - Skills with People

"People skills have really helped me to grow in confidence and to have a much smoother life day to day. If you think about it, almost everything we do involves other human beings, interacting with them and working with them. Getting better in social situations is not that difficult but take my word for it, it makes a mighty difference." VE

The Most Important Transferable Skill - Skill with People (aka interpersonal skills)

For some of us, building relationships and creating rapport comes easily. For others, it is something they may need to work on - but we can all improve.

As people who are often judged for our past mistakes and who may face some barriers to employment, it is very important for us to stand out in a positive way and work hard to make a good impression.

'Creating rapport' simply means getting along; it is a sense of comfort, similarity and familiarity that two people experience. Sometimes rapport is natural. We can all remember someone who we just 'clicked with' straight away. What many people are not aware of is that we can also deliberately create and maintain rapport by working with human nature and by inspiring cooperation.

Many experts from a wide range of backgrounds consider skills with people to be the most important thing to develop. There is little evidence to suggest that any other skill set can have such dramatic effects on almost every aspect of a person's life (particularly employability).

People skills maximise the potential of any interaction and of each relationship.

Skills with people are important because when presented with a choice, people do business with people they like. We want employers and other people to feel comfortable with us and to choose to work with us.

IMPORTANT - Using people skills is not:	X	✓
	Sucking up.	Instead it is to **make people comfortable** and bring the best out of our everyday interactions.
	Gaining leverage.	
	Appeasing people.	
	Manipulating others.	

As you learn people skills and begin to implement them, you will find that people warm to you more and quicker; that they tell you more and that you learn more.

If you make an effort with other people you will correspondingly see that people, make a big effort with you and your whole life will take on a new positive energy.

Daily Diplomacy™, literally developing good skills with people does not mean that you need to change who you are as a person; you just need to become consciously aware of the dynamics of human interactions, to learn a few simple shortcuts and strategies, and make a sincere effort with other people.

40

People Skills really are the most important Transferable Skills - you can use them anytime, anywhere and with anybody.

I am going to share 30 important People Skills with you - one to practise each day for every day of the month. I call this *Daily Diplomacy*™.

Imagine if more people went through their lives trying to be diplomatic with other people. Would these **daily diplomats** be more or less likely to attract support from other people? Would they achieve more in the workplace and business arenas? Would things be more or less likely to work out for them?

You intuitively know the answers to these questions.

Here is your **Daily Diplomacy**™ to practise and each one is explained after the list:

Daily Diplomacy™	1	**MMFI** - **M**ake **M**e **F**eel **I**mportant.
	2	**Use 'WE'** - 'I' isolates, 'We' wins.
	3	**Reply promptly** to communications.
	4	Use and **remember people's names**.
	5	**Control distractions** and be attentive.
	6	**Respect people's time** and your own.
	7	**Empathise** and find things in common.
	8	**RAP** - Recognise, Appreciate and Praise.
	9	**Apologise quickly**, in passing and move on.
	10	**FORM** - Family, Occupation, Recreation and Me.
	11	**Be patient** with other people, try not to rush them.
	12	**Be polite** and save swear words for rare occasions.
	13	**Physical Position** - Do not oppose, dominate or trap.
	14	**Shrink your ego** - Do not be arrogant or overbearing.
	15	**Have a relatable image**, be clean and well-groomed.
	16	**Conduct yourself** in a relatable (not outlandish) way.
	17	Understand and adapt to **different personality** types.
	18	Be aware of your **body language**; aim for congruence.
	19	Control what you say to other people; **your outer voice**.

Daily Diplomacy™	20	Control the things you say to yourself; **your inner voice**.
	21	**Excellent eye contact**, in balance with the other person.
	22	**Be present** and interested, concentrate on the moment.
	23	Use and **vary the volume, tone and speed** of your voice.
	24	**Explain things** to people and avoid unfamiliar terminology.
	25	**Offer your hand** and give a warm and confident handshake.
	26	**Balance your mood** and understand your own body clock.
	27	**See potential** - avoid judging by appearances or first impressions.
	28	Remind yourself **'2 ears + 1 mouth'**; listen twice as much as you talk.
	29	Acknowledge **important dates** and diarise events in front of people.
	30	The most important **Daily Diplomacy**™ of all is to **SMILE**, a lot.

1. **MMFI** - **M**ake **M**e **F**eel **I**mportant.

   Imagine that everyone you meet has MMFI tattooed on their forehead - this stands for **Make Me Feel Important**.

   Everyone wants to feel valued and important; consider their needs and respect their opinions. If you treat every human being with decency, respect, courtesy and patience, (including those people that others consider to be insignificant), they will appreciate you and you will be rewarded.

2. **Use 'WE'** - 'I' isolates, '**We**' wins.

   Use '**I**' as little as possible, try to say 'you' and 'we', framing things from the other person's perspective.

   This stops people shutting their ears and thinking to themselves "Blah blah blah, he's going on about himself again!" Become aware of how often we say '**I**' and try to replace '**I**' as much as you can e.g.

   Instead of saying "I will teach you this on Saturday" (which is really saying "I am a big shot and very important, I know more than you"), say "we will cover this in detail on Saturday" or "that is fine it should have been explained better but everyone will understand this after Saturday's role play session."

   Instead of saying "I will not offer you that much", say something like "It wouldn't be viable for us to pay the price you are asking, we would like to help if possible but would need to offer you slightly less."

   So, try to reduce the number of times you use '**I**' in conversation and use 'we' as much as possible. "I isolates whereas 'we' inspires cooperation and support.

3. **Reply promptly** to communications.

It can be a bit overwhelming in the modern age having so many forms of communication but the more routes of communication you allow people to have with you the more open you will appear - It is like having the door open to your office, people see you as more approachable.

It is good practise to reply to Voicemails, SMS (Texts) and IM (Instant messages) within about 6 hours, emails within about within 24 hours and posted letters within 72 hours.

Prompt replies are important because they show that the person corresponding is important to you and it is a sign of respect.

If you need more time to draft detailed responses, it is absolutely fine to send a holding reply/ an acknowledgement. Something along the lines of "Thank you for your email. Please leave this with me for a couple of days and I will come back to you with my detailed reply." This is polite and courteous to the other person and does not make you feel rushed into any decisions. After this, reply within the timescale you have promised.

If you are going to be unavailable or away, set up an automatic-reply within email settings and a voicemail greeting so that people know that they are not being ignored and that you will come back to them upon your return.

4. Use and **remember people's names**.

There is a magic word which if used in the very early stages of getting to know someone will help to build trust.

This magic word is their name.

Use people's names several times in the first five minutes of meeting someone to help with rapport building and so that you can 'put the face to the name' in future.

Never allow yourself to say "*I am bad at remembering names*" because this is just giving yourself permission to forget someone's name. You cannot give yourself permission or excuses to forget names because they are too important!

Practise repeating each person's name in silent to yourself, like a mantra so that you remember it.

"I have been practising my people skills and the results have been mind-blowing! I didn't realise what a difference simple techniques could make to the way other people respond. I feel less nervous; I am more confident in my ability to communicate well with other people." RA

5. **Control distractions and be attentive**.

   In the early stages of a relationship, the Bridge-Building or honeymoon period, it is important to not allow yourself to be distracted or appear distracted when with the other person.

   It speaks volumes if you demonstrate to the other person that you will not allow yourself to get distracted e.g. if the phone rings, look at it, reject the call, turn the phone off and say, "sorry about that, what were you saying?" This makes the other person feel very respected and valued.

   Studies have demonstrated that the quality of conversations is adversely impacted just by the presence of mobile phones, even if they are left on a table between two conversationalists. So just keep them out of sight and out of mind to prevent the other person from thinking that the conversation might be interrupted at any time.

   Think about other possible distractions that may occur and take steps to prevent them, ideally do this in front of the other person so that they feel good that distractions are minimised.

6. **Respect people's time** and teach them to respect yours.

   Try not to keep people waiting, arrive early to the general area but turn up where you are meant to be exactly on time. Some people are very precise and get irritated or take offence if they are made to wait; fortunately, not everyone is like this, but we should still be aware that any negative first impression can set the tone for an unsuccessful meeting.

   When visiting people leave 10 minutes before they want you to leave and keep people wanting more (avoid overstaying your welcome).

   Likewise, do not leave immediately as soon as the business is finished but do invest a little time with people getting to know them and making small talk.

   When you phone someone clear the time slot first, by asking "Have you got 5 minutes to talk". When they phone you, if they don't ask you the same question then early in the conversation say something like "I am happy to talk now but I do only have 10 minutes because I have a scheduled call coming in/ I am on my way out of the door/ I am about to go into a meeting."

   If you make sure that people value your time, they will appreciate your input more and will listen more intently to what you have to say.

"No one had the courage to point out to me before that I was intimidating people because of my bad habit of dominating. It was putting people off and I had a lack of opportunity as a result. I listened and took it on board and now I sit quicker, don't block people in and talk a little quieter so that people feel less threatened. Now things are going better for me in a whole load of areas." IS

7. **Empathise** and find things in common.

A large percentage of people have a beaten down self-image and frequently feel inadequate, so they often wear masks that hide their real selves. Life can leave scars that are not obviously apparent, and many people live like shadows of who they really are or put on a big show of bravado. Many are scared to expose themselves or reveal any vulnerability. Their inner-most selves are hidden in a secret place where few people are allowed to go.

By finding common ground i.e. things we have in common and points of agreement, we can literally build bridges that lead to that real person.

It is important to be subtle; do not run in shouting like '*a bull in a china shop*', but perhaps pleasantly say:

"Oh, wow, my uncle used to take me fishing too, do you go very often?"	*"Yes, I like reading John Grisham books too, have you got the new one yet?"*	*"Sadly, I lost my dog three years ago too, so I really understand how you feel."*

NB: Only say things if they are true, do not just say them to try to relate to the other person, you will soon be exposed as a phoney!

The important point is that we are proactively seeking out and then pointing out areas where we are alike.

"We are both on the same side in wanting the best outcome here.

"I think it is important to mention that we both can agree on these points."

We all have more things in common than differences. If you focus on areas of mutual interest and points of agreement, it encourages support and co-operation from other people.

One of the very best ways of helping people to realise that they are on the same side is to use **Feel, Felt, Found** - If you are genuinely empathising with someone you can say *"I know how you **feel**, I **felt** the same way, I **found** (conclusion or solution)."* If used sincerely, this is an excellent way to build rapport.

Empathy is something which is hard to fake, but you can genuinely get better at it. Your empathy muscle can be trained by imagining yourself 'in the other person's shoes'. Don't just think about how you would feel in a similar situation but try to go beyond that to really imagine that you are that person, what is it like to be them? To experience the things, they have and are experiencing? How would you handle it?

Real empathy exposes us to pain and raw emotion; it takes a lot of courage to do. I say 'do' because empathising takes deliberate action. It is different from listening, nodding in agreement but not actually allowing yourself to FEEL.

A good way to test your current level of empathy is to watch programmes like *'you've been framed'* and when someone hurts themselves (perhaps by falling astride railings) do you say "Ouch, ooh, I bet that hurt!", or do you laugh like most people?

45

Choose a time to deliberately watch *'You've Been Framed'* and instead of laughing instinctively, imagine that you are the actual person in the clip; you will most likely be shocked at how different your reactions become.

Feeling real empathy and showing it is a skill. Like all skills, you can get better and improve with deliberate, conscious effort.

Empathy makes a huge difference to how successful you are at relating to other people and at helping them to relate to you.

8. **RAP** - Recognise, Appreciate and Praise people.

Go through life looking for the good in other people and acknowledging it.

Praise works wonders, it builds - Criticism does not, it damages.

Anyone can be a pigeon that goes around pooping on statues of other people, but there are not many people who sculpt statues, or who are worthy of a statue.

It is a simple choice do we want to be a pigeon-person or a statue-person?

Behaviour that we praise or criticise grows because it is focussed on more. If we want the good behaviour and good features of a person to grow, then we need to praise and encourage it. We should become "good finders". Remind people of when they did well; do not remind people of their past failings.

Compliment people's achievements and things that they have control of, for example gaining a degree is an amazing achievement with all credit going to the student. Having nice long fingers is not really an achievement but long finger nails are an achievement if someone has been relentlessly biting them in previous years due to anxiety.

Complimenting people for their achievements is sincere and this is different from flattery to 'butter someone up'.

Recognition is an important human need, take the time to acknowledge other people's achievements and appreciate their contributions and they will go out of their way to help and support you.

9. **Apologise** quickly, in passing and then move on.

If you slip up (which we all undoubtedly do from time to time), apologise quickly in a light-hearted and easy-going way and without making a big issue out of it then move on.

People appreciate it when they and their feelings matter to you enough for you to say sorry. Sorry means that you understand where you went wrong and that you do not intend to make the same mistake again in future. It goes without saying, do not apologise unless you mean it.

Forgive yourself and other people too, we are not perfect; we will make mistakes and we will miss or lose some opportunities. Let it go.

10. **FORM -** Family, Occupation, Recreation and Me.

Keep conversations flowing by using of the acronym FORM.

Always be on FORM - this stands for **F**amily **O**ccupation **R**ecreation **M**e (my life and my message).

People love to talk about themselves and if you talk about them, they will think you are the brainiest and most interesting conversationalist they have spoken to in a long time.

Ask questions, being genuinely interested in the other person, but not rapid-fire, interrogation style, just easy and relatable prompts to keep the conversation flowing.

Usually one or two questions are enough to start the conversational ball rolling. We just then need to keep the conversation rolling. With the addition of "Ooh", "Ah", "Wow", "I see," "Right", "Yes", "I understand".

<u>F</u>amily e.g. Have your mum and dad always lived here? Do you have any brothers or sisters? Have you got any children / grandchildren?

<u>O</u>ccupation e.g. "What do you do for a living?" (Slightly raised voice at the end of the sentence to show interest), "Oh that's interesting". Have you been doing it long?" "What made you decide to do that? Did you have to train for a long time to get that role?

<u>R</u>ecreation e.g. "So, what do you like to do in your spare time?", "What's your hobbies?", "Do you follow any sports?", "Oh yeah I played tennis too". I played golf before but wasn't any good at it. What tips would you give to improve golf?"

<u>M</u>e, my life and my message e.g. Share some information about your life to make the conversation less one sided and find a link/bridge to any message you want to leave them with.

Use open ended questions which lead into a series of further thoughts, explanations and elaboration because this is what makes a conversation.

For example, "how did you feel when that happened?"," What did you do then?"

Avoid closed questions which just give a *yes* or a *no* answer and potentially kill the conversation dead. Be careful not to question people in such a way that they feel defensive or that you are making them justify things.

For the rest of our lives, we should never have awkward silences. Like all muscles your conversation muscle needs regular workouts. Practise **FORM** to stay on top form when it comes to conversations.

"FORM really worked for me; I have used it a lot recently and this has helped me to overcome years of shyness." WJ

11. **Be patient** with other people, try not to rush them.

Do not rush people or pressurise them. Try to talk, think and explain things at their pace.

Take pride in holding yourself to a higher standard and not being easily rattled. Stay calm, professional and easy-going keeping a long fuse (not showing irritation or annoyance) at all times.

If you struggle to deal with certain people a trick may be to imagine what they were like as a small child. Inside each of us is still that small child that is unsure, fearful, stressed sometimes and that likes to get our own way - that child would usually receive more patience and understanding.

Give them the benefit of the doubt, other people will soon put them in their place, it does not have to fall to us to do that.

12. **Be polite** and save swear words for rare occasions.

Use please and thank you frequently, hold doors open for people, when people thank you say, "you're welcome."

Take the time to use basic manners because they do make a big difference to the way that people interact with us. Also encourage and expect the other person to thank you by saying "I hope that is helpful to you" or dropping similar reminders.

Do not show your bad habits when you are with other people; develop the self-discipline not to sniff, resist the habit to scratch or adjust (men), try not to yawn when anyone else is talking, do not pick your nose. If you blow your nose do not look at the contents of your tissue afterwards, hold in farts, definitely do not spit.

Swear-words should only be used occasionally; they can actually be very effective and have been proven to inspire trust but only if used occasionally rather than habitually and in very small measure.

Social etiquette may sound obvious to many of us, but some people have never been taught or have become lazy with personal habits.

"I always thought that if people didn't want to be around me then it was them who had the problem. I understand human nature more now and I realise that it was me who had the problem. I was the one missing out on chances to live a richer life because I was not approachable and likeable.

It takes effort to get in the habit of making an effort **with people, but these tips are simple, and it is well worth it."** EL

13. **Physical Position** - Do not oppose, dominate or trap.

In order to get people to remove their barriers, you need to have gained their trust, so that their guard is not up.

The subconscious mind is our internal guidance system. Someone positioned directly opposite you will intuitively feel like you are an obstacle, a competitor or a threat.

If people are feeling uncomfortable then you will not be able to build rapport, influence and help or guide them.

If you have no choice, but to be positioned directly opposite someone, then as soon as possible move yourself to be sitting, standing alongside or at an angle to the person you are talking to. In this position the other person will see you as physically "on their side." Try not to allow prolonged periods of time to pass with you sitting or standing exactly opposite to the person you're talking to.

Avoid standing over someone because they will feel dominated or intimidated When you are standing up in someone else's company, you might want to consider sitting instead. If the other person is sitting on a chair, you might want to sit on the floor, even if it is only for a few minutes (that is an extreme case). Also avoid blocking doorways because people subconsciously feel trapped.

Be careful not to invade people's personal space too; keep a respectable distance so that you do not begin to infringe on their more intimate zone, which is reserved for close friends and family. Standing or sitting too close to someone in the early stage of a relationship will make them feel nervous and uncomfortable and to think that you are too forward and pushy. Look out for physical signs of discomfort such as people moving away to reset their boundaries.

14. **Shrink your ego** - Do not be arrogant or overbearing.

Tame your ego, become its master, rather than its slave, so that it does not take over and make you behave smugly or full of self-importance.

When sitting down, tilt your head or sit lower so that your head and eye level is slightly lower than the other person's attentively listening.

Confidence is good; it is professional and appealing but an arrogant bullying ego that continues to assert its power over others can be very off-putting.

Practise demonstrating humility with confidence.

Do not talk constantly about how amazing you are. People will be more impressed with you if you take the time to understand and listen to them and they can gradually find out how amazing you are over time.

Of course, there are times where it is appropriate to sing your own praises, e.g. if you are trying to explain your expertise to someone who needs encouragement to listen or if you are selling yourself in an interview situation.

Nevertheless, these can still be done with confidence and a smile rather than trying to beat people up with a boastful running commentary of 'I'm better than you'.

15. **Have a relatable image**, be clean and well-groomed.

First impressions are important; people instinctively judge the value of a product by the packaging.

Personal grooming counts.

If your teeth are in a bad condition, see a dentist and have the necessary work done. If you have bad breath, use mouth-wash and keep better oral hygiene. If you smell, change your diet, wash more regularly and use deodorant. Wash and brush your hair.

Wash and iron your clothes, brush dog hairs off your coat, polish your shoes. Pull your trousers up; no one wants to see your underwear outside of the bedroom!

Give some thought to how you present yourself to the world. People will make quick decisions about whether you are worthy of respect sometimes based on whether you respect yourself.

Do not walk with an edgy swagger or point your nose in the air aloof to other people. Do not hold your head down or shoulders hunched as if you are ashamed of yourself. Instead hold your head straight and in a balanced way walk like you are someone who matters, with somewhere to go that also matters.

Likewise dress appropriately for the occasion and the audience/ people you are likely to meet. Do not turn up in leather trousers to a job interview and likewise do not turn up in a suit to a motorbike rally!

16. **Conduct yourself in a relatable (not outlandish) way.**

It is fine to have a fun or eccentric personality but if you know that you can be a bit "hyper" sometimes, tone it down when you first meet someone. This allows people to get used to you gradually.

Likewise, it is fine to be quiet and subdued sometimes but when you first meet someone perk up a bit and come across as happy and relatable.

We all know people who brighten up a room - *when they walk out of it!* We do not want to be that person; we want to be the person that people look forward to meeting and to seeing for the second and third time.

People do judge by first impressions, so try your best to make your first impression relatable (seem like someone that other people can identify with) and do not reveal any extreme personality traits in the early stages of a relationship.

This is not to say you must be a clone of other people; on the contrary, your real personality can show through when you give people a chance to get to know you better, without them being put off at the first meeting.

"No one taught me these essential life skills, I went through life bumping and bumbling my way. Now I have instructions to follow - it's brilliant." OS

17. Understand and adapt to **different personality types**.

Many studies have demonstrated that there are four primary personality types and each one learns, performs tasks and interacts with other people differently.

The type of personality one has, depends on whether someone is more outgoing (extrovert) or reserved (introvert) and whether they are more people-oriented or task-oriented. People have one of the following primary personality traits:

	OUTGOING (extrovert)		
TASK ORIENTATED (Achievement focussed)	Outgoing and task-orientated, RED (aka high 'd' personality). Characterised by leadership, efficiency and high achievement. Should be alert to their tendency to take-over and dominate even appearing railroading or aggressive to some people.	OUTGOING and people-orientated, YELLOW (aka high 'I'). Characterised by popularity, enthusiasm, persuasiveness, liking attention and limelight. Should be alert to their tendency to overlook important details and over-promise to other people.	**PEOPLE-ORIENTATED (Relationship focussed)**
	Reserved and task-orientated, BLUE (aka high 'c' personality). Characterised by being methodical and highly organised with great attention to detail and thoroughness. Should be alert to their tendency to procrastinate and avoid tasks indefinitely because things are not perfect.	Reserved and people-orientated, GREEN (aka high 's'). Characterised by dependability, generously supporting other people and listening well. Should be alert to their tendency to be passive, exploited by others, not speaking up early and not taking care of their own needs.	
	RESERVED (introvert)		

People cannot be pigeon-holed into a single box and they can change their personality to suit the situation and environment (for example a fun outgoing person could force themselves to be more disciplined and make the time to work through this book), but it is helpful to understand your own primary personality type and that of the most important people in your life.

Developing an understanding of the personality types will allow you to work with those people who want to get straight down to business as effectively as with those people who want to have a cup of tea and chat for an hour first. For now, it is a good idea to be aware that not everyone responds or thinks in the same way and we need to adjust and modify our approach with different people.

You may want to read 2 books called *'Personality Plus'* by Florence Littauer and *'Positive Personality Profiles'* by Dr Robert Rohm.

18. Be aware of your **body language**; aim for congruence.

Develop an awareness of your Body Language; it is speaking even when you are not.

Congruence means that your body language should match the words that you are speaking and the impression you are trying to make. If you do not show congruence, then people intuitively become suspicious and distrusting.

Body language says so much more than physical language. It runs alongside what is being said almost like background music and impacts on the way anything we say is received and interpreted.

Use folded arms rarely because it makes you appear unapproachable and defensive whereas open arms show honesty and acceptance. Lean forward to demonstrate listening intently. Only lean back when trying to appear relaxed and comfortable in the other person's presence, but not to show arrogance.

Become aware of your own thoughts which accompany each body language gesture - this is generally the thought that is transmitted to the other party, until you control it and learn to be an actor when necessary.

A good introduction is to read the book "Body Language" by Allan Pease.

19. Control what you say to other people - **your outer voice**.

When we are talking aloud make a concerted effort to never say anything negative or off-putting.

When other people hear what we are saying, our language often becomes a self-fulfilling prophesy.

For example, sitting outside an interview and saying, "I don't think I'll get the job." will obviously not inspire confidence in the people interviewing you (as per point 20, it will not help you to be confident either).

Some people think that they need to be realistic and cautious, but this does not help when you are trying to break out of your comfort zone, and it does not inspire support in other people. Ban certain words from your vocabulary, e.g. can't (can if you try), impossible (I'm possible).

Do not try to score points with others by putting them down or making them feel small. Do not make negative jokes about other people, they are not funny to them and if they laugh it is usually only because they feel like they must - inside it erodes their confidence a little each time.

Many people actually have very literal interpretation of what you say so be careful not to use sarcasm or put-downs because they often do not understand the humour.

Make sure that you begin and end meetings on positivity so that you are associated/ anchored with good thoughts. People will not always remember what you said but they always remember how you made them feel.

20. Control the things you say to yourself - **your inner voice**.

Our brains operate a system of internal dialogue, this helps us to understand, to problem solve and to plan. This dialogue continues 24 hours a day and 365 days a year.

It is often known as self-talk and is generally carried out sub-consciously; that is below the level of our consciously realising we are doing it. It is important to monitor what you are saying to yourself otherwise we are just like a leaf being blown by the storm with little control of our relationships, our interactions with other and over the success and failures of our lives.

It is possible however to direct this self-talk, just like channelling a powerful river. Eventually, with effort and persistence, the river will automatically follow the new course you have designed for it.

Our brains work the same way, we can design and programme a direction using positive self-talk and mantras that begin to rewrite old programming.

Positively leading self-talk was pioneered and proven to be effective in 1901 by Dr Emile Coue who taught his patients to repeat:

Every day in every way, I'm getting better and better.

Every day in every way, I'm getting happier and happier.

Every day in every way, I'm getting healthier and healthier.

His patients recovered from illness and injury faster and lived more fulfilling lives.

Now ALL famous sports achievers use self-talk to imagine, visualise and magnify their results. You can and should be doing this too.

In many cases our self-talk does not serve us well but instead acts as an undercurrent trying to drag us back to our comfort zone, to our lower levels of achievement and it feeds our fears and doubts.

But why should we allow external influences, uncontrolled fears or random intrusive imaginings to control our thoughts, actions and results?

Develop your own positive self-talk and mantras which you say repeatedly to silence the voice of doubt in your head.

Keeping self-talk positive and upbeat is a constant challenge and one we should rise to. Use affirmations to help your brain default to good self- talk.

Your self-talk shows up on your face; people like to be around positive happy people and will be more co-operative with you.

I strongly recommend reading a book entitled '*What to say when you talk to yourself*', by Shad Helmstetter.

21. **Excellent eye contact**, in balance with the other person.

Eye contact tells people that you are sincere and that they matter to you. People who hide their eyes, who do not make initial and regular eye contact, can come across as insincere, shifty and not to be trusted.

It is more important that the other person can look into your eyes and read them than for you to read theirs. If you are shy or feel nervous, develop the habit of looking at the top of people's noses instead. This has the same effect as making good eye contact because the other person can still see into your eyes.

Briefly breaking eye contact to gather your thoughts or to show that you are considering what the other person has said can help a lot.

Eye positions give insights into people's thoughts, because our brains are accessing different information areas, and these are very hard to fake. As a simple introductory example, right handed people look to their left if they are remembering and right if they are creating. This can tell you if someone is honestly remembering or if they are making up a story.

More importantly, if we show our eyes, it allows other people to intuitively have access to some of our thoughts and feelings.

Human beings evolved in communities which relied heavily on unspoken language, including eye signals and facial expressions, before we learnt to talk. It is very difficult to empathise, or build rapport, without eye contact.

You may have heard of mirroring the other person (using similar gestures, posture and body language), to help build rapport. This is most important with eye contact.

EQUALISE | the amount of eye contact | **EQUAL EYES**

Maintain consistent eye contact but be in balance with the other person. If you are dealing with a person who is shy and reserved, their eye contact will be a little bit less, so you must not force them to give more, until they are comfortable with you. Also withdraw your gaze earlier to help them gradually become more confident.

This is better than forcing them to meet your gaze and leaving them feeling uncomfortable and pressurised, but without them knowing why. Eye contact is not a staring competition! Manic staring is intimidating to other people.

We want to appear confident, positive and easy to relate to, so give balanced eye contact.

"I am much more aware of making an effort and deliberately showing respect and courtesy to other people. This is even more important when trying to gain employment and do well in the workplace." AL

22. **Be present** and interested, concentrate on the moment.

When you are with someone else you must have the strength of mind to remain present even if you have serious issues on your mind or you are emotionally upset. Concentrate on the matter at hand. Do not let personal situations or challenges show through, if the meeting is about something or someone else.

People can sense insincerity and if you are not really "with it", not listening or paying attention when they are trying to talk to you. If you do not have time, then politely explain:

"I am sorry, but I have to get this finished, can I call you later?"

"I am sorry, but I am really working to a deadline can we catch up another time?"

Multi-tasking can be great, but it does not work with people; people do not like to be multi-tasked they appreciate undivided attention, courtesy and respect.

Have the strength of mind to remain present and concentrate on the matter at hand and the people you are with at them time. If you struggle with this, pick up a book on Zen or Mindfulness and begin to enjoy living in the moment more.

23. Use and **vary the volume, tone and speed** of your voice.

The words you say are just one part of what you say.

For example, you could tell someone "You're terrible!" and it will mean two totally different things depending on the tone and volume of your voice.

The volume of your words is very important, it affects how people listen. If you speak at a lower volume, then people will listen more intently and believe that what you are saying is serious.

Speed and tonality also affect how people interpret the words you say - if you talk slowly or in a grave tone this will emphasise an important point. If you speed up your voice and talk fast, you sound excited and positive. If you shout, then people may be less likely to hear what you are saying because they are instinctively worried about aggression.

Practise and see what a difference changing the volume, tone and speed of your voice can make.

"I make a lot more allowances for other people than I used to, and I know that we are all very different. We think differently and interpret and understand things differently. It is this diversity that makes teams strong." KV

24. **Explain things**, avoid using unfamiliar terminology and unnecessarily big words.

Avoid using unfamiliar terminology with people because this can cause embarrassment, dislike or a loss of credibility.

If you are teaching something or telling someone something, they may not be aware of then explain everything, particularly abbreviations.

Consider the following examples:

a) I am qualified in PTS, Personal Track Safety so I am able to work on the railways.

b) I need to install an RCD, this stands for Residual Current Device, which is a safety feature.

Try to talk in basic language that everyone can understand.

Einstein is credited with saying that if you cannot explain a concept in a simple enough way that anyone can understand it, then it is likely that you have not grasped it properly yourself.

Don't try to impress but do try to express better and build bridges to understanding.

Also avoid using unnecessarily big words (*'Brobdingnagian utterances'*).

Do not try to score points with pomposity, aimed at embarrassing the other person or making them feel small.

25. Offer your hand and **give a warm and confident handshake**.

Volunteer your hand because this is a confident and appealing gesture which demonstrates that you value the other person.

A positive handshake:		
✓ IS perfectly vertical, which indicates mutual respect and the ability to work together.	X	IS NOT palm-up, which shows submissiveness.
	X	IS NOT palm-down, which dominates the other person.
✓ IS a warm grip which shows that you are interested in the other person and that you care enough to make an effort.	X	IS NOT a vice like grip that hurts and cripples the other person.
	X	IS NOT a lifeless passive 'floppy fish' that indicates a lack of personality.

Also, make sure that your hand is not sweaty or wet before you shake someone else's!

56

26. **Balance your mood** and utilise your body clock to be at your best.

Be aware of things that affect our mood and our emotional states such as hunger, tiredness, hormone imbalances and distressing life situations.

There is no point trying to deny the fact that sometimes we are not at our best, we can all be grouchy when we are tired or hungry, the trouble is that it often other people who bear the brunt of these mood swings.

They will not understand that this angry, emotionally upset or physically distressed person is not the real you, they will just not want to be around you.

Mood swings and emotion imbalances are problematic, and they cost us in missed opportunities. It is not fair on the other person if they must deal with roller coasters of unpredictability; it is not fair on you either, when it affects your professionalism and ability to build rapport with other people.

Balance your peaks and troughs, as much as possible by eating regularly (carry a banana or cereal bar for emergencies), drinking enough fluids, getting a good night's sleep (avoid coffee in the evenings), taking enough time out for yourself and learning emotional management strategies. If things get really bad of course see a doctor; do not try to manage everything on your own; you could just end up more stressed and isolated.

Try to do your most important work and meet with other people when you are at your best times as much as possible. For example, I personally know that I am not going to perform well if I have skipped breakfast and not given myself enough time to wake up properly, so I try to hold important meetings after 10am. Everyone has daily, monthly and annual cycles where they are able to interact best with others. Some of us are night-time people (aka owls) and others are best in the morning or afternoon (larks).

Stay away from all non-prescribed drugs; the effects are far too unpredictable for them to be a part of any positive life and treat alcohol with great care too - it is proven to do two things:

1) Make you crave more of it; even the most well-intentioned people who start out thinking they will just have one drink can end up having five or six or more.

2) Reduce all inhibitions and increase basic, primitive (brain-stem) urges. People end up doing things that they would never normally do, and which are completely out of character. Very often things said and done under the influence of alcohol become a source of great regret for years afterwards.

Alcohol is one of the most dangerous drugs available in our society; although it is legal, many of the after-affects and consequences are illegal. Be wary of going out for serious drinks with business associates or work colleagues, they may see a different side to you and you to them.

To mitigate the risk of you losing control and saying or doing things that cause embarrassment in future, drink one glass of water in between every drink, you will still enjoy yourself, but this will help to dilute the alcohol and you will be more alert to possible problems.

It goes without saying, do not drink alcohol (certainly do not get drunk), the night before an important meeting, you will be dehydrated, and your brain function will be massively impaired. The time to celebrate is <u>after</u> a successful meeting or event, at least then you will feel that you have earned it and you will not be putting your future success.at risk.

Understanding your own body, respecting it and working with its natural cycles and rhythms will help you to be more efficient and productive and you will naturally be better with other people when you are at your best times.

27. **See potential** - avoid judging people by appearances or first impressions.

See and imagine the potential, not just the person, when you first meet someone.

Everyone has the ability to change and we do not always see people at their very best. Imagine that you are wearing magic 'possibility' glasses when you are looking at people; glasses that let you see what they could be and what they could achieve.

Very often people will rise or sink to the level of other people's expectations and treatment of them. Each person is unique, everyone has incredible potential within them, and we all change and grow as we progress through life. Sometimes all it takes is the seed of a goal or dream to be planted and nurtured (through positive action and support of other people).

You can count how many seeds are in an apple, but you can never count how many apples can come from a single seed.

Give people the benefit of the doubt; do not make the mistake of judging by our incorrect assumptions and first impressions. These are so frequently proven wrong as you get to know the real person.

28. Remind yourself **'two ears/ one mouth'** - Listen twice as much as you talk.

This old saying does have a lot of relevance in the modern world. We should listen twice as much as we speak. NOT 'paying lip service' but REALLY listening with a goal to not talk until we have internalised, digested and acknowledged what the other person has said.

If it was important enough for them to say it to you then we should give their words, the respect they deserve. If we don't agree or understand, that is ok - we can at least try to understand the thought processes and the circumstances that generated it.

When you **really listen** to someone else, it is both life-affirming and transformational. Many people almost never truly get listened to and if you do listen to them, they appreciate it and remember it.

29. Acknowledge **important dates** and diarise events in front of the other person.

Diarise important dates and write notes of important information.

Family members will particularly value your commitment to noting dates in your diary and **making things that are important to them also important to you.** I sometimes actually say to my children, "if it is important to you, it is important to me" and I see their faces light up because of it.

Additionally, making some occasional small notes as someone talks is often appreciated because it shows you are really interested in what they are saying.

I once wrote to a very important person asking permission to quote them from a brief talk they had given; he felt very complimented that I had taken the time to accurately make a written record of his words and he has been a huge support and an ally to me ever since.

Remembering dates goes a long way, for example I still get a wedding anniversary card from a lady who came to our wedding in 2000; every year she remembers the date without fail - it means a lot.

30. The most important **DAILY DIPLOMACY**™ of all is to **SMILE**, a lot.

Smiling disarms and reassures the other person.

It also has an almost magical effect on your own mood and your own problem-solving abilities. It enhances the quality of your life. The most charismatic and appealing people generously share their smiles with those around them (even when they do not feel like it).

When you meet someone, smile and greet them enthusiastically.

Consider your facial expression particularly when looking at other people, sometimes we might be buried in thought and frowning but if you look at someone with this expression, they will automatically think that your face is their fault - be aware of this phenomenon.

If you begin to smile more often, you will start to physically develop smile lines instead of frown lines on your face which helps people to see you as friendly and approachable.

Practise smiling more often to:

- Lift your mood
- Appear more approachable

and

- Gain a lot more support from all the people who cross your path.

"I read the chapter on people skills before my job interview which I think went very well. Now I am going to follow the 30-day test and see what happens." GD

Treat each human interaction as a learning opportunity and a chance for you to improve. These techniques are not to use, manipulate or exploit people, but are to help them be more open and to improve quality of life for both of you.

"A deficiency in skills with people is responsible, long-term, for more social isolation, depression and poverty than any external circumstances will ever be." PM

The more you practise your people skills, the better you become and eventually once you have mastered these skills, they can become instinctive. You will begin to see that, as you become a more people-orientated person and as these people skills become habitual and natural, more opportunities for advancement will present themselves and life will become a lot more fulfilling.

Developing people skills, connecting with other people and creating rapport leads to:

- Increased productivity.
- Support from other people.
- Better problem-solving abilities.
- More motivation from all parties.
- Confidence and easiness about life.
- Less confusion and clearer understanding.

Opportunities, agreements and cooperation from other people will flow much better.

Practise saying "Hello" and "How are you?" to people you do not know, to strike up conversations with people and watch them interacting with you with no effort at all.

"The quality of your life is the quality of your relationships." Tony Robbins

Building or improving a relationship leads to increased productivity, better understanding on both sides and a rarely found easiness about life and working together. All relationships will encounter problems; it is how we respond to them that makes the difference. Some problems are caused by:

- Lack of motivation and effort.
- Lack of understanding and empathy.
- Hunger or tiredness affecting communication.
- Challenges with physical and/or mental health.
- One person being too aggressive or too passive.
- External pressures e.g. financial challenges or changing life stages.
- Failure to clarify expectations or having unreasonable expectations.

By practising these 30 People Skills and by building rapport, all your relationships will improve, especially if these skills develop into habits. Make a conscious decision to focus on one each day for the next 30 days and then go back to the beginning.

These will enable you to bring the best out of the people you interact with and the best out of each relationship.

"Using skills with people and practising Daily Diplomacy™ is like pouring oil on the gears and cogs of life, making everything run easier and more smoothly." PM

These are general people skills that apply when meeting new people and in the earliest stages of a relationship; the *'bridge-building'* period.

Once you have built rapport and when there is trust and understanding in place, then you will understand each other better and you can be more daring in pushing the boundaries; you can be more forthright and forward, without coming across as overbearing and without making the other person uncomfortable because they already know you by then.

Cole's Law of human relationships teaches us that **'when individual people, ingredients or ideas are successfully blended together, the result is substantially better and more valuable than the individual parts.'** (coleslaw!), PM

Claiming a Daily Diplomacy™ Skills with People Award

I personally challenge you to practise **Daily Diplomacy™** and embrace the massive difference it can make to your life!

If you keep a diary of your experiences, (using the template on the next few pages), it will make you more aware of your interactions and help you to noticeably improve.

To receive a certificate of completion of your 30-day challenge, email a copy of your diary to info@ex-seed.co.uk or post to Philip Martin t/as Ex-seed™ 5 Crabtree Drive, Northampton. NN3 5DR

Award - for studying skills with people and successfully completing a 30-point implementation and reflection diary.

Your Name Here   21st January 2020

Congratulations and Well Done!

R. Martin

Philip Martin
Content writer and
submissions verifier

Daily
Diplomacy™
AWARD

Once you receive your certificate, you can legitimately add a new entry on your CV with wording as follows:

"Daily Diplomacy Skills with People award for studying skills with people and successfully completing a 30-point implementation and reflection diary."

My Daily Diplomacy™ Diary

For 30 days from _____ (insert today's date), I will give this people skills project 100% effort and commitment and I will record my experiences in this diary at the end of each day, signed _____

Day	People Skill	My experiences and reflections on the difference this made
1	**MMFI** - Make Me Feel Important.	
2	**Use 'WE'** - 'I' isolates, 'We' wins.	
3	**Reply promptly** to communications.	

4	5	6	7	8	9
Use and remember people's names.	**Control distractions** and be attentive.	**Respect people's time** and your own.	**Empathise** and find things in common.	**RAP** - Recognise, Appreciate and Praise.	**Apologise quickly**, in passing and move on.

10	**FORM** - Family, Occupation, Recreation and Me.
11	**Be patient** with other people, try not to rush them.
12	**Be polite** and save swear words for rare occasions.
13	**Physical Position** – Do not oppose, dominate or trap.
14	**Shrink your ego** - Do not be arrogant or overbearing.

15	16	17	18	19
Have a relatable image, be clean and well-groomed.	**Conduct yourself** in a relatable (not outlandish) way.	Understand and adapt to **different personality types**.	**Be aware of your body language** and aim for congruence.	Control what you say to other people - **your outer voice**.

20	21	22	23	24
Control the things you say to yourself - **your inner voice**.	**Excellent eye contact**, in balance with the other person.	**Be present** and interested, concentrate.	Use and vary the **volume, tone and speed** of your voice.	**Explain things**: avoid unnecessarily big words and terminology.

25	**Offer your hand** and give a warm and confident handshake.		
26	**Balance your mood** and understand your own body clock.		
27	**See potential** - avoid judging people by appearances or first impressions.		
28	Remind yourself **'two ears/ one mouth'** - listen twice as much as you talk.		

29	Acknowledge and **diarise dates** that are important to other people.
30	The most important **DAILY DIPLOMACY**™ is to **SMILE**, a lot.

I _____ (insert name), confirm that I practised all 30 of the people skills and that the reflections in this diary are honest. I understand that meeting the expected criteria for the issuing of Daily Diplomacy™ Skills with People Award is at the sole discretion of Philip Martin, the content writer and submissions verifier. I consent to Philip Martin t/as Ex-seed™ processing and storing my personal data in accordance with the privacy policy on page 357 of this book.

Signed _____, Date _____

Address for issuing of certificate:

Any other comments:

To receive your certificate, email a copy of your completed diary to info@ex-seed.co.uk or post to Philip Martin t/as Ex-seed™ 5 Crabtree Drive, Northampton. NN3 5DR

Chapter 3 -
Disclosing
a
Criminal
Record

"We are not so interested in what you have done in the past but what you can achieve in the future, by building on your positive attributes and experiences, not those you regret. We have the opportunity to help each other to do things right, not do things wrong."

Simon Catford, Regulatory Director - Viridor

Disclosure Explained

Disclosure simply means *telling someone something*.

In this case, it means telling a potential employer about your criminal record.

N.B: Disclosure is also required for some financial products such as insurance and mortgages and the same rules do apply.

Many people with criminal records unnecessarily fear the disclosure process.

In fact, a Personal Disclosure Statement (PDS) can be a very useful tool. Well-worded PDS's have been proven to impress forward thinking employers, who provide long-term job placements, as well as training and personal support.

Disclosure of convictions to potential employers is compulsory, for everyone who:

  a) Has an unspent conviction.

 and

  b) Is asked whether they have any criminal convictions.

Most employers have a tick-box or will ask you whether you have a criminal record/ any unspent convictions.

If you are asked, then you **must** disclose your unspent criminal convictions.

Not disclosing would be a new offence of fraud and a breach of licence conditions, potentially leading to recall.

Disclosure must therefore be considered essential, but it can work to your advantage (as explained later in this chapter).

You must disclose **ALL** of your unspent convictions, not just the one you were most recently sentenced for.

If you are not asked by a potential employer, then you do not have to disclose; but not being asked is very rare indeed (and it can also result in later problems).

If you are self-employed as a sole trader or employed by your own company (only allowed if you are not also subject to a Director's ban as part of your sentence) then clients will not usually ask you to disclose criminal convictions.

If you are asked, however, then the same obligations will apply.

"Using the templates provided in this book, I created a Personal Disclosure Statement that removes the awkwardness of explaining my past. I feel confident that I can compete on a level playing field with other applicants (and win!)." MB

Spent Convictions

After a certain period (called a rehabilitation or buffer period), some convictions become "spent". This means that they do not have to be disclosed when requested/required, because you are considered fully rehabilitated.

The table provided below shows the rehabilitation periods under the Rehabilitation of Offenders Act 1974 (amended 2014).

Sentence Type and Length	When the Conviction becomes Spent	
	Aged 18+ when convicted	Younger than 18 when convicted
Fines	12 months after conviction	6 months after conviction
Community Order	1 year after order expires	6 months after order expires
6 months and under	2 years after LED	18 months after LED
From 6 months and a day to 30 months	4 years after LED	2 years after LED
30 months and a day to 4 years	7 years after LED	3.5 years (42 months) after LED
Any sentence over 4 years	Never Spent	Never Spent
Any indeterminate sentence (parole required for release)	Never Spent	Never Spent
LED = Licence Expiry Date. This means that rehabilitation periods are calculated from the expiry date of the full sentence length handed down by the courts and not from the halfway point.		
N.B. This table is subject to the **important considerations** on the next page.		

Important Considerations

We can see from the table on the previous page that some criminal offences are classed as spent after a "rehabilitation period". These include sentences of 4 years and less, fines and community punishments.

If your convictions are spent then you are no longer obliged to disclose them, they may still show up on the highest level of Disclosure and Barring Service check and a **Personal Disclosure Statement (PDS)** can help significantly if this is the case.

You must consider the following 6 important points when calculating when your convictions will be spent:

	Rule	Example
1	**Suspended sentences are treated the same** as prison sentences.	A 20 month Suspended Sentence will become spent 4 years after the 20 months have passed.
2	**Remand time does not count** towards the rehabilitation period, even though it counts towards the sentence.	The full duration of remand time must be added to the timescale in the table shown. Be aware that some online tables calculate from date of conviction and avoid clarifying this point.
3	**Concurrent (at the same time) sentences are treated only as the longest sentence** and the rehabilitation period runs from LED + remand time.	A 3-year sentence + 2 years concurrent is treated as a 3-year sentence. As per the table, the sentence would become spent 7 years after LED (+ remand time).
4	**Consecutive (one after another) sentences are treated as a total sentence** and the rehabilitation period runs from LED + remand time.	A 3-year sentence + 2 years consecutive is treated as a 5-year sentence. As per the table, this sentence will never be spent because it is over 4 years.
5	**If you are convicted of a new offence whilst an earlier conviction remains unspent,** then neither conviction becomes spent until both do.	If the new sentence is more than 4 years, then it will never be spent - but neither will the earlier one, even if it was for less time.
6	**If you have an outstanding court order** related to a conviction, for example a crime prevention order, then the conviction (s) will not become spent, until the order is satisfied.	If you have an unpaid confiscation order (even if a default prison sentence is served), the associated conviction(s) will never become spent until and unless it is paid.
	If you unsure when your conviction(s) will become spent, then I recommend using the free tool at www.disclosurecalculator.org.uk (kindly provided by *'Unlock'* charity).	

The Disclosure and Barring Service (DBS)

Many employers do not rely solely on disclosure but instead pay for a **DBS** - formerly Criminal Records Bureau (CRB) check.

DBS checks are in place primarily to protect children and vulnerable adults from harm. They also ensure that only the most suitable people can operate in responsible positions such as financial services or law and work in high risk jobs such as the police or military.

The highest level of check, called "enhanced" is required for the highest risk positions, e.g. school jobs. This draws on additional information including spent convictions and police intelligence, among other sources.

Even if your convictions are spent and you are no longer obliged to disclose them, they may still show up on the highest level of Disclosure and Barring Service check and a **Personal Disclosure Statement (PDS)** can help significantly if this is the case.

An accurate PDS forewarns the employer about convictions that show up on Disclosure and Barring Service checks. It may save them money and it will also save you both time, if your conviction(s) would make you unsuitable for the role.

Employers are urged by **NACRO** (The National Association for the Care and Resettlement of Offenders) to consider 3 factors when thinking about whether to employ an ex-offender:

1. The seriousness of the crime(s).
2. The circumstances of the offence.
3. The relevance of the conviction to the job.

As opposed to implementing a blanket policy of not employing ex-offenders. www.nacro.org.uk

"We believe very much in second chances and that people should not be judged on their past mistakes providing they are genuine in wanting to turn their lives around. If the applicant is keen to learn from past mistakes and has the ability and desire to change, there is no reason why they should not be part of our team."

Paul Crossman - Genuine Solutions Group

The Benefits of Upfront Disclosure

There are ten benefits to a *Personal Disclosure Statement* (PDS).

A considered and well written PDS:

1. Demonstrates honesty and transparency.

2. Provides a written record, proving that you have disclosed fully.

3. Inspires employers and makes you stand out from other applicants.

4. Explains negative search engine results and social media commentary.

5. Forewarns the employer about convictions that show up on DBS checks.

6. Saves a huge amount of time by filtering the employers who are willing to consider looking beyond your conviction(s).

7. Allows you to prepare what you are going to say in advance, rather than being caught unprepared and 'put on the spot'.

8. Enables other decision makers to read it (rather than just verbal explanations being passed across, which may lose accuracy).

9. The process of writing your PDS gives you a better understanding of your past mistakes and will help you to avoid relapsing or slipping back into problems.

10. Your commitment to making a PDS serves as a clear separator between the past and the present; it indicates that you have started a new and more fulfilling chapter in your life.

Upfront and honest disclosure is the best way, by far. The time investment required to follow the Disclosure Builder system (pages 86 - 112) is around 2 hours (less with help) and it really pays off.

"I was petrified of attending a job interview and having to explain my conviction. Having created a Personal Disclosure Statement, I know that the embarrassing bit is out of the way in advance. I have been invited to an interview and I am not worried about what to say. I can just focus on my skills and the company, rather than trying to explain my past." JP

From my experience I can honestly tell you that hundreds of people have already proved the following statement to be true…

An ex-offender who gives a clear, honest and comprehensive disclosure early in the recruitment process has an equal or greater chance of being offered the job that they are applying for (and for which they are qualified, and which is unrelated to their convictions), as someone who has no criminal record.

This is so important that I recommend that you read it again to let it really sink in....

An ex-offender who applies for a job:

> *a) Which is unrelated to their conviction(s), and*

> *b) That they are qualified, skilled or experienced enough to perform, and who*

> *c) Provides clear, honest and comprehensive disclosure, early in the job application process.*

Has an <u>equal</u> or <u>greater</u> chance of being offered the job that they are applying for, as someone who has no criminal record.

An effective Personal Disclosure Statement (PDS) is a document in which you tell potential employers your story. In this story you can explain the things that went wrong and why they are unlikely to reoccur in future i.e. how much you and your circumstances have changed and the lessons you have learnt.

50% of employers surveyed said they would consider employing an ex-offender. (Source: YouGov 2016)

25% of employers surveyed said they would not use a disclosed conviction to reject, or discriminate, against an ex-offender applying for a job. (Source: Working Links, "Prejudged" 2010)

We are aiming to reach those employers who do not immediately prejudge applicants based on their previous convictions. These employers have more of a social conscience; they appreciate honesty and value applicants who show that they have changed and are trying to better themselves.

"This book has all of the answers I wanted and when I wasn't sure how to put things into words, I was able to use the template examples. I have just got a new job back in IT. My criminal record stopped being a <u>barrier</u> to employment and instead it became a <u>bridge</u> to employment. Thanks." AP

If we provide an explanation (a background story), then these more compassionate employers are better able to understand what took place and see the prison sentence in the context of a larger set of circumstances.

These circumstances are highly unlikely to reoccur if you are employed.

Potential employers will be more confident that giving you a chance to prove yourself through work will not put them or their company at risk.

For clarity I call this **the 5 R's**.

1. **Remorse** - express **remorse** for your crime(s).
2. **Reasons** - explain the **reasons** why it happened.
3. **Responsibility** - show that you accept **responsibility** for your mistakes.
4. **Rehabilitation** - demonstrate how you have changed for the better.
5. **Reconciliation** - make plans to re-join society and contribute.

We explore each of these R's in detail on pages 80 - 83.

"Following this system, whilst I was still in prison and just before my release, I sent my Personal Disclosure Statement and CV to an employer who was not even advertising any job vacancies. Here's what they replied:

> *'Thank you for your recent letter, whereby you enquire about possible employment opportunities with us.*
>
> *Having reviewed your personal disclosure statement, I would like to thank you for your honesty. I appreciate it is a very difficult position you have found yourself in, and it's clear from the way you write that you are looking to draw positives from the experience and use the time to improve your prospects moving forward.*
>
> *With this in mind, if we are able to, **we would like to support you back into employment**. We would like to arrange for you to come in and have a chat about opportunities that you may be suitable for. In the meantime, if there is anything you need me to do with regards to paperwork for the prison service, please let me know and I will be happy to assist.'*

The Personal Disclosure Statement lived up to the promises made in this book. I now have an interview lined up and I will now make sure I follow the tips in the interview chapter too! I will keep you informed."
AG

The Consequences of Failing to Disclosure

A person, who states that they have no convictions when they do have a conviction or convictions, which are unspent, is lying for personal gain.

This would be a criminal offence prosecutable under the Fraud Act.

A person who is serving the remainder of their prison sentence on licence in the community can be recalled (returned to prison) by probation if they commit or are suspected of committing, a new offence.

Ex-offenders who are on licence are required to inform their Probation Officer and ask for approval before undertaking paid or unpaid work. It is not unusual for Probation Officers to speak with employers regarding disclosure.

Reminder: Spent convictions do not need to be disclosed, they are considered to no longer exist and you are legally allowed not to disclose them.

Failing to disclose can mean that you lose your job when the conviction is discovered. They are often discovered by an internet search, revealed when there is a need to travel or when someone from the past tries to sabotage someone's success.

"I was never asked about my criminal conviction:

> Unfortunately, when I was seen to be working, someone who knew me rang my employer and I was dismissed from my job. This was despite having me having been working there for 4 months without any problems." FL

"I was asked about my criminal record, but I did not disclose:

> When I was released from prison, I wanted to turn my life around. I got a job that I really enjoyed as a general labourer and technician in a music studio. Unfortunately, I had failed to disclose my conviction, I still wasn't being honest. The owner was so pleased with my job performance that he offered me an opportunity to help him open a studio in America. At this point, because of travel laws I had to come clean about my conviction. He fired me on the spot. I had rebuilt my life, I had a son, a flat and a car and didn't know where to turn - I felt like I had failed, yet again. I became a criminal again, but I didn't want to be. When I got caught again, I knew that I had to change. All the potential employers had been asking me whether I had experience and qualifications, so I made prison my chance to change for the better. I worked hard and gained qualifications and in future I will be honest and upfront with any potential employer." JP

When and How to Disclose

The recommended disclosure process is different for advertised and un-advertised jobs, as follows:

Unadvertised Vacancies

Where you are applying directly to employers and not in response to an advertised job, I recommend that you post or email all three of the following documents TOGETHER as a set:

- Personal Disclosure Statement (PDS) (chapter 3).
- Curriculum Vitae (CV) (chapter 4).
- Application Letter (AL) (chapter 5).

It is so much better to be upfront from the beginning, this avoids wasting your time unnecessarily and employers also appreciate the upfront approach.

If you follow the system for creating an effective PDS, you will find that you get more replies from employers than an average person writing into a company.

Your communication is dealt with differently by Human Resources departments. It changes from "Oh here's just another CV" to "Let me think how best to progress this this interesting application". More of the right people take an interest and you will be surprised at the response.

Professor Richard Wiseman (Psychologist) analysing statistical research conducted by Jones and Gordon from Duke University (Timing of Self-disclosure and its Effects on Personal Attraction) explains that:

Presenting weakness early turns a weakness into a unique strength and makes us more relatable. People feel more comfortable with us and building rapport is easier.

When disclosure happens early in the process, employers believe that they are dealing with someone who has the strength of character and integrity to relate personal difficulties first and who is not trying to mislead them.

Presenting weaknesses early is seen by employers as a sign of openness. (Source: 59 Seconds by Professor Richard Wiseman)

"We believe passionately that everyone should be given a chance to shine in life. To this end we have committed to recruiting the very best people based on their aptitude, not their past. We focus on what people can offer now and, in the future, rather than looking back. This allows us to provide greater opportunities for people looking to start a new chapter in their lives." Karen Brookes, HR Director, Sir Robert McAlpine Construction

Advertised Jobs

Most advertised job applications are now done by way of an online form and many of these have a tick-box for initial disclosure of criminal records.

You have a legal obligation to disclose your criminal record when you are asked by a potential employer; **you must not lie or leave such a tick-box un-ticked.**

In some cases, you will get the chance to elaborate within the form, if so, then you can copy *(keyboard shortcut ctrl-c)* and paste *(ctrl-v)* your PDS or retype it into the relevant section of the form.

Usually, however there is no opportunity to write supporting information within the form. In these cases, the tick-box results in those forms being dismissed altogether.

It is important that your application does not get filtered out by the box.

To get a fair chance and avoid this happening to you, where there is a tick-box, submit a postal or email application to the company with the CV, PDS and AL together as a set instead.

There has been a national campaign called "Ban the Box" which encourages companies to remove the tick-box from application forms and to ask about convictions later in the recruitment process.

For the most up to date list of employers signed up to Ban the Box visit www.bitc.org.uk/programmes/ban-box or ask a family member or librarian.

My opinion of Ban the Box is that it is a good thing that this campaign is raising awareness of the value of hiring ex-offenders, however I would rather know as early as possible if a person or company, is going to be prejudiced against me.

I would rather not waste anymore of my time or their time and resources if they have a blanket policy of not hiring ex-offenders anyway.

There are thousands of jobs available and some of them will be perfect for you.

The UK currently has 800,000 unfilled job vacancies. (Source: BBC News 12/9/2018)

"The thought of disclosure was stressing me out as I did not know how to deal with it. I followed the guidance in this book. I just thought 'try it, what have I got to lose?' Well that worked because I have just left a job interview where the boss praised me for my honest disclosure and said he wants to give me a chance; Thanks for the inspiring guidance!" TI

Mind-set Milestones - The 5 R's of Change

There are several **Mind-set Milestones** that a prisoner or ex-offender must go through to effect a real change and to live a law-abiding life.

I call these **Mind-set Milestones** the 5 R's and explain them as follows:

- **R1 Remorse**

  I am sorry for what I did, for the impact of what happened, and I do regret my crime(s).

- **R2 Reasons**

  I now understand the reasons/ triggers why I committed my crime and the circumstances around it.

  I have a clear insight into the circumstances, my thought processes and my emotions at the time.

  I know exactly where I went wrong.

- **R3 Responsibility**

  I admit that it is my fault, I am not passing the blame and neither am I minimising the impact of my crime.

- **R4 Rehabilitation**

  I will not do it again; I have learnt lessons and changed.

- **R5 Reconciliation**

  I want to make up for what I did wrong and contribute.

  I am committed to living a rule following and law-abiding life.

  I have goals for the future, and I consider the impact of my goals on other people and society.

  There are people in society that will accept me. I know that there is a place for me in my community and that I can have a job and a home and a chance of a fresh start.

"If all the 5 R's of change - Remorse, Reasons, Responsibility, Rehabilitation and Reconciliation, are adopted by an individual, then change can be as permanent as if it was set in concrete." PM

I have learnt the following 2 important considerations:

1. The **5 R's of change** are each of equal importance, to secure lasting change.

2. People can be helped and encouraged, but not forced, to discover each of the **5 R's of change.** They must be ready.

Achieving **all 5** of these Mind-set Milestones guarantees them a more positive future in which they are not weighed down by guilt or shame from the past, not recalled back to prison and not convicted of new offences.

The previous chapter will clearly end and a completely new one will begin.

John's story, which follows, includes and demonstrates all the 5 R's.

As you read it, tick each one that you can spot:

Mind-set Milestone		Tick
R1	Remorse	
R2	Reasons	
R3	Responsibility	
R4	Rehabilitation	
R5	Reconciliation	

I was sentenced to 12 years' imprisonment for being involved in a conspiracy to supply drugs. This meant spending 6 years in prison and 6 years under supervision in the community.

I would like to share some background, not to justify what happened, but to explain a little.

I have always been a hard-working person. At the time of committing my offence I was working as a Construction Site Manager.

My partner and I married and had 2 beautiful children. We bought a modern car and our first home all within a very short space of time. As my expenses grew, it was clear that I had taken on too many financial commitments in this short space of time before my wife could return to work.

I got myself into a lot of debt and I tried to deal with it all by myself instead of discussing things with my family or seeking proper advice (which I now realise I should have done). I was working as many hours as possible in my job but was unable to get in front. I became fearful that we could lose our family home.

I confided in someone I thought was a friend who introduced me to a couple of people with a "business opportunity". They were in fact drug dealers. At first, I was shocked by this, but it is only years later that I can now admit to myself that I felt excitedly "naughty" and like a big man meeting these criminals.

Really my attitude was immature and irresponsible; looking back I am ashamed. With hindsight, it is clear that I should have said no straightaway, but in my desperation, I thought I saw a way to get out of the problems I had put my family in, and I got involved in the conspiracy.

Predictably, I was caught after just a couple of months. I put my hands up, accepted responsibility and pleaded guilty. My crime was totally out of character for me. This was my first offence. I apologised to my family and to the judge and I decided to face my prison sentence courageously and as a positive opportunity to change my outlook and my life.

Whilst in prison, I have committed to self-improvement, continued my work ethic (my CV still has an unbroken work history despite coming to prison) and tried my best to help other people in difficulty or distress.

I voluntarily completed an accredited Victim Awareness course called Sycamore Tree, as well as other personal development programmes. I met victims of crime and I learnt about the huge impact drugs have on society as a whole.

I became a drug and alcohol peer mentor where I saw first-hand the nightmarish struggles that drug addicts go through. I supported users through detox and helped them to understand their risks of relapse. I also made referrals and signposted them to healthcare and to mental health teams.

With formal training from the Samaritans, I trained as a prison "listener" and helped other people, whilst they were at their lowest points, (self-harming or contemplating suicide).

I am now a more understanding and humbler person. My intention is to build a productive life and put the past behind me. I really regret my previous criminal activity and I have learnt many lessons; I am a different person now.

I have just finished the custodial part of my prison sentence and I have been reunited with my family. We currently live in Stevenage; Hertfordshire and I am willing to commute or even relocate for the most suitable employment opportunity. I know that I can contribute to the community as a decent and law-abiding citizen again and I have every intention of doing so.

Hopefully you can see that the Mind-set Milestones, the 5 R's form part of "John's" journey and they are embedded throughout this person's experience.

John will be highly unlikely to ever re-offend again because he has instinctively and now consciously hit all the 5 Mind-set Milestones.

John also has 2 of the 3 most important elements for successful resettlement namely **Support from Family** and **Long-Term Accommodation.**

The other important element being **Stable Employment** was being worked towards at the time of writing the letter.

By way of an update, **"John"** is now working full-time again **(November 2019).**

**"Forgiveness and reconciliation are possible
in an enlightened society."** PM

The 5 R's of Change

Remorse, Reasons, Responsibility, Rehabilitation and Reconciliation

It takes a lot of courage to be honest and open about your offence(s). Fear and discomfort are normal and expected when you are doing something different for the first time, or which is outside your comfort zone.

Understanding how you ended up in prison and accepting what happened are both important if you want to start a new chapter in your life.

"Leave any feelings of shame or anger in the past; these will not help you in the future." PM

Provide a narrative (explain the story) and cover these 5 R's in an upfront and honest Personal Disclosure Statement and you will gain support and respect from prospective employers.

R1 Remorse	I am sorry for what I did and I do regret my crime(s).
R2 Reasons	I understand the background circumstances and my personal buttons/ triggers well enough that I can explain to others if necessary.
R3 Responsibility	I admit that it is my fault, I am not passing the blame and neither am I minimising the impact of my crime.
R4 Rehabilitation	I will not do it again; I have learnt lessons and changed.
R5 Reconciliation	I want to make up for what I did wrong and contribute.

Disclosure Information Capture Form

The following information will be required in order to create an effective Personal Disclosure Statement (PDS). It is helpful to gather this together and think about the points before building a PDS for yourself or for the person you are helping.

What was the crime?	Offence(s):
	Offence period (duration):
What was the punishment?	Date of Sentence/Remand:
	Sentence Type and Length:
What are the reasons? What is your story?	Reasons/ Background to Offence:
	Any mitigation put forward to court:
Do you accept responsibility for what went wrong?	Did you plead guilty?
	First offence or details of previous offences:
	Do you feel more responsible now than you did at the time of the offence?

Why won't it go wrong again in future?	Praiseworthy prison conduct e.g. Mentoring, Listeners and Support roles:
	Drug or alcohol rehabilitation courses and processes undertaken:
	Self-improvement courses completed and how they affected you:
	Victim Awareness course completed and any impact it had on you:
	Overall, how have you changed?
The Future:	Release date/ next parole:
	Current prison category:
	Release area or home area if no longer in prison:
	Who supports you?
	What are your goals?

'Disclosure Builder' - Creating Your Personal Disclosure Statement (PDS)

Following these 15 steps will lead to the creation of a sincere, professional and effective Personal Disclosure Statement.

Put some time and effort into creating this important statement.

If you invest 2 hours (or half the time if you have help) following these instructions, your PDS will:

- Truly reflect you and your story.

- Give you a feeling of hope for the future.

- Give you confidence to send it to employers.

- Make you feel proud of how much you have changed.

- Be interesting to read and will inspire employers to invite you for interview.

Your PDS is a formal document, to be laid out traditionally and similar to the examples included at the end of this chapter.

Step 1, Contact Details	Type your personal details in the top right corner. **If you are currently in prison -** then use your prison number, prison address and no telephone number or email address. **If you are at home, or shortly returning home -** then use your home address, home telephone number and an email address. There are many free services such as Outlook and Gmail that make it easy to set up an email address Ensure that your email address is clear and professional so that it makes a good impression such as firstname.lastname@serviceprovider.com.		*Name* *Address* *Postcode* *Telephone* *Email* *Date as Postmark*
Step 2, Greeting	Insert the following text on the left-hand side: *Re: Personal Disclosure Statement* *To whom it may concern* *Dear Sir/ Madam,*		

	Begin your letter with the most applicable of the following sentences:

Step 3, Introduction

For a single unspent conviction		*I am writing this letter to accompany my CV and to inform you that I have been convicted of a criminal offence.*
For multiple unspent convictions		*I am writing this letter to accompany my CV and to inform you that I have a criminal record.*
If you were aged 25 or younger at the time of offence and it was more than 10 years ago		*I am writing this letter to accompany my CV and to inform you that when I was _____ (insert age at conviction) years old I was convicted of a serious criminal offence (I am now aged _____ (insert current age).* **So when it is complete the sentence will be similar to:** *I am writing this letter to accompany my CV and to inform you that when I was 20 years old, I was convicted of a serious criminal offence (I am now aged 36).*

Step 4, Sentence Details

State the prison sentence and the crime(s), worded accurately in plain English.

You are obliged to disclose all your unspent convictions (see guidance on spent convictions pages 71 - 72).

SHORTCUT - Choose the wording from the examples below that most applies to your own sentence and edit it to reflect your personal circumstances:

For a determinate / straight sentence	*In _____ (insert the month and year that you were first remanded or sentenced) I was imprisoned for _____ (insert offence(s)). I received a sentence of _____ (insert sentence length), which means that I had/have (delete one) to spend _____ (insert halfway length) in prison followed by the same amount of time under supervision in the community.* **So, when complete the paragraph will be similar to:** *In March 2018, I was sentenced to 4 years' imprisonment for fraud and forgery. This means that I must spend 2 years in prison followed by 2 further years under supervision in the community.*

Step 4, Sentence Details, Continued	**For IPP sentences**	*In _____ (insert the month and year that you were first remanded or sentenced) I was imprisoned for_____ (insert crime(s)). I was sentenced to imprisonment for public protection (IPP) - this is a type of life sentence that was handed out at the discretion of the judges but has since been abolished. This sentence means that I must serve all the time, instead of half and that even then I can only be released after approval from the parole board. I was sentenced to serve a minimum tariff of _____ (insert tariff), but, like many other IPP sentenced prisoners, I have not yet been granted parole and am currently over tariff, having served _____ (insert actual time spent in prison) so far. I have a parole hearing in (insert the month and year of your next hearing) with a view to release back into society.* **So, when complete the paragraph will be similar to:** *In December 2005 I was imprisoned for GBH with intent (S18). I was sentenced to imprisonment for public protection (IPP) - this is a type of life sentence that was handed out at the discretion of the judges but has since been abolished. This sentence means that I must serve all the time, instead of half and that even then I can only be released after approval from the parole board. I was sentenced to serve a minimum tariff of 2 years and 4 months but, like many other IPP sentenced prisoners, I have not yet been granted parole and am currently over tariff, having served 10 years and 6 months.*
	For multiple unspent convictions	*I was sent to prison for _____ (insert all offence(s)). In _____ (insert the month and year that you were remanded or sentenced on your most recent prison sentence) I received a sentence of _____ (insert sentence length), which means that I had/have (delete one) to spend _____ (insert halfway length) in prison followed by the same amount of time under supervision in the community* **So, when complete the paragraph will be similar to:** *I was sent to prison for Assault, Burglary and Robbery. In 2015 I received a sentence of 8 years which means that I must spend 4 years in prison followed by the same amount of time under supervision in the community.*

Step 4, Sentence Details, Continued	**For life/ indeterminate sentences**	*In* _____ (insert year) *I was imprisoned for* _____ (insert crime(s)). *I received a discretionary/ mandatory* (delete one, if unsure leave out) *life sentence with a tariff (minimum time to serve) of* _____ (insert tariff). *I have served* _____ (insert actual time spent in prison) *so far and have a parole hearing in* (insert the month and year of your next parole hearing) *with a view to release back into society.* **So, when complete the paragraph will be similar to:** *In 1995 I was imprisoned for murder. I received a mandatory life sentence with a tariff (minimum time to serve) of 18 years. Having served 24 years so far, I have a parole hearing in January 2020 with a view to release back into society.*
	For EDS sentences	*In* _____ (insert the month and year that you were first remanded or sentenced) *I was imprisoned for* _____ (insert offence(s)). *I received an Extended Determinate Sentence of* _____ (insert sentence length), *which means that I must spend a minimum of* _____ (insert 2/3rd length) *in prison followed by a period of time under supervision in the community.* **So, when complete the paragraph will be similar to:** *In January 2018 I was imprisoned for GBH Section 18 and Criminal damage - recklessly endangering life. I received an Extended Determinate Sentence of 4 years, which means that I must spend a minimum of 32 months in prison followed by a period of time under supervision in the community.*
	Additional explanation - For certain charges it may be helpful to your reader to briefly explain what the terminology means. It is up to you whether you think this will help in your case. Read these simple explanations below and if necessary, add an explanation after you state your offence(s).	
	GBH - S20 means unintentionally causing injury to someone.	
	GBH - S18 means deliberately causing serious injury to someone.	
	Fraud by false representation means telling lies for personal gain.	
	Manslaughter means that I was responsible for the accidental death of another person.	

Step 4, Sentence Details, continued	*Conspiracy means being involved in plotting and planning with other people to do an illegal act.*
	Converting criminal property means trying to legitimise illegal money; similar to money laundering.
	Joint-enterprise means that I wasn't the person who actually committed the crime but by being there I was considered to be an accomplice.
	Being part of a conspiracy meant that I was working with other people to distribute drugs. I hadn't really thought of these wider implications before.

"Creating an honest disclosure document is tough because it takes a lot of soul searching and honesty. The process really pays off though, just reflecting on lessons learnt and being able to explain to others makes a big difference. If you follow the clear structure in the book you can't go wrong." JF

Next, we will cover the 5 R's of Change - Remorse, Reasons, Responsibility, Rehabilitation and Reconciliation (Read the guidance on pages 80-83).

Step 5, R1 - Remorse	**Remorse**	Leave a line space and begin the introduction to your personal story. This sentence demonstrates your **remorse**; that you regret what happened. Remorse is not a fiction story; if you don't genuinely feel remorseful, please don't pretend, this book is not for you!
	If the crime was something that you did	*I deeply regret my crime and I am writing this personal statement to explain where I went wrong and the lessons I have learnt.*
	If it was a set of circumstances that happened	*I would like to share some background, not to justify what happened, but to explain a little. I deeply regret my offence which arose because...*
	If you committed multiple crimes over a long period of time	*I feel that it is important that I share some background, not to in anyway justify what I did, but because I understand so much more about my past than before.*

"I was more confident after following this guide. I felt better about my situation and that I could show my good side and not just my past offences to an employer. I just left my job interview and the employer said to me 'You were so honest and remorseful in your disclosure letter and it was so well written that I feel like I definitely should give you a chance.' It could not have gone any better, thanks to this guide." PT

Reasons

Reasons are different from excuses. They show that, with hindsight, you have a better understanding of what took place and that you are unlikely to make the same mistakes again. They also help prospective employers to understand what happened.

Think back to any mitigation that your barrister put before the judge, this may be an appropriate time to mention it again. This part of your PDS is your chance to put across your side of the story, **not to contradict what has previously been reported as fact**, but to explain why you made the decisions you did and why you would do things differently now.

Consider what was reported in newspapers and online. Nowadays, all employees search Google and Social Media, such as Facebook, before making hiring decisions and often before even deciding who to interview. If your PDS does contradict what has been reported by reputable news channels, people will assume that you are in denial or trying to pull the wool over their eyes; it is better to leave out points of disagreement and stick to your honest perspective.

Each story is personal to you and it is for you to explain your story; it may be helpful however to have a chat with someone who is able to help you clarify your thoughts.

The examples below will give you some ideas about how you could put your own story into words.

I had just received a phone call to tell me that my Grandfather had sadly died. I rushed to get home to my family, too fast and went through a traffic light that had just changed to red. I caused a collision in which a lady got hurt. Fortunately, the lady has made a full recovery, but I am truly sorry for causing this accident.

I struggled for many years with an alcohol addiction. I was working but my car became unreliable, I was unable to get to work and I lost my job. I then became depressed and relapsed into drinking again and ultimately lost my flat too. It really was that stereotypically awful spiral that we hear about with alcoholism. This time, it was happening to me, I did experience homelessness. I lived in my car for two months, which was freezing and felt that I had nothing to lose. I do regret what I did, and I am very sorry.

"I have used my time in prison to improve myself and become better; my disclosure statement was my chance to explain that." AC

I have come to a clear understanding of where I went wrong, it started when I was 15 years old and in year 10, I struggled to fit in at school and was labelled as a problem child. I was kicked out of school and left to fend for myself with no further support. I ended up living 'street life' and joined a group of older men. At the time I felt accepted and wanted; with hindsight I know that they influenced me and used me. I was sucked into a gang culture that made crime feel like an adventure. I know that being a 'road man' appeared to be glamorous and that rap music made it seem cool, but with an adult's maturity I can see how dangerous and negative such a life can be.

I was a very active father to two young children when my partner unexpectedly fell pregnant with our third child. We were very happy at the news, but inside I also began to worry about how I would provide. I had not long gained my formal plumbing qualifications and I was finding my feet working full time in my new job. When my new baby son was born, I was in awe of him and of my partner. Our relationship was good, and our family was complete. I knew that my son needed so many things and I was as stretched as I could be in work. In a moment of weakness, I discussed my fears and worries with some associates I knew. They told me about how I could make money by 'working' with them. I should have said no and walked away but I gave in to the temptation to ignore the law to make money.

My wife and I had been married for more than 10 years and had two lovely children. Unfortunately, we entered a very difficult stage of our marriage when my wife began a relationship with another man. She kept telling me that she would break it off but never did and continued to string me along. I became clinically depressed and suffered from anxiety and insomnia. Additionally, the medication I was prescribed resulted in me suffering from blackouts and worsening mental health. My wife became progressively more controlling, manipulative and aggressive and our arguments escalated, she often threatened to commit suicide. I realise now that this pattern of behaviour is called coercive-control. I wanted to leave but she wouldn't let me leave and continued to see this other man. One evening, I was not being compliant, and she was not pleased with me, I wasn't behaving as she wanted, and she became violent towards me. She was hitting me and in shock and fear I overreacted and grabbed her around the neck. I had a blackout and awoke to find her unconscious on the floor. I called an ambulance and the police. My wife sadly died in hospital.

"Without this system I would not have known where to start and been able to produce a clear disclosure statement. The templates are helpful and very professional so now there is nothing to stop me getting back into work!" PJ

92

Responsibility

I recommend that you use different wording depending on whether you pleaded guilty or not guilty and if not guilty, whether you are maintaining your innocence.

Accepting responsibility means that you:

- Admit your mistakes.
- Have learnt from them.
- Are in control of your decisions and actions.
- Are unlikely to make those same mistakes or bad decisions in future.

There is usually some element that you can and should accept responsibility for, even if you can't accept responsibility for the entire sequence of events.

Denial of any responsibility whatsoever speaks volumes about taking ownership of events and whether you have any control over whether you break the law again in future.

Bear in mind that it is hard to show responsibility, or that you have changed when maintaining innocence. The general public are sadly misinformed and believe that criminal trials are based solely on evidence.

"Most people are highly sceptical about alleged miscarriages of justices and believe that maintaining innocence is the same as refusing to take responsibility." PM

Most employers and the wider population have very little experience (or accurate opinions) of the Criminal Justice System and treat guilty convictions as irrefutable facts.

It is also in your best interests to discover where you went wrong, where mistakes were made and what you could have done better. This will help to ensure that you do not return to prison.

SHORTCUT - Choose the wording from the examples below depending on whether you pleaded:

a) Guilty.

b) Not-guilty and now accept responsibility.

c) Not-guilty and are maintaining your innocence.

Step 7, R3 - Responsibility, Continued	**If you pleaded GUILTY**	**Begin with the following sentence:** *I accepted responsibility by pleading guilty.*
	and **If this was your first offence use one of these paragraphs**	*My crime was completely out of character for me. I have never broken the law before and I am embarrassed by my behaviour.*
		Committing any crime is completely out of character for me. This was my first offence of any kind. I am a mature person with a family myself and a strong work ethic.
		My crime was completely out of character for me. This was my first offence. I am actually a mature person with a strong work ethic, and I am ashamed of my past actions.
		This was my first ever offence and this will definitely be my last because I do not see myself as a criminal at all, in fact this chapter of my life has been completely out of character.
		I have never been in trouble with the police before and certainly never been to prison so getting caught and being charged was a massive wake up call to me. To maintain my personal integrity and salvage any element of decency, I had to put my hands up and admit to my crime.
		This was my first offence. I am ashamed of what I did and I would like to apologise to my victim(s). I am usually a hard-working person myself and I can only imagine how I would feel if it happened to me. I would be angry and upset and very sad at the world. The thought that I created these feelings and this harm in other people spurs me on to want to change.
	If this was not your first offence but it was your first prison sentence	*My crime was completely out of character for me. I have never been to prison before. I am a considerate and respectable person, with a strong work ethic and I am ashamed of my past actions.*
	If you have been to prison before	*I am now a much more mature person with a strong work ethic, and I am ashamed of my past actions.*

Step 7, R3 - Responsibility, Continued	**If you pleaded NOT GUILTY and you now accept responsibility, use one of these sentences**	*I do accept full responsibility for what I did, and I am very sorry.*
		I do accept full responsibility, and I am ashamed of my past actions.
		I accept full responsibility for my reckless behaviour and when I came to prison, I knew that I needed to change.
		I do accept full responsibility, I am now a more mature, considerate and respectable person and I am ashamed of what I did.
		I take full responsibility for my offences; since coming to prison I have done a lot of soul-searching and I made a series of very personal and deliberate decisions to turn my life around.
	If you pleaded NOT GUILTY and continue to maintain your innocence, give an explanation	**Begin with the following sentence:** *I am maintaining innocence of my crime.* **Then explain the situation and provide any information that supports your innocence.** Read the examples below to give you an idea of how to put your circumstances into words.
	I did not profit in any way from this 'crime' as evidenced by the fact that I had no proceeds of crime/ confiscation proceedings.	
	I admit that I should have ceased trading prior to my bankruptcy but that I was guilty of the civil breach known as Insolvent Trading rather than the crime of Fraudulent Trading.	
	My case is currently being investigated by the Criminal Cases Review Commission (CCRC) because there were a number of injustices and inaccuracies during my trial.	
	It was stated by the judge that this was a circumstantial case, the jury could not agree unanimously, and two people believed me to be innocent, but the judge accepted a majority verdict as being enough to convict me.	

Step 7, R3 - Responsibility, Continued	*After a lengthy and gruelling trial, my barrister read out a statement saying that "no well-directed jury could find me guilty of any offence, that there is no case against me and no evidence whatsoever of any wrongdoing". (Please see supporting document attached). The jury did however return a guilty verdict and I was sent to prison.*
	I was sentenced under 'Joint Enterprise' (which is now interpreted very differently by judges). I was with a former friend when he got into an argument with another man, we both knew. To my complete shock my friend had a knife and stabbed the man in the leg. I didn't know how serious the injury was at the time, but the victim sadly died. I was not the person who committed this violent crime, I did not encourage it and I didn't know about it until it was too late.

"I pleaded not guilty because I did not believe that I was guilty of the charges as suggested. I was however guilty of irresponsible and dangerous behaviour that led me to this point. I had to accept responsibility otherwise I knew that I could never change for the better. I had to take a long look at myself and get to the point where I said, 'It's my fault' only then could take control of my future." RA

Step 8, R4 - Rehabilitation	**Rehabilitation**	This means explaining how you have changed for the better and demonstrably reduced your risk of re-offending.
		It may include how you understand and now avoid your triggers, how you have improved your thinking and behaviour, the courses that you have completed and what will stop you committing crime in future.
		Use wording similar to one or two of the following examples which will give you an idea of what your own journey of rehabilitation may have included.
	I completed a victim awareness course, put myself in other people's shoes and grew in empathy and understanding.	
	I have worked hard to completely detox from drugs, I am no longer an addict and I am fully rehabilitated from substance abuse.	
	Before I came to prison, I broke my drug addiction and one thing I am proud of is that I have been drug free for more than 2 years.	
	The first time I was offered counselling was when I came to prison. I accepted this help and I have now come to terms with my past.	
	I completed a victim awareness course which made me face up to my actions and how they had a big impact on my victim and the wider community.	

I am worried about my children and I phone them every day. I have promised them that I will never coming back to prison or commit crime ever again.

I have held 3 different and highly trusted catering roles in prison; drawing on my previous catering experience and developing my skills further.

This was a unique set of circumstances which could never reoccur. I had never been violent prior to meeting this man and I am truly sorry for what I did.

I have taken a long hard look at myself and reminded myself constantly that I was here because of my own decisions. I have been inspired to change for the better.

I have arranged to attend driving awareness courses and tell my story to warn other people of the dangers of phones and other distractions whilst driving.

I sought help for my addiction and have now recovered. I no longer gamble. I have joined Gamblers Anonymous who provided me with help to beat my addiction.

I have become a better person in prison, I am more considerate of others, I have developed better communication skills and I choose my associates more carefully.

I have gained educational qualifications and yes, I am now even doing a degree! That is something that would have been unthinkable for me a few years ago.

I have embraced the concept of self-improvement and changed my thinking and behaviour. I have completed work related courses and gained many qualifications.

I have completely turned my life around. I have completed a number of accredited self- development courses and I have broken ties with undesirable past associates.

I sought help for my addiction; I am now clean of drugs. I have subsequently studied relapse prevention so that I know what warning signs to look out for and so I can help other people.

I have seen first-hand the problems that drug supply creates and how it messes people up and destroys lives. I really regret my involvement in the 'disease' that I now realise that drugs are.

I have completed numerous psychological courses, interventions, drug and alcohol and victim awareness courses. I know first-hand that crime and revenge creates a never-ending 'ripple effect' into society.

I have proven worthy of trust and responsibility by leaving the open prison, going to work and returning on time each day. I have been praised by my employer for how hard I have worked and for my reliability.

I wanted to improve myself and so I completed several progressive courses in prison which have helped me to gain vocational qualifications and I am beginning to reset positive goals for the future.

I have completely turned my life around. I have committed to self-improvement, both physically and mentally. I consistently pass all drug tests; I have no interest in drugs and no longer even smoke.

I committed to personal growth and self-development. I have self-studied and matured, gaining numerous qualifications from GCSEs to my crowning achievement - BA (Hons) Humanities with Philosophy.

I completed several personal development programmes which helped me to learn about managing conflict, improve my communication skills and self-esteem and to plan for more positive, community-based living.

I completed a very inspiring course called Building Better Relationships which has helped me a great deal to build relationships with both my birth-mother and my step-mother as well as with other family members.

I voluntarily completed an accredited Victim Awareness course called Sycamore Tree and other personal development programmes. I met victims of crime and this gave me profound insights into the harm of crime.

I completed 5 years of therapy in a secure therapeutic community, this helped me to come to terms with my traumatic past, to deal with my thoughts and emotions and to communicate and manage relationships better.

I took part in a life changing course called Alternative to Violence Project (AVP). I gained a certificate in understanding and handling conflict. I related so much to the course that I mentored and helped other people too.

I completed courses called 'Positive Lifestyles' and 'Personal and Social Development' which gave me a framework to improve my thinking. I also learnt about the long-term effects of both crime and drug supply on society.

It has been a struggle, but I have been drug free for a number of years. I completed a 'psychosocial workbook' in which I logged my determination to change, my goals for the future and I studied urges, triggers and relapse-prevention.

I have completed several personal development courses which have helped me to understand myself and to consider the long-term effects of my actions better; basically, my thinking and my attitude have improved tremendously.

When I came to prison, I was very shocked and dejected - wracked by guilt and I regretted getting involved with the people I did. I looked in the mirror and decided to take personal responsibility for my life and to change for the better.

Before I came to prison, I completed my electrical qualifications, so that I would have a stable future. It was a shock coming to prison and losing so many years of my life. I knew however that I had to get through it and use the time to improve.

I secured a place on a carpentry course which gave me a purpose for six months and led to me gaining formal qualifications. This new focus means that I can now gain legitimate employment and stay away from criminals and criminal activities.

Drug use and dealing has brought nothing but pain and loss. I now understand the wider implications on society and how the harm spreads out into our communities. I am very sorry for my involvement and I am determined to change.

Whilst in prison, I have always worked or studied to improve myself. I gained Numeracy (Maths) and Literacy (English) Level 2 qualifications which are equivalent to good GCSE passes; I also completed several vocational courses which will help me in employment after my release.

I have gained additional vocational skills in prison and I have become a fully qualified bricklayer. I have even shown other people how to build fireplaces, garden walls, cavity walls, piers and window frames. I am looking forward to following my clearly defined career pathway when I am released.

When I came to prison, I completed a Victim Awareness course called 'The Forgiveness Project'. I learnt a lot from this, particularly about improving relationships and understanding other people. After completing this to a high standard I became a mentor and helped other students to graduate.

I have completed several personal development courses which have made a big difference to my outlook on life and my plans. The one that really stands out for me was called Plan B Mindfulness; on this course I learned about long term benefits of better decision making and keeping calm.

This was a unique set of circumstances which could never reoccur. I have subsequently completed many personal development courses to enable me to understand other people better, to channel my emotions and to come to terms with my past. I am a different person now; I regret what happened every day.

I completed a comprehensive work programme called Addressing Alcohol Related Offending (AARO). This helped me to understand why I drank and why drinking changed my behaviour. Alcohol magnifies emotions and it does increase the likelihood of criminal behaviour, hence why I no longer drink at all.

I have completed a victim awareness course and learnt about the terrible affects that drug supply has on individual users and on society. It was only after completing this course that I realised just how many victims are created and how many crimes are driven by a user's desperation to get money for their drugs.

In the 12 years I have served, I have also worked through 3 years of therapy in which I learnt and changed a lot. I now understand where my patterns of behaviour originated and my intense need not to be 'disrespected' as I saw it then. I do accept responsibility for the angry young man that I was back then.

In the 6 years I have been away from my family I have missed so much. Many milestones in my children's lives have been and gone. I know that drug supply creates victims and I also made my own family into victims. Not a day has gone past that I do not feel remorse for what I did. I will never commit crime again.

Since coming to prison, I have completely changed my mind-set and sorted my head out. I have completed many courses and I have also had the courage to ask for help both personally and for my wife. Now my wife is more supported, and I know that things will be so much better this time when I am home again.

Being in prison has been very traumatic for my family, due to my recklessness they have lost the family home and had to move away from family and friends. My teenage daughter has fallen into the grips of anorexia as a result of me being away. I will never commit crime and cause so much distress to my family in future.

I am ashamed. I now realise how stupid my behaviour was and how serious the consequences of my actions were. Previously I had always been there for my wife and children but now my wife must manage everything by herself and my children are suffering without me being there. Crimes such as mine can have far reaching impacts into society too. I know that I needed to mature and change.

I have completed many personal development courses and engaged wholeheartedly with these, frequently being praised for my commitment. I waited years to access a 6-month intensive programme called "self-change" and I completed it to a high standard. My thinking is different now. I have positive goals for the future and a better understanding of the building blocks of a positive life.

When I came to prison I was fortunate to have been given counselling and therapy which helped me to come to terms with my traumatic past, to deal with my thoughts and emotions, to communicate and manage relationships better and to reflect on and understand the harm that I had caused to individual people as well as society. I am truly very sorry for what I did, and I am crime-free for good.

I spent 7 years in therapy which was life changing for me. I learnt to express myself and explain things better and began to understand what drove me. Until I came to prison, I had neither the ability nor the courage to talk through my experiences. I spent most of my life not being able to trust people, I would ruin relationships myself, not believing that I could be worthy of authentic love and affection.

When I came to prison and I had to leave my two young children and my wife, I was devastated. My baby son was only 6 weeks old at the time. I was in a bad way mentally and emotionally for several months, but I knew that I had to stop feeling sorry for myself. I decided to learn from my mistakes, and I began to plan for a positive and legal future. I completed Victim Awareness and Understanding Motivations courses to a high standard, and I will never break the law again.

I deserved to come to prison for what I did but I knew that it would be possible to change my behaviour and get help for my drinking. I completed a range of courses including Thinking Skills, 12 Step Programme, Alcohol Dependency, Victim Awareness and others, all of which changed me and my attitude from the inside. I grew and developed so much that I studied further and gained a Level 4 DIPLOMA in Drug, Solvent and Alcohol Abuse Counselling issued. I even have letters after my name now - S.A.C.Dip and I am able to help people whose lives have been affected by drugs, alcohol, solvents and violence.

"Disclosure Builder made producing a Disclosure Statement easy. I followed the instructions and have now gained an apprenticeship." KG

Step 8, R4 - Rehabilitation, Continued		*In order to demonstrate how genuinely sorry I was, I met the victims of my crime through a Restorative Justice Service. I admire them so much for coming to see me; I can only imagine how they must have been feeling. They handed me a letter from their young son and in it he asked me never to do it again and I was moved to tears. This wasn't me; I am a good-hearted person who cares. When I saw and understood first-hand what drug addiction had pushed me to do and had become acceptable to me, I was raging with myself. The couple were so compassionate to me, I was shocked. They invited me to visit for coffee in the future. I am inspired to live a good life for them and truly grateful for their understanding and forgiveness.*
		I engaged wholeheartedly with a self-change programme called 'Kaizen' which taught me anger management and mindfulness techniques as well as how to stay clean of drugs and alcohol. This really helped me to turn my life around and I learnt so much; the person who graduated was not the same person who enrolled on the course. I feel so good and positive now; I discovered the power of self-talk and positive thinking, considering consequences, managing emotions, choosing personal associations carefully and other life skills that I can use. After I completed the Kaizen, my family were invited to attend the awards day. I am so pleased that they saw how much I have progressed. They have agreed to give me a second chance and I will not let myself or my family down again.

"I am more confident going forward; I feel like explaining my story has helped me to understand where I went wrong and draw a line under my past." JG

Step 9, R5 - Reconciliation	**Reconciliation**	This means explaining the positive contributions you have made; giving back to communities and society.
		It is a good opportunity to explain who you have helped and how you have helped them.
		Mention those things that you are most proud of including any personal insights or exemplary conduct whilst in prison.
	Begin with one of these introductory sentences...	*I had to see prison as a turning point in my attitude and my life.*
		I completed my community service wholeheartedly and went the extra mile, doing even more than was expected of me...
		Whilst in prison, I have always worked, studied to improve myself and helped other people via the following initiatives:

Step 9, R5 - Reconciliation, Continued	**Introductory sentences - continued**	*I worked all the time during my prison sentence and did a great deal of studying to improve myself. I also helped the prison community.*
		Although I am ashamed of where I ended up, I decided to see my sentence as a positive time. I committed to work, self- improvement and contributing to help other people.
		Whilst in prison, I am proud to have maintained my unbroken work ethic; I have no employment gaps in my CV, I kept my existing skills up to date and even gained some new ones. I also volunteered because I wanted to help.
		I looked around at the overwhelming and oppressive environment and the vulnerable people that I saw and decided to contribute and help other people. I dedicated my time to several worthwhile initiatives.
	Then continue with wording similar to one or two of the examples	The following examples will remind you of the kind of things that you may have achieved during your time in prison or whilst doing community work.
	I mentored and helped young men to steer away from gangs and violence.	
	I worked as a Charity Advisor, liaising between prisoners and a housing charity.	
	I saved a man's life by performing CPR for several minutes until the paramedics arrived and was highly commended.	
	I voluntarily helped and supported many people in the gym and with personal coaching to help them to live healthier lives.	
	I have held a number of trusted positions where I have always proved worthy of the trust placed in me. Please see my CV for further details.	
	I served as a Health and Wellbeing Champion and provided emergency health care assistance and personal support to vulnerable people.	

Step 9, R5 - Reconciliation, Continued	*I became an Information, Advice and Guidance provider in prison also known as an "Insider". I helped and supported many desperate people.*
	I speak sign language, so I helped deaf people to communicate regarding urgent personal matters as a key member of the equalities department.
	I served as segregation orderly where I worked alongside officers to help and support isolated prisoners who were very often in difficulty and distress.
	I have worked hard and gained many vocational skills and qualifications, please see my CV for full detail of these. I do have a demonstrable work ethic.
	I gained a 'Restorative Approaches' certificate in communication, conflict management and mediation. With my new-found skills I prevented several arguments escalating into violence.
	I became a Prince's Trust Mentor and guided young people away from crime and gangs and instead help them to educate themselves and become employed.
	I completed Applied Suicide Intervention Skills Training (ASIST) and became able to help people who were struggling to cope with the impact of imprisonment.
	Whilst attending a 6-month personal development programme, I helped many other prisoners who struggled to express themselves fully or had difficulties with reading and writing.
	I qualified in Health and Social Care Awareness which enabled me to support elderly prisoners. I have found that by taking the focus off myself I can be of most value to others in need.
	I became an Education Orderly, signposting people on to courses that would help them to progress. I also informally helped less articulate people to word letters to family and professional contacts.
	I facilitated Business Enterprise classes in which I shared my experiences with people who have their own small business ideas, such as being self-employed tradespeople, or starting online ventures, upon release.
	With extra training I became an Equalities Coordinator and developed procedures with Officers, Prisoners and Civilian Staff to ensure that all nine protected characteristics of the Equalities Act were complied with.
	I gained numerous positive comments from prison staff for my contributions to the prison community and for those times where I helped new people arriving into prison in my highly trusted role as Reception Orderly.

I trained and qualified with the Samaritans. I became a prison "listener" and supported other people, whilst they were at their lowest points, (self-harming or contemplating suicide). I served in this voluntary role for 10 years.

I have guided and supported many people to progress personally; I now speak to small groups and larger audiences (my last presentation was to 150 people) about the power of positive change and the value of education.

I have used my skills to improve the surroundings for others, undertaking cleaning, cooking and maintenance tasks, completing all of these to a high standard (even winning an award for fully refurbishing a prison wing).

I set up a drug mentoring programme which helped drug addicts to detox from drugs and to understand their risks of relapse. I met with Ministry of Justice dignitaries who were interested in the good work I was doing.

I was a representative for over 50s. I identified numerous problems faced by the growing elderly population in prison and develop initiatives with management to improve conditions, communications and quality of life.

I served as a functional skills peer-mentor. This is a type of classroom assistant who offers a high level of personal, one to one support to people who are struggling or who have fears around classrooms and education.

After studying to gain relevant qualifications I became a drugs and alcohol Peer Supporter who provided a high level of guidance, direction and personal attention to people who were often in distress or coping with mental health challenges.

I created and facilitated my own courses which educated people of the risks of New Psychoactive Substances (NPS) and general drug use. I personally taught around 500 people in my classes and I am proud to have made such a difference to the lives of so many people.

I developed a love of art and the ability to inspire other people. I am now a Koestler award winning and published artist having featured in Matthew Meadows book "Inside Art". I used my talent and skills with people to teach therapeutic art classes to other prisoners.

I served on the Prison Council and helped to improve relationships between prisoners and staff. I regularly met with the Governor and I personally helped to implement several 'Rehabilitative Culture' initiatives designed to reduce reoffending and assist in the resettlement of ex-offenders.

Whilst serving my sentence I have proven worthy of trust and worked in support roles including that of visitor centre orderly. In this important position I was able to prepare the visits hall and make the distressing experience of visiting someone in prison easier for first time visitors.

I served as a Health and Wellbeing Champion and personally contributed to helping a man stop self-harming. I continued to mentor this person until he was released. I also gained additional qualifications and provided emergency health care assistance and personal support to vulnerable people.

I joined a "Buddy Action Team" which is a voluntary project to help others in partnership with the healthcare department. I assisted and cared for people who, through ill-health or infirmity, required assistance with day to day activities, such as washing, dressing, laundry, library or basic mobility.

With extra training and guidance, I served as a Violence Reduction/ Safer Custody representative. I was a mediator between officers and prisoners and often between prisoners themselves. In my role I am proud to have prevented many serious incidents and stopped disagreements from escalating into violence.

I helped people to complete courses and gain qualifications. I inspired people to use their time to achieve something worthwhile instead. I was personally responsible for helping people to enrol on and complete scores of distance learning courses which can have long term positive impacts on their future lives.

I qualified as a Yoga teacher (Level 4). Whilst in prison, I established my own classes which were very well attended by both residents and staff. My classes help people to improve their physical wellbeing and to find balance and peace. I have written a 10-week Yoga and Mindfulness course so that I can reach more people.

I served as a lead facilitator for a charity project called "Keep Out". I worked with deprived young people who were identified as being at high risk of engaging in crime and I discouraged them from crime by explaining the awful consequences, how to avoid negative peer pressure and how to set goals for a crime-free life.

As an experienced first-aider I recognised the symptoms of a man who was having a heart attack. He had basically died but I gave him CPR and chest compressions. It was wonderful when he started to breathe again and when the emergency nurse came, she told me that I had saved his life. He recently wrote to thank me.

I served as a Rehabilitative Culture representative. This is a national awarding body which is accredited by the Ministry of Justice and which encourages and recognises custodial establishments that support positive change. I worked hard in this post and developed efficient processes and meaningful relationships.

I like helping other people and I used my time in prison to contribute to the community and support others. I had a room-mate who had never learnt to read so over a period of several months I taught him the basics. It is such a simple thing that we all take for granted but to him it was life changing. I feel proud to know that he learnt how to read and reply to letters from his family.

I have served other people in prison and learnt humility. I have taught other people to read, following the system created by a very positive charity called the Shannon Trust. I went through training with them to be able to help other people in this manner and it is rewarding teaching adults to read. They never knew what they were missing out on or what an essential life skill it was, until they discover what all these letters and words mean!

I trained as a volunteer with Shannon Trust charity and taught people to read. I had always taken reading for granted but it really opened my eyes to how difficult it must have been for some people to go through their life unable to read. I committed to this and helped people to write letters home to their children and families. The look of joy and happiness when they were able, with my help, to read the replies from their children spoke volumes.

I volunteered in a range of roles to help people in a worse position than myself; I became a Listener, this is a support service provided by the Samaritans to help people in distress and struggling to cope with a wide range of problems including mental illness, despair, self-harming or having suicidal thoughts. I embraced the opportunity to train with such a well-respected organisation as the Samaritans and I volunteered with them for more than 10 years, helping and supporting numerous people in that time.

I stopped a man from committing suicide; he had wrapped a ligature around his neck and was about to jump off a railing to hang himself. I grabbed him just in time and talked him round. I helped him to realise that he still has a future; no one knows the possibilities that lie ahead. I was commended for my actions. I have heard from a third party since that he has come to terms with his prison sentence and is doing much better now. I do take some comfort and pride from having saved someone life. Perhaps there was a bigger reason for me being in prison.

I used my skills and qualifications to help other people in remedial gym sessions. These were special classes and coaching sessions for people who have been physically injured in car accidents, recovering from operations or addiction, or struggling to retain their independence during old age. I showed patience and compassion and received references for my contributions to helping others. I became a GP Referral Fitness Instructor which is a prestigious accolade in recognition of the consistent results which I helped my "clients" to achieve.

Step 9, R5 - Reconciliation, Continued	*I served as a 'Veterans in Custody' support representative. I was the first point of contact for new arrivals in to a secure residential establishment. I liaised between veterans and service charities including Soldier, Sailor, Airforce Families Association (SSAFA) and Care after Combat (CAC). I conducted initial interviews, provided practical help (such as writing letter and completing forms), organised clothing parcels and signposted to other helpful organisations. I used my communication, mentoring and organisational skills to improve the wellbeing of veterans struggling both in prison and with earlier trauma they experienced.*
	I volunteered to become a Wing Wellbeing Representative, this was a new idea that I came up with. I gave up my own time to help vulnerable and distressed people. There was one young lad I met who was a serial self-harmer, I had many conversations with him and spent a lot of time with him. He had no family support and was facing a long sentence; he felt that he had no future. I tried to give him support and encouragement. I helped him plan goals for a positive life after release. He did take strength from our friendship. When I last saw him, he hadn't self-harmed for 9 months which was a big milestone for him. I got a letter from him a few days ago and he has now hit 12 months without any self-harm. This is a big difference for someone who was self-harming most days. I take comfort and feel a little pride that I have been able to make a difference to others. I do feel like I am putting some good back where there had been harm from my reckless behaviour before.

Step 10, Summary	If you genuinely regret your crime, then state again that you do and that you have had time for self-reflection and personal growth. **Begin with the following sentence:** *I very much regret my crime and I have learnt many lessons, I am a different person now.*	
	And then compose a similar sentence to one of these examples	*The time I have had for self-reflection has not been wasted and I still have much to offer to the employer who gives me an opportunity to work for them.*
		Although my conviction will never be spent, the mind-set which created it has been spent. I have much to offer to the employer who gives me an opportunity to work for them.
		I have had a lot of time for self-reflection and personal development; I am a more positive person, in a better place mentally and physically than when I committed my offence. I am determined to start a new chapter in my life, free of crime and contributing to society.

Step 10, Summary Continued	**Examples continued**	*I have worked throughout my prison sentence and used my time to gain even more work skills. I am reaching out to you to respectfully request that you put my criminal convictions in the past and take me at face value. I am, and have always been, a hardworking family-orientated person and I have been loyal to every employer I have worked for.*
		I have matured and changed a lot since I selfishly committed my crimes. I know that people who leave prison without qualifications get drawn back into the streets, 'cuddled back' because it is where they feel accepted; they need to fill their time with something and earn money. I don't want this so I have turned my back on that life and gained many qualifications and skills so that I can be legally employed upon release from prison and turn my life around.
Step 11, Workplace	If your conviction(s) did not happen in the workplace, then **Insert the following sentence:** *My conviction would not create a risk of any problems in the workplace; in fact, employment is a proven stabilising factor which would form the solid foundation of my future life.* If your conviction(s) did happen in a previous workplace or in connection with a previous job, then disregard this sentence and move on to Step 12.	

"I really did not want to face up to disclosure, but eventually I realised that it was an important part of me moving to the next stage of my life. After writing my story down it has helped me to get two job interviews in two weeks!" RH

Step 12, Support network	Explain your **support network** and any **goals** for the future.	You can use wording similar to these examples below (taken from multiple PDSs): **Begin with the following sentence:** *I intend to build a productive life and put the past behind me.*
	Continue with wording which is appropriate to your circumstances like these examples	*I am fortunate to have support from my family and law-abiding friends.*
		I have an ambition to be a family man with a partner and children as well as build a career around the gym and fitness industry.
		I am grateful to my partner who has steadfastly continued to believe in me, and I will never let her or my children down again.

Step 12, Support network, Continued	**More examples of Support Network and future goals**	*I am fortunate to have help and encouragement from my mum, as well as a support network of friends and strong ties to my faith community.*
		I have a goal to gain permanent employment and live a stable life where I can be there for my family the way that they have been there for me.
		I have nieces and nephews and one day I want to be a parent myself. I want to be there to watch them grow up and to be actively involved in their lives.
		I have broken all ties with past criminal associates and have formed a support network of family and friends who all live decent, law-abiding lives.
		I am looking forward to being reunited with my partner and our children. After all these years I do still have the love and support of my partner and we have plans to get married after my release.
		Since those early years, I have grown and matured a lot. With children of my own and a long-term partner, I am more determined than ever to be a positive role model and to live a crime free life.
		I am fortunate to have a stable home life and a supportive family. My wife and I have been married for 38 years and I am looking forward to being re-united with our children and grandchildren.
		I gained a clear vision for my future which is to help those young people who are most at risk of engaging in crime to change direction before it is too late. My mission is to catch those young people before they are excluded from school or before they look to gangs as their family.
		I reconnected with a wonderful person who I knew from school and she is now my partner. She is a professionally qualified accountant and has been a stabilising influence in my life. I am deeply committed to living a crime-free life for her, for my young son, for myself and for society.
		I am determined to re-enter the workplace and prove myself. I am reaching out to you to respectfully request that you put my criminal convictions in the past and take me at face value. I am, and have always been, a hardworking family-orientated person and I have been loyal to every employer I have worked for.

Step 13, Release and Resettlement Details	Now we will explain to the reader where you are in terms of your prison sentence.
	
	Give details of:
	
	a) Whether you have completed community orders or been released from prison.
	
	b) If you are still in prison, whether you are in open conditions.
	
	c) Relevant dates, including:
	
	    i) Release date (if not already released).
	
	    ii) Eligibility date for training placement (usually last 18 months).
	
	    iii) Eligibility date to work full-time in the community (usually last 12 months).
	
	d) Home area.
	
	Use wording similar to these examples and according to your personal circumstances

I have completed the custodial time required and I am no longer in prison.
I completed the community service that I was ordered to do, and I am available for full-time employment.
I served my prison sentence and now live in Swindon; I am willing to travel for work and will be loyal, committed and dedicated.
I have a parole hearing in October 2019 with a view to release back into society. I will live in Northampton, near my family upon release.
I will be released in January 2020. I have taken the responsible decision to start the new chapter in my life in a new area, Tunbridge Wells, Kent.
I will be released in May 2019 to my home area of Leicester on a curfew tag which simply means that I must be in my house between 7pm - 7am.
I have completed the custodial time that I had to serve, and I am no longer in prison. I am subject to a Home Detention Curfew (HDC) until May 2020 which simply means that I must be in my house between 7pm - 7am.
I will be released in June 2020 to my home area of Colchester, Essex. In the meantime, because I have proven myself worthy of trust and responsibility, I can live and work in open prison conditions. I am eligible to apply to attend interviews and work outside the prison on special licence.

Step 13, Release and Resettlement Details, Continued	**Further examples of release information**	*I have a parole hearing in March 2020 with a view to release to my home area of Northampton. In the meantime, because I have shown myself to be entirely trustworthy, I am allowed to live and work in open prison conditions and to apply for community work, training placements and full-time outside employment.*
		I will be released in May 2020 to my home area of Sheffield. In the meantime, because of my exemplary conduct whilst in custody, I am allowed to live and work in open prison conditions. I am eligible to apply to work outside the prison on special licence at a training placement from October 2019 or full-time employment from June 2020.
Step 14, Closing Sentences	**Finish the letter/statement professionally using these sentences**	*I know that I can contribute to the community as a decent and law-abiding citizen again.* *Thank you for your kind attention,* *Yours faithfully,* *John Smith BA (Hons)* (Your own full name and any qualification letters)
Step 15, Signature	**Signature**	Sign in-between Yours faithfully, *Sign Here* Your name

Ex-offenders need clear advice about disclosure ... and to prepare and practise their disclosure statement. Often the most important thing employers want to see is remorse and that people have moved on. (Source: The Forward trust, Bridging the Gap report)

Congratulations on working through this process!

Your Personal Disclosure Statement should now be comparable to the following examples.

Example Personal Disclosure Statements

Example PDS 1

Charles Change
Hope Prison
Any town,
AB1 2CD
12th November 2019

Re: Personal Disclosure Statement

To whom it may concern,

Dear Sir/ Madam,

I am writing this letter to accompany my CV and to inform you that I have been convicted of a criminal offence.

I was given a mandatory life sentence in 2002 and have served 16 years so far. I have a parole hearing in December 2018 with a view to release back into society.

I would like to share some background, not to justify what I did, but to explain a little. I really regret my offence, which arose because when I was 23, I developed a problem with alcohol and got in a fight when I was drunk. I punched a man in the face, he fell and hit his head; he sadly died a week later. I have regretted what I did every day and will continue to regret it. I wrote to the man's family to express my sincere remorse and I cut alcohol out of my life.

When I came to prison, I was very disappointed with myself and became depressed. I pushed through these feelings, increased my motivation and made a deliberate decision to use the time to change for the better.

Examples of my achievements in prison include:

- I completed an inclusion (drug and alcohol) recovery programme. On this course I learnt about how to access personal support, identifying personal triggers and resisting temptation to relapse.

- I voluntarily completed an accredited Victim Awareness course. I gained certification in the Restorative Justice Process (reducing crime in society). The course and my commitment to complete it had a profound effect on me.

- I have worked consistently throughout my sentence and demonstrated my work ethic and my determination to remain employed despite my incarceration.

113

- I gained many new vocational skills which increase my employability and appeal to potential employers.

- I trained as a volunteer with Shannon Trust charity and taught people to read. I had always taken reading for granted but it really opened my eyes to how difficult it must have been for some people to go through their life unable to read. I committed to this and helped people to write letters home to their children and families. The look of joy and happiness when they were able, with my help, to read the replies from their children was, honestly indescribable.

- With extra training and guidance, I served as a Violence Reduction/ Safer Custody representative. I was a mediator between officers and prisoners and often between prisoners themselves. In my role I am proud to have prevented many serious incidents and stopped disagreements from escalating into violence.

I very much regret my crime and I have learnt many lessons, I am a different person now. The time I have had for self-reflection has not been wasted and I still have much to give back to the employer who gives me an opportunity to work for them.

I am now 39 years old and a more mature individual. I am a good natured and calm person. I intend to build a productive life and put the past behind me. I am fortunate to have an extended family that does support me, although my parents passed away during my time in prison. Once I am released, I will be living with my family in Market Harborough, Leicestershire.

I very much regret my crime and I have learnt many lessons. I am a different person now. Although my conviction will never be spent, the mind-set which created it *has* been spent. The time I have had for self-reflection has not been wasted and I have much to offer to the employer who gives me an opportunity to work for them.

Thank you for your kind attention.

Yours faithfully,

Charlie Change

Charles (Charlie) Change

Example PDS 2

Jane Doe
1 New Beginnings
Hope Avenue,
County
Date as Postmark

Re: Disclosure

To whom it may concern,

Dear Sir/ Madam,

I am writing this letter to accompany my CV and to inform you that I have a criminal record. In December 2017 I was imprisoned for Conspiracy to Rob. Conspiracy means being involved in plotting and planning with other people to do an illegal act. I received a sentence of 8 years and 1 month, which means that I must spend just over 4 years in prison followed by the same amount of time under supervision in the community.

I would like to share some background, not to justify what I did, but to explain a little. I was 21 years old at the time of my offence and I was doing well refurbishing properties. I was ambitious and I started a side-line exporting goods, but my ambition clearly turned to greed and I exported some stolen goods. I was 23 years old when I came to prison. This was my first offence and I have never been to prison before.

I do know that I have been too loyal to friends and that I allowed myself to be easily influenced. I had to look at my life and realise that I can't be led to by anyone else in future. I do not blame anyone else however and I accept full responsibility for where I went wrong, I knew that I had to do a lot of soul searching and that I needed to change. I studied to improve myself and gain additional qualifications. I completed a Restorative Justice Programme called 'Restore' where I learnt about the wider impact of crime on individuals and society and this was a real eye opener for me. I have also worked throughout my prison sentence and helped many other people in mentorship and orderly roles.

A long prison sentence is unimaginably hard to handle, particularly because it meant being taken away from my young son. It is very hard trying to be a parent from prison. I have matured a lot and I want to make up for the time I have missed by being a good mother. I very much regret my crime and I have learnt many lessons, I am a different person now. The time I have had for self-reflection has not been wasted and I still have much to give back to the employer who gives me an opportunity to work for them.

I do intend to build a productive life and put the past behind me. I will be released in January 2022 when I will be returning to Cardiff, South Wales. In the meantime, because I have shown myself to be entirely trustworthy, I can live and work in open prison conditions. I am eligible to apply to work outside the prison on special licence. I know that I can contribute to the community as a decent and law-abiding citizen again and I hope to be given the opportunity to prove this.

Thank you for your kind attention.

Yours faithfully,

J Doe

Jane Doe

Example PDS 3

Mr A New
Address
Town
County
Postcode
Date as Postmark

Re: Personal Disclosure Statement

To whom it may concern,

Dear Sir/ Madam,

I am writing this letter to accompany my CV and to inform you that I have a criminal record. I have been sent to prison for conspiracy to steal and rob. In June 2014 I was sentenced to 13 years. This means that I must spend 6 years and 6 months in prison followed by the same amount of time under supervision in the community.

I would like to share some background, not to justify what I did, but to explain a little. I grew up never knowing my dad. My mum did an excellent job of raising me on her own and I will always be grateful to her. Unfortunately, at the age of 15 I fell in with a bad crowd of older men. I felt very grown up, wanted and accepted but they were using me. They got me involved in car theft and I came to prison for the first time. Coming to prison meant that I didn't gain any GCSEs or later A levels like my peers in school did. When I left prison I hadn't changed, in those days, prisons were not about rehabilitation and helping people to improve, they were more about warehousing people and I was basically locked up most of the time and left to my own devices. Still lacking leadership and direction in my life, with no father figure, once I was released, I went straight back to those same men. Now I felt even more like a big man. I look back and realise how foolish I was and how I would do things so much differently in future.

As a mature adult, this sentence was a big wake up call for me. I have made a promise to myself and to my mum that I will never commit crime or come back to prison again. I also have a family to think about and I am determined to be present for my children in future. I don't want to be an absent father like my own dad was.

So, I was, and I remain, heavily motivated to change. I have completed an intensive course called TSP-Thinking Skills Programme. This is a widely recognised and praised programme it really is a game changer. It woke me up to the idea that I could live a crime free life, that I can be better than I have been, that I can make better decisions and that I deserve a chance of happiness and normality too. I worked hard on this programme and I was highly praised for my commitment to engage wholeheartedly and complete the course.

Whilst in prison, I have always worked, even if people called them menial jobs, I didn't. I worked every day whether it was cleaning, serving food or guiding other prisoners in Orderly roles. I have got a good habit of work and I always give 100% effort to my job. On top of my work and on a voluntary basis, (with formal training from the Samaritans), I trained as a prison 'listener' and helped other people, whilst they were at their lowest points, self-harming or contemplating suicide.

I continue to gain work related skills and study, filling in those gaps in my education and gaining vocational qualifications. I have goals for my employment and my future crime free life. I really regret my crimes and I have learnt many lessons, I am a different person now. The time I have had for self-reflection has not been wasted and I still have much to give back to the employer who gives me an opportunity to work for them. I do intend to build a productive life and put the past behind me. I will be released in December 2020 to my home area of Birmingham.

I know that I can contribute to the community as a decent and law-abiding citizen again and I hope that I can be given the opportunity to prove myself. Thank you for your kind attention.

Yours faithfully,

Andrew New

Mr A New

Example PDS 4

Mr Horatio Honest
7 Interesting Road
Employment
Norwich.
NR1 2AB
24th July 2020

Re: Disclosure Letter / Personal Disclosure Statement

To whom it may concern,

Dear Sir/ Madam,

I am writing this letter to accompany my CV and to inform you that I have a criminal record.

In January 2018, I was imprisoned for burglary. I received a sentence of 7 years which means that I have to spend 3 years and 6 months in prison followed by the same amount of time under supervision in the community.

I deeply regret what I did, and I am writing this personal statement to explain what I did wrong and the lessons I have learnt.

A few years earlier, I had been kidnapped by a gang of youths. I was not in a gang myself, but I knew a couple of people who were gang affiliated. The gang made taunting videos and distributed them on social media. I was rescued by the police when someone who knew me saw the videos and reported it. I was in a distressed state when I was found. I suffered from anxiety and flashbacks, but I didn't get help or counselling when I should have done. I tried to be strong and independent. Unfortunately, keeping my feelings and problems to myself meant that I became withdrawn and distant. I started to gamble as an escape from reality and a release for my feelings. After a while, my gambling became an addiction, it wasn't about winning or losing, or fun, it was just about the need.

I was low, I felt that I was failing, and I was letting my family down. I was not providing properly for my children. I wasn't being a good father, but I could not express my thoughts and feelings properly either. I am ashamed to say that it was in this time of chaos and personal weakness that I committed my offences.

It took me a while to get to this point of accepting personal responsibility. At first, I had been blaming other people and looking for excuses. When I came to prison, I was angry and upset. I was remanded for 12 months and remand prisons have very unsettled communities and very harsh regimes. It was not easy to cope but it did give me the time I needed for self-reflection and to sort my head out.

I was fortunate that I met a Prison Training Officer (Simon) who ran a horticulture course and he became a mentor to me. I was able to talk to Simon and he cared enough to listen, he inspired me on the path of self-improvement.

With his help I went on to mentor other people and I gained a qualification in Learning Support and Peer Mentoring. Simon coached me and I worked hard to gain a range of vocational qualifications (including garden machinery, forklift truck and CSCS card). I believe that this man helped me to change my life for the better.

I have engaged with support services to beat my gambling addiction for good and I have completed several personally challenging courses. The course that had the biggest impact on me was called Thinking Skills Programme (TSP) this lasted 6 weeks and it covered so many helpful life skills like positive thinking, managing emotions, problem solving, improving communication and setting future goals. I feel much stronger than I did when I was 'on the road'. I have changed my former social circles and I am now keeping to a small number of good and law-abiding friends. My personal goals are to gain employment, look after my children and stay crime free. I want to be happy and live a normal life and certainly never hurt anyone else through my selfish actions again.

Ultimately, I would like to be a voluntary youth worker. I would like to teach the young ones that crime is not the way and that they need to be careful of what they allow into their heads. Music does influence the youth a great deal and much of it is aggressive and damaging. They also need to be careful of who they hang around with. I have been down that road with the wrong people on the wrong path. I have a lot of experience that I can pass on to other people. When you are in the thick of this kind of life it is hard to see a way out or listen to other people. But just like Simon, that mentor who I had in prison, if I can help even one young person to change for the better, I will be happy about that. I am sorry for my crimes, I do regret them, and I believe that I am a different person now. The time I have had for self-reflection has not been wasted and I still have much to give back to the employer who gives me an opportunity to work for them.

My conviction would not create a risk of any problems in the workplace; in fact, employment is a proven stabilising factor which would form the solid foundation of my future life. I will be released in September 2020 to my home area of Central London. I am fortunate to have a stable home life and a loving and supportive family. I know that I can contribute to the community as a decent and law-abiding citizen again. Thank you for your kind attention.

Yours faithfully,

H.Honest

Horatio Honest

Example PDS 5

Example Ex-offender
Address
Town
Postcode
Date as Postmark

Re: Personal Disclosure Statement

To whom it may concern,

Dear Sir/ Madam,

I am writing this letter to accompany my CV and to inform you that I have a criminal record.

In February 2018 I was imprisoned for possession of prohibited firearms. I received a sentence of 6 years, which means that I have to spend 3 years in prison followed by the same amount of time under supervision in the community.

I would like to share some background, not to justify what I did but to explain a little. I was 19 years old and studying at Leeds University. I met up with some childhood friends and after some persuading I foolishly agreed that they could leave a duffel bag in my home. When I was arrested, my fingerprints were not present; I had never been in involved in any criminal activity. I pleaded guilty to the charge of possession because that was my fault and I had to accept responsibility. Being so young, my mum was devastated, and she blamed herself. I come from a good family (I achieved good grades in my GCSEs and A Levels) and never wanted to get involved in any criminal activities. When I came to prison, I was devastated but I knew that I had to make the best of it and that with my faith, my upbringing and my positivity I could improve things for people worse off than me. Despite having to leave my degree course I enrolled with the Open University, determined to continue my studies and to eventually gain my degree.

I spent the first part of my sentence at a very challenging place called Aylesbury Young Offender's Institution, but I stayed out of any trouble and made it clear that "this is not me". I served on the Prison Council and helped to improve prison conditions and relationships between prisoners and staff. As a Prison Council member, I regularly met with the Governor and I personally helped to implement a number of 'Rehabilitative Culture' initiatives. These were designed to reduce reoffending and assist in the resettlement of ex-offenders. With formal training from the Samaritans, I also trained as a prison "listener" and helped many other people in distress.

I very much regret my crime and I have learnt many lessons, I have grown up a lot and improved myself. The time I have had for self-reflection has not been wasted and I still have much to give back to the employer who gives me an opportunity to work for them.

I will be released in February 2021 to my home area of Nottingham, East London. In the meantime, because of my exemplary conduct whilst in custody, I am allowed to live and work in open prison conditions. I was the first prisoner in 12 years to achieve D-Categorisation directly from Aylesbury prison. I am eligible to apply to work outside the prison on special licence. I know that I can contribute to the community as a decent and law-abiding citizen again. I do intend to build a productive life and put the past behind me.

Thank you for your kind attention

Yours faithfully,

J G Example

Example Ex-offender

Example PDS 6

Mr Ralph Responsible
7 Interesting Road
Employment
Norwich.
NR1 2AB
24th July 2019

Re: Disclosure Statement

To whom it may concern,

Dear Sir/ Madam,

Further to my application for an employed position with yourselves, I am writing this letter to accompany my CV and to inform you that I have a criminal record.

In August 2018 I was imprisoned for Possession with intent to supply Class A drugs.

I received a sentence of 6 years and 6 months. This means that I have to spend 3 years and 3 months in prison followed by the same amount of time under supervision in the community.

I deeply regret committing crime and would like to share some of my personal background, not to justify what I did but to explain a little. I was raised in a happy and stable home in Rwanda, when suddenly war came upon us. There were two ethnic tribes in my home country, the Hutu and the Tutsi. As a Tutsi family living on the outskirts of our capital, my family were at risk of being killed. I saw houses burnt down, whole families that had been killed and heard bombs being dropped. I could literally feel the fear in the air. We fled our home and ran at night time, staying with cousins and relatives until we reached the safety of a neighbouring country, Uganda. My dad sadly died and for a very long time despite being in a relatively safe place, I experienced nightmares about bombs and gunshots. My brothers and I stayed with my aunt in Uganda and my mum left for Europe to find us a new home. After 8 months we were reunited with my mum. We spent a few weeks in Sweden before being accepted into England in 1998 when I was a teenager.

Coming to the UK was so good, I remember cycling and swimming. I worked helping a lady in an office and doing cleaning work. I gained some GCSEs. I never did have time to grieve for my dad and for all we had lost. We had left our home with nothing; no photographs or personal possessions.

Now I know that when you survive something as traumatic as the genocide, you need counselling. My mum's way of coping was working all the time to provide for us children. She was busy preparing food, helping with homework and working several jobs. In my culture men don't really talk openly about feelings, fears or concerns. I now understand that it is not a sign of weakness to talk but is in fact a sign of strength. Unfortunately, I had found my solace and my escape by smoking cannabis instead.

120

My elder brother and I started smoking cannabis regularly as a coping mechanism; a way to forget all of the terrible things we had seen.

The relationship with my mum started to deteriorate and she told me I had to stop smoking, so we argued and I left. Now I had no adult guidance, I sought out other older men locally for companionship and they were all into selling drugs.

I thought that I could make money this way and also feed my own habit. Peer pressure and influence are so very important. Now I know the value of listening to the right people.

I have read a lot of books and studied hard in prison. I do believe that we become most like the 5 people we spend the most time with. I had let the pressure of built up grief, anger and distress get the better of me. I kept it all inside without seeking help and I had allowed myself to be too easily influenced by other people.

I am a more positive and determined person now. Before I came to prison, my partner gave birth to our baby son. He has now just turned 3 years old. I want to be there to teach my son about his heritage and never leave him without his father.

I am determined never to come back to prison but to live a crime free life, contributing to society and to my community.

To this effect I have worked hard to gain new skills and qualifications and also completed several personal development courses. I believe that I am a better, more balanced person for having used my time in prison effectively.

I have stopped smoking cannabis and also tobacco. I just completed a 5k mile run in 24 minutes so I know that I am in good health again. Mentally and physically I am in good shape and ready to begin this new, positive chapter in my life. This new chapter will be one in which I am an involved and present father to my son and where I am a good partner to his mum, working legitimately and providing legally for my young family.

I very much regret my crimes and I have learnt many lessons, I am a different person now. The time I have had for self-reflection has not been wasted and I still have much to give back to the employer who gives me an opportunity to work for them.

My conviction does not create a risk of any problems in the workplace in fact employment is a proven stabilising factor which would form the solid foundation of my future life.

I do intend to build a productive life and put the past behind me. I am no longer in prison and have recently resettled back to my home area of Norwich, Norfolk. I know that I can contribute to the community as a decent and law-abiding citizen again.

Thank you for your kind attention

Yours faithfully,

RN Responsible

Ralph Responsible

Example PDS 7

Positive Peter
Hopeful Prison
Any town,
AB1 2CD
23rd October 2019

Re: Disclosure

To whom it may concern,

Dear Sir/ Madam,

I am writing this letter to accompany my CV and to inform you that I have a criminal record. In February 2018 I was imprisoned for Fraud. I received a sentence of 5 years and 8 months which means that I must spend 34 months in prison followed by the same amount of time under supervision in the community.

I would like to share some background, not to justify what I did but to explain a little. I had a legitimate business which began to struggle due to an under-availability of stock. I began to mislead customers into the legitimacy and provenance of items, in the misguided belief that I wasn't doing any harm and was in fact filling a need and keeping customers happy. I really regret what I did and to be honest, it just snowballed, and I couldn't really stop when I started the habit. I am truly sorry for what I did, and I do regret my behaviour. I know exactly where I started to go wrong, I was trying to maintain a reasonable lifestyle and provide for my children at a time when my business was struggling. I know with hindsight that I would never repeat my dishonesty and I would secure a proper job and not keep trying to sustain an unsustainable business.

I regret my crime and I have learnt many lessons, I am a different person now. I have completed a number of personal development courses which helped me to understand my thoughts and emotions better. I also took part in programme called Becoming Victim Aware (BVA). This really hit home to me the impact of crime on other people and how crime negatively impacts communities and society. I was determined to also use my time to help other people, so I studied and completed two Peer Mentoring courses and gained qualifications in helping and supporting students in functional skills and vocational skills.

Barnardos children's charity would come in on a regular basis to operate family visits days and I held the trusted position of Visits Orderly. I committed as much time as possible to working on behalf of this brilliant charity. I ensured that the overall experience for visitors, (many of whom have travelled long distances) was pleasant. I cleaned and prepared the room, tables and chairs before visits started. During the visits I served customers hot drinks, food and snacks. I used my good communication skills and friendly nature to make nervous or first-time visitors feel comfortable and welcome. Before I left that prison, I rewrote the visitor's manual which is still being used today to guide visitors. Whilst in prison, I have worked consistently and have gained additional skills. The time I have had for self-reflection has not been wasted and I still have much to give back to the employer who gives me an opportunity to work for them.

I will be released in December 2020 to my home city of Manchester. I am fortunate to have a stable home life and a loving and supportive family. I know that I can contribute to the community as a decent and law-abiding citizen again and I have every intention of doing so. Thank you for your kind attention,

Yours faithfully,

P.Positive

Positive Peter

Example PDS 8

Owen Up
1 New Beginnings
Hope Avenue,
County
Date as Postmark

Re: Personal Statement/ My honest disclosure

To whom it may concern,

Dear Sir/ Madam,

I am writing this letter to accompany my CV and to inform you that I have a criminal record.

In August 2016 I was imprisoned for GBH Section 18 with intent (this means causing serious injury to someone). I received an extended determinate sentence of 8 years which meant that I had to spend a minimum of 5 years and 4 months (2/3rd) in prison, followed by a period under supervision in the community.

As part of my sentence I spent two and a half years in a secure therapeutic community, which helped me to better understand where I went wrong and why I thought and acted the way I did. I had a violent upbringing, a childhood where I had to protect my 2 younger siblings from harm. As a young adult I continued to want to be the protector and I joined the Army. I served for 8 years and as part of a rapid deployment force I was deployed to a number of volatile places and warzones including Northern Ireland, Rwanda, Kosovo and Zaire (now DRC). As an infantryman soldier, I grew up quickly, but I also saw some horrific sights, which even after therapy are hard to talk about. I did suffer from complex PTSD, but I do not blame the Army; that was my job after all. My crime happened when I visited some friends who were very dear to me. They seemed withdrawn and quieter than usual and when I asked them what was wrong, they explained to me that their two children had been sexually abused by a local youth. I was still in protector mode; my emotions got the better of me and I took matters into my own hands. I am sorry for what I did; I pleaded guilty and I accepted personal responsibility. I understand now that I should have let the police and the justice process take its own course. I should just have been there to support my friends as this awful crime wreaked the destruction it did on their family. My involvement and my actions did not help them in any way.

When I came to prison, I wanted to contribute and help other people. I completed many personal development programmes in addition to graduating from my intensive therapy course. I also gained a BSc (Hons) Degree in Sport and Fitness Coaching with the Open University.

Most personal to me, I became a SSAFA (Soldier, Sailor, Air-Force Association) representative and in this role, I helped and supported many veterans in three different prisons. I have worked to improve the wellbeing of veterans struggling in prison by providing personal contact and practical support as well as signposting to other organisations and agencies.

I am sorry for committing my crime and I have learnt many lessons, the time I have had for self-reflection has not been wasted and I still have much to give back to the employer who gives me an opportunity to work for them.

I do intend to build a productive life and put the past behind me. I am no longer in prison and live in Dudley, West Midlands and I am currently available for full time work. I know that I can contribute to the community as a decent and law-abiding citizen again. Thank you for your kind attention.

Yours faithfully,

O Up

Owen Up

Example PDS 9

Guy London
1 New Beginnings
Hope Avenue,
County
Date as Postmark

Statement of Intention and Disclosure

To whom it may concern,

Dear Sir/ Madam,

I am writing this letter to accompany my CV and to inform you that I have a criminal record.

In December 2019 I was imprisoned for GBH Section 18 with intent, this means causing serious injury to someone. I received a sentence of 6 years which means that I must spend 3 years in prison, followed by the same amount of time under supervision in the community.

I deeply regret what I did and I am writing this personal statement to explain what I did wrong and the lessons I have learnt. I am a graduate in Business and Management and was working full-time as an IT professional. I was out for a birthday meal with my girlfriend, after which I met up with some friends in a local pub where we watched a live rugby game. This was not a raucous evening and we were not planning to get drunk. I am a professional person; this was meant to be a respectable and sophisticated evening out. Unfortunately, the next thing I knew was waking up in a police cell. I was distressed to see where I was and I felt extremely ill and disorientated. I was seen by a nurse who said that I had clearly taken drugs and my heart rate was 148bpm. Unfortunately, no blood test was ever taken, which would have helped my defence because it is apparent that at some point my drink had been spiked. I was told that I had been helped back home by my friends but that at home I had attacked my housemate. I did plead guilty to the GBH charge but not to the intent, knowing that I must have caused injury, but that I hadn't ever intended to do so. This would have made it S20 instead of S18. My belief and the reasoning of my legal team was that, although I must have hurt my housemate, I had not done so deliberately. To this day, I still have no recollection of what happened. Nevertheless, I am so terribly sorry for hurting my housemate. This is extremely out of character for me and I have never been in any trouble with the police before. A drug specialist spoke as an expert witness on my behalf during my trial and he did explain that some of the drugs typically used to spike drinks can, in collaboration with alcohol, cause aggressive responses. However, without a blood test or drug tests, it is impossible to tell. As a result of this vital evidence being unavailable, the jury found me guilty of the S18 charge.

The period before coming to prison was very challenging, being on bail and all the uncertainty that went with it made it very difficult to focus and to make any plans. Coming to prison, although unexpected, at least meant that it was all over, and I could put my head down and get on with things.

I served the greater part of my prison sentence as a classroom assistant teaching functional skills (literacy and numeracy) to people who missed out on formal education as well as providing IT support to both officers and prisoners. Working alongside the College heads, I even used my IT background and experience to build a College Intranet which improves accessibility to important course and sentence planning materials.

Despite coming to prison and my crime, I felt that my positive attitude was important and to be guarded. I treated the time as an educational sabbatical and continued to learn and study. I taught myself new IT languages and also gained additional vocational qualifications.

I know that my crime was wrong and that my victim was hurt, and I am so sorry. If I could turn the clock back, I would. The evening out had life changing consequences for me and my family. My dad was diagnosed with cancer and sadly died within 3 weeks of the diagnosis. I was fortunate to be able to have seen him a couple of days before he passed away and to have attended his funeral, albeit in handcuffs on both occasions. I telephone my mum every day to try to offer her every support that I can and after my release I will be there for her the way she has been there for me for so many years.

I very much regret my crime and I have learnt many lessons, I am a different person now. The time I have had for self-reflection has not been wasted and I still have much to give back to the employer who gives me an opportunity to work for them.

I do intend to build a productive life and put the past behind me. I will be released in December 2022 to my home area of Kenilworth, Warwickshire. I am loyal and hardworking and even willing to relocate for the most suitable opportunity. In the meantime, because I have shown myself to be entirely trustworthy, I am allowed to live and work in open prison conditions. I am eligible to apply to work outside the prison on special licence.

I know that I can contribute to the community as a decent and law-abiding citizen again. Thank you for your kind attention.

Yours faithfully,

Guy M London

Guy London

Example PDS 10

Benny Fishall
HMP Establishment
Any Location
Any Town
AB12 34CD
Date as Postmark

Re: Disclosure Letter/ Personal Statement

To whom it may concern,

Dear Sir/ Madam,

I am writing this letter to accompany my CV and to inform you that I have a criminal record.

In May 2017 I was imprisoned for conspiracy to defraud HMRC and UK clearing banks and money laundering. I received a sentence of 9 years altogether, which means that I have to spend 4 years and 6 months in prison followed by the same amount of time under supervision in the community.

I would like to share some background, not to justify what I did, but to explain a little. I came through the care system and experienced a lot of volatility and uncertainty growing up. I left school early and without qualifications but I was determined to live a better life and not let my children experience any of those same hardships. I became a very motivated businessman and ultimately founded an electronics distribution company that at its peak employed many dozens of people and achieved a substantial sales volume. The company experienced some challenges primarily around sales margins and I carried out a series of illegal acts with the intention of maintaining profitability. I take full responsibility and admit that my crimes were my own fault.

Coming to prison was unimaginably hard both for me and my family; surprisingly it brought back all the difficult memories of being in care. I had thought that I had left those difficult times in the past but here I am as an adult going through it again. This time it was worse because I brought it on myself and as a result my family have had to suffer too. It has been hard for them to cope; they have lots of practical problems and also suffered prejudice and embarrassment within our community too.

I am very sorry for what I did and I regret my crime. I have never been to prison before and I am intelligent enough not to repeat any of the same mistakes again in future. I am humbled by my time in prison and I have changed a lot. In prison I helped a lot of people with advice and sign posting when they were most distressed and in need.

I do intend to build a productive life and put the past behind me. I will be released in December 2020 to my home area of Bristol and I hope to start a new job shortly after release. I know that I can contribute to the community as a decent and law-abiding citizen again.

Thank you for your kind attention

Yours faithfully,

Benny Fishall

Benny Fishall

126

Example PDS 11

Liberty Start

12 The Willows

Fresh End

Sea Town

Date as Postmark

Re: Personal Disclosure Statement

To whom it may concern,

Dear Sir/ Madam,

I am writing this letter to accompany my CV and to inform you that I have a criminal record. In July 2014 I was imprisoned for causing death by dangerous driving and received a sentence of 4 years and 8 months.

I would like to share some background, not to justify what I did, but to explain a little. I was a professional driver of Heavy Goods Vehicles (HGV1 articulated lorries). I had been driving HGVs for more than 15 years, without incident. In recent years I had been working for a plant and fork-lift hire company. I attended a regional festival to collect two pieces of heavy machinery and as I was about to exit the site, a vehicle came down the main road overtaking two cars at speed. The driver suddenly braked and pulled in erratically to turn left into the road I was exiting from but of course he was unable to do so because my lorry was positioned to turn.

I waved at the man to reverse out but for some inexplicable reason he got out of his car and walked to the back of my lorry talking with the site security guards and shouting at me. After waiting a few moments, I got into his car and reversed it safely so that I could perform my manoeuvre. When I returned to my lorry and started to drive it out, the man started shouting at me and stood in front of my lorry. He then went to the side, so I assumed that he had got out of the way. I checked my mirrors and cameras and saw a man in the mirror who I thought was him. I started moving at no more than 2-3 miles per hour and suddenly my lorry lifted. Unbeknownst to me the man had slipped over and as I moved forwards he was under the front wheel. I stopped immediately to check and saw that he had been injured. I immediately telephoned for an ambulance and the police and the man was airlifted to hospital.

The man sadly died in hospital a few days later. This was a tragic accident and there was certainly no deliberate intent on my side. I had a choice to plead guilty or not guilty and although this was a terrible accident, I did not want the man's family to suffer more than they already had and so I took full responsibility and pleaded guilty.

The accident itself and the after effects of coming to prison was a big shock; I had been advised that I may not go to prison due to the mitigating circumstances of this tragic event. The shock of leaving my partner and our two children hit me hard. I did ask for counselling, but in the restricted circumstances of prison, this was never facilitated. After a few weeks I began to come to terms with what had happened and as I looked around me I saw people in truly desperate situations. Their lives were a long way off-track and in many cases they had endured many hardships and desperate times themselves before coming to prison. Some would self-harm and others suffered severe mental illness. I decided to use my time as much as possible to help other people. I served as a reception orderly which is a highly trusted position within prisons. I was able to sit with people when they first come to prison and offered them guidance and support.

I particularly remember a man with autism who I have spent a lot of time with personally. I helped keep him focussed on positive aspects of his life, such as relationships and his future and I helped keep his mind off of the things that would make him most anxious and distressed. I still keep in touch with him and I am pleased to have taken the time to understand his special needs. I think if more individualised help and support were made available then there would be far fewer victims of crime.

For my own part, I deeply regret the terrible accident that I was involved in. The time I have had for self-reflection whilst in prison has not been wasted and I still have much to give back to the employer who gives me an opportunity to work for them. My past conviction would not create a risk of any problems in the workplace; in fact, employment would help me to build the solid foundation of my future life. I know that I can contribute to the community as a decent and law-abiding citizen again. Thank you for your kind consideration of my application.

Yours faithfully,

L. Start

Liberty Start

Example PDS 12

F. Oughtless-Lee
Hope Cottage
Example Town
Example County
Date as Postmark

Re: Personal Disclosure Statement

To whom it may concern,

Dear Sir/ Madam,

I am writing this letter to accompany my CV and to inform you that I have a criminal record.

In November 2015 I was imprisoned for causing Grievous Bodily Harm without intent (Section 20). This means causing serious injury to someone by accident. I received a sentence of 4 years, which means that I have to spend 2 years in prison followed by the same amount of time under supervision in the community.

I would like to share some background, not to justify what happened, but to explain a little. I had gone out for a quiet drink with my long-term partner when two men became troublesome in the pub. They had been drinking heavily and it looked to me as if they were being aggressive due to drug use. I told my girlfriend to sit down and stay away and I asked them to stop picking on us and on everyone else. I thought I was doing the right thing by telling the bouncers but they didn't take any action. One of the men grabbed me by the hand and tried to hit me. I picked up a pool ball to protect myself but the bouncer threw that man out and I put the pool ball down. The man who remained in the pub wouldn't leave me alone so I hit him once and then the man who had been thrown out smashed the window and started calling me to come out. I was charged with two other offences alongside the GBH S20 namely 'possession of a weapon' (this was the pool ball that I had picked up and put down without using) and assault by battery for punching the man in the pub.

The man outside was goading me and being very abusive and I know that I should have waited for the police but by this time adrenaline had taken over. I was feeling stressed and I could not tolerate the thought of being bullied; it was a trigger for me because of certain things that happened when I was younger and so I overreacted. I went out, punched the man once and he fell to the floor. Tragically he hit his head and suffered severe damage.

I had never intended to hurt my victim so badly; the CCTV showed that it really was only one punch. I accepted responsibility by pleading guilty to the charges. I was so sorry for the impact of what happened that night. I don't wish that on anyone it was just a terrible set of circumstances. I realise that it could just as easily have been me who had hit my head so hard.

129

When I came to prison, I was determined to change for the better and so with a huge amount of effort on my part, I graduated from a 12-week, 26-session, intensive programme called 'Resolve' and I am literally far better equipped to manage and resolve difficult situations calmly. I now look at the bigger picture and consider things much more carefully.

The impact of coming to prison has been devastating personally. It has upset family members and I also sadly suffered the break-up of my long-term relationship. I had to take a long hard look in the mirror, and I decided to use the time away as an opportunity to change for the better.

I very much regret my crime and I have learnt many lessons, I am a different person now. The time I have had for self-reflection has not been wasted and I still have much to give back to the employer who gives me an opportunity to work for them.

Whilst in prison I have continued my work ethic and also gained additional skills and work-related qualifications. My conviction would not create a risk of any problems in the workplace; in fact, employment is a proven stabilising factor which would form the solid foundation of my future life.

I do intend to build a productive life and put the past behind me. I am no longer in prison and have resettled successfully into my home area of Congleton, Cheshire. I know that I can contribute to the community as a decent and law-abiding citizen again.

Thank you for your kind attention

Yours faithfully,

F. Oughtless-Lee

F.Oughtless-Lee

"I received 2 job offers within one week after following the system in this book! I am now off to work for Taylor Wimpey. Thank you." FF

Chapter 4 -
The Curriculum Vitae (CV) Guide

"I invited someone to interview solely because he used the CV template from this guide and wrote an honest disclosure letter. It showed that he had thought about his skills and attributes and that he cared enough to make an effort. He had the right experience for the job, but he wouldn't have achieved the interview without getting that CV in front of us first."

GL deputy C.E.O. regional employer

The Purpose of a CV (Résumé)

CV is short for "Curriculum Vitae" which originally meant in Latin "course of life" or more recently "**life story**".

Whilst employers do not actually need your life story, they do need relevant information about applicants, so they can choose to invest their time and money with the most suitable people. Recruitment mistakes are expensive, and it can be problematic if new employees work out as expected.

Employers receive many CVs, and this is their first filter (excuse) to eliminate applicants.

The purpose of a CV is not to get a job.

The purpose of a CV is to get an interview.

A CV is a marketing document. It should be drafted to present you in the best possible light, but it must also be honest and accurate.

Just like wearing a suit for a wedding, instead of jeans and a t-shirt, this is our chance to present the best possible image of ourselves, to shine our shoes and look good in photographs of the big day.

This is a traditional, formal document which follows a conventional format so that employers can compare different applicants' features at a glance.

"Your CV is probably the most important personal document that you will ever create." PM

Applicants are expected to make an effort, or to seek help, to create their CV. A high-quality CV requires a time investment of two - four hours to produce from scratch; it should not be rushed; it is worth spending the time to create.

"I have been in prison for a long time and not having done a CV for a while, this book has given me a greater understanding of how I am to present myself in writing and in person, it has given me the necessary pointers where acquiring employment is concerned and some of the skills that would aid me in an interview. I feel so much more confident now." DS

'CV Builder' - Your CV Framework

Following this 'CV Builder' and Do and Don't List, guarantees the creation of a professional and impressive CV.

Insert:
Name
Address
Postcode
Telephone
Email

'CV Updated - *(insert date)*'

Profile:

Read the guidance on page 137

This section is a summary of top strengths as an employee

SHORTCUT - Choose 3 or 4 personal attributes from pages 137 - 138.

Key Skills:

Read the guidance on page 139

This section is a summary of top vocational skills

SHORTCUT - Choose your top 3 or 4 key skills from pages 139 - 146.

Preferred Role (<u>Optional</u>):

Read the guidance on page 147. This section is not required for most people.

Experience:

Read the guidance on page 148.

This section is a summary of multiple years of work experience, listed with most recent first and working backwards in time, 15 - 20 years.

Duties and responsibilities should be clearly explained as well as knowledge, skills and experience gained

SHORTCUT - Prison job templates, pages 150 - 166, conventional job templates 167 - 196 and explanations for gaps in employment pages 197 - 198

'Please note: dates listed, and the timeline are approximate.'

'Previous work experience includes' *(insert a one-line phrase summarising earlier work).*

133

Professional Memberships (<u>Optional</u>):

Read the guidance on page 199. This section is not required for most people.

Qualifications:

Read the guidance on pages 200 - 201. This section lists your educational and vocational qualifications, as well as personal awards gained.

SHORTCUT - Refer to the examples of Academic and Vocational Qualifications, outside prison on pages 202 - 206 and inside prison on pages 207- 215

'Currently studying to achieve' *(insert something that you are currently studying or are about to start studying)*

'Fluent in' *(insert languages that you speak well)*, 'I also speak passable' *(insert languages that you can just about hold a conversation in)*

'Holding a full driving licence' *(if you do, along with any extra permissions)*

'Right to work' documentation in hand' *(check that you have your long birth certificate or passport AND a document containing your National Insurance number such as a letter from HMRC, a P60 or a P45)*

Other Achievements (<u>Optional</u>)

Read the guidance on page 216. This section is not required for most people.

Personal Interests:

Read the guidance on page 217.

This section gives brief insights into your favourite activities and interests.

SHORTCUT - Choose your favourite 3 or 4 personal interests with suitable wording from pages 217 - 227

References are available upon request.' (Optional)

This phrase is often excluded from modern CV's - Only include it if you know that previous employers will give you a good reference. Do not include it (or check with previous employers first) if unsure. An alternative is to offer personal references from Probation, Offender Supervisor or Support Worker:

'Personal references are available upon request.'

Your CV should now be comparable to the examples included on pages 228 - 235

CV - Do and Do Not List

Following this Do and Do Not List will ensure that your CV makes a positive impression on potential employers.

DO:

☑ Type your CV on a computer, or arrange for someone to type it for you, so that it can be saved and amended.

☑ Use font size 11, 11.5 or 12, no larger or smaller.

☑ Use good quality (at least 80gsm), white, A4 paper.

☑ Insert the date at the top e.g. '*CV - Updated 24th July 2019*'.

☑ Justify the text to the left and right margins, to make it appear neater.

☑ Insert your name, address, telephone and email in the top right corner.

☑ Reserve the use of **bold** or <u>underline</u> for headings, not within the text itself.

☑ Space out the sections so that the document is easy to read and looks clean.

☑ Use a clear, sans serif (without flicks) font, like Arial, in black only, which is easy to read whether on screen or printed.

☑ Aim for two pages (this is preferable), or three pages at the most. Do not only write one page as this is far too short and conveys a poor impression.

☑ Adhere to a traditional framework similar to the 'CV Builder' which follows. This highlights your best features first and allows for easy comparing.

☑ Be honest. Your CV must be familiar to you. You should be prepared to answer personal questions about it and explain points at job interviews.

☑ Number the pages 'page 1 of 2' and 'page 2 of 2', insert your name in the bottom of each page (footer) alongside the page number so that it looks like this '*John Smith - CV - page 1 of 2*'.

☑ Save the file on a computer as '*firstname.lastname.CV.*' - Not just 'CV' (like many people do). This way it is easy for employers to find it amongst all the other CV's.

☑ **<u>Prepare a specific, targeted CV for different job roles</u>**. The examples shown in this book are general CV's which are great for uploading to careers portals (websites like Indeed, CV-library, 'Job serve' etc.). When you are applying for a specific role however it is better to highlight the skills, qualifications and experience which are most relevant to that role.

☑ Spelling mistakes are not acceptable. Refer to a dictionary and check spelling and grammar in MSWord by pressing F7 key.

Do not rely on spellcheck entirely because it will not correct all words appropriately. For example, job or jot, frog and fog which are both spelt correctly, but mean different things.

The noun 'licence' is spelt licence not license (which is a verb meaning "to licence"). Having a dictionary to hand will prove helpful as will making sure that your computer is set to English (UK) rather than English (USA).

☑ It is traditional, (but not essential), to end a CV with one of the following simple phrases:

1) *Professional references available upon request* - *Only state this if you know that previous employers will give you a good reference. Do not include it (or check with previous employers first) if you are not sure.*

2) *Personal references available upon request* - *An alternative is to offer personal references from Probation, OMU or Support Worker.*

3) *References in hand* - You can use this phrase if you have some testimonials, references and letters of recommendation in your possession already.

I recommend that you ask for a "to whom it may concern" reference letter each time you leave a job or complete an education course. These can prove helpful in the future when contact people will have changed, memories fade, or companies are no longer trading.

☑ Once you have written and checked your CV, come back to it again the next day. Also ask a professional friend or associate to check and comment on it.

☑ Update your CV regularly as new qualifications are gained, new achievements noted, and new job roles started.

DO NOT:

☒ Do not use words or phrases that you don't understand.

☒ Do not claim experience that you don't have or misrepresent anything.

☒ Do not include a photograph, unless specifically asked to do so in certain image conscious roles, such as modelling.

☒ Do not use coloured paper because it does not photocopy well, and employers often need extra copies for other staff members.

☒ Do not experiment with unconventional layouts or do other things to try to draw attention; these make it more difficult to compare like for like features and recruiters expect a good CV to stand out for its content alone.

Profile - Personal Attributes

This section is a brief introduction to you as a potential employee.

The profile section is sometimes called *'Personal Attributes'* and you can call it this if you prefer.

This is your chance to get the interest of a prospective employer in the first few moments of glancing over the CV. There are two options for this section as follows.

Option 1	If you are good with words and know exactly what you want to say, you can write an introductory paragraph about yourself, similar to: *I am a positive and loyal person. I am looking for a new opportunity in which I can commit to an employer for the long term. In return for this opportunity, I will work hard in my new role, work cooperatively within the team and I will be willing to learn any new skills required. I am fit and healthy, enthusiastic and also open minded about my next job role.*
Option 2 (preferred)	Choose **3** or **4** features that best describe you and write an appealing sentence about each. Avoid using vague or confusing words like "passionate" or overused phrases like "team player". There are pre-written examples below which have been used very successfully. If you use these then make sure that you choose sentences that definitely apply to you.
Begin with **one** of these	*A flexible worker with numerous vocational skills and qualifications and I am open minded about my next role/ challenge.* *I am reliable, loyal to any employer and hardworking; I take pride in my work and I enjoy the satisfaction that comes from completing a task well.*
And then add **two** of these (continued overleaf)	*I am an adaptable, positive and resilient person.* *I have the ability to add value in all environments.* *I am efficient, organised and able to forward plan.* *I am great at analysing systems and improving them.* *I am reliable, loyal to my employer and hardworking.* *I have the ability to multi-task and prioritise work flow.* *I enjoy learning new skills and working alongside other people.* *I am calm and collected under pressure and an asset to any team.*

Additional examples of personal attributes	*An inspiring team player who creates a co-operative atmosphere.*
	A dedicated worker with a refreshingly positive and focussed outlook.
	I am positive and professional, and I help and support other people.
	Dependable and determined to meet targets and exceed expectations.
	I am loyal, hardworking and conscientious and I work to an excellent standard.
	I am goal orientated, totally dedicated to the current project and its fulfilment.
	I am an excellent problem solver and overcome all obstacles to get the job done.
	I know how to train, motivate and monitor other people and bring the best out of them.
	I am flexible and very good at organising environments and designing efficient systems of work.
	I am a polite and respectful person; I treat everyone equally with patience and understanding.
	I am compassionate, with a strong sense of empathy and I bring the very best out of other people.
	I am very organised and reliable; people and companies who depend on me are never disappointed.
	I am dependable, reliable and responsible having maintained trusted positions including key holding.
	I am conscientious; I take pride in my work and enjoy the satisfaction that comes from completing a task well.
	I am an original and creative thinker with a solution orientated and structured approach to solving problems.
	I have a superb work ethic; I hold myself to a high standard and conduct myself professionally at all times.
	I am dependable and trustworthy, able to work on own initiative and be relied on to deliver the results required.
	A superb problem solver who thrives in challenging situations, when given hurdles to overcome and targets to meet.
	I am an organised and professional employee who can prioritise work flow, make a good impression and work to a high standard.
	I have strong commercial awareness with the ability to price contracts, negotiate well to include profit and also ensure that there is a margin of flexibility for contingencies.
	I am enthusiastic and a fast learner. I ask questions; invite comments and ask for help if needed and I happily pass my knowledge on to others in the form of best working practises.
	I am a very capable and motivated individual who works independently and on own initiative and also thrives as part of a team. I also have some team- leading and supervisory experience.

Key Skills

This section highlights, at a glance, your top skills.

Cherry-pick **3** or **4** skills only and write an explanatory sentence about each.

Although bullet points are used below, avoid using them in your CV. It will look neater if you simply leave a line space between each of your key skills.

If you are not sure what key skills you have, then the skills listed below may remind you and help you to think of your own top skills. You do not have to use the pre-written wording - use as much or as little from the examples.

Make sure that you are completely accurate and honest when listing your skills.

Begin with two of these	*Excellent communication, organisational and functional skills.*
	Many vocational skills gained, please see experience section below.
	An excellent communicator with an intuitive ability to build rapport.
	Till trained and experienced at using retail software and technology.
	Competent in Microsoft Office suite, online applications and general PC use.
	A superb problem solver; able to manage and resolve the most challenging of situations.

And then add **one** or **two** further work-related skills similar to these pre-written examples (listed in alphabetical order)

Work Skills A - Z	An **Advertising Executive** specialising in sales, marketing and media/ communications planning.
	A qualified and recognised **Art Teacher**. Experienced in teaching classes at all skill levels from beginners to advanced students.
	A highly skilled and qualified **Asbestos Removal** specialist, able to handle the safe removal and sealing in-situ of asbestos in all environments. Able to train and supervise teams of workmen.
	An experienced and qualified **Baker** and Pastry Chef. Known for hard work and meeting production targets. Supervised in multiple establishments.
	A qualified **Barber** with a proven ability to perform all hair services to a high standard and also train apprentices.
	A qualified **Barista** with a full range of skills including coffee processing, brewing, creation of all coffee types (latte, espresso, cappuccino, macchiato, flat white, mocha, Americano), equipment care, health, safety and hygiene.

An experienced **Block Paving** and surfacing contractor. Knowledgeable about pathways, driveways, drainage and street works.

A qualified **Bookkeeper** with substantial experience within a diverse range of industry sectors including construction and food production.

A skilled **Bricklayer** with a thorough approach and enthusiasm for all aspects of brickworks.

A highly experienced **Builder**. Experienced in property refurbishment and construction of single storey and double storey extensions.

A highly experienced **Business Consultant** with accountancy qualifications and a wealth of knowledge in Human Resources, employment law, business structures and funding requirements.

An experienced and skilled **Butcher** able to undertake all forms of butchery and meat processing including cutting, cooking, curing, boning, cleaning.

A **Bicycle Mechanic**, experienced in manufacture, maintenance and repair of a wide range of bicycles.

A **Cable Puller**. Installs LV cables in buildings and HV onto the outside. Worked on new-build sites and refurbishments.

A qualified and highly experienced **Carpet Fitter** and flooring specialist.

An experienced, qualified and skilled general **Carpenter** and Bench Joiner. Skilled in design, manufacture, repair and installation of wooden fixtures.

A commercial shuttering **Carpenter** familiar with building frames, outside of walls and lift shafts ready for concrete.

An experienced **Car Wash Manager**. Competent in pre-wash preparation, jet washing, polishing, internal vacuuming and valeting.

A highly experienced **Caterer**, Chef, kitchen porter and waiter with knowledge on all aspects of the food service and hospitality industries.

A qualified Assistant **Chef** (NVQ Levels 1 and 2, HACCP Level 3) and **Kitchen Porter**, with many years of experience working in commercial kitchens, as well as preparing and serving food.

A highly qualified **Chef** (7061 7062 City and Guilds) experienced of working in French and Brazilian restaurants, hotels and within private catering firms.

A **Childcare** specialist; having looked after children from a young age, possessing a natural way with children and young people, and with an acute awareness of safeguarding (as well as health and safety).

A **Classroom Assistant**/ Learning Mentor. 5 years of experience working with children aged 5-12. Primarily focussed on supporting under privileged children, with learning difficulties or experiencing personal upset.

A specialist **Coachbuilder**, wheelwright and technical woodworking machinist.

A **Construction Worker** with a wide range of competencies.

An empathic **Counsellor** experienced and qualified in drug, solvent and alcohol abuse counselling, teaching vulnerable people to read and supporting people in crisis with information, advice and guidance.

A **Customer Service Professional** who serves and helps people in a positive and friendly manner and encourages additional purchases to maximise revenue.

An experienced **Customer Service Adviser** able to support clients both face to face and over the telephone. Demonstrably represents the company in a positive and professional manner in all situations.

A **Demolition Engineer** with over 20 years' experience in the safe demolition of commercial and residential properties; from attendance on site and securing the area, to demolition, clear down and removal, leaving a flat site.

A **Diamond Driller** experienced in all types of concrete drilling and cutting, including using a wide range of power tools such as gas saws, diesel saws, hydraulic track saws for floor cutting, bursting and crunching and qualified to use all tools of the trade.

A popular **DJ** specialising in Reggae and Dancehall. A confident and enthusiastic performer who exceeds expectations and delivers high quality events to audiences of all sizes.

An experienced and qualified **Door Supervisor and SIA Security Officer**, contracted to work at superstores, nightclubs and events.

A qualified and experienced **Drainage Specialist**. Able to join and lay drainage pipe-work, build manholes and undertake concrete finishing.

A highly experienced **Duct Engineer** skilled installing and maintaining all types of ducting in a wide range of establishments and settings.

A commercial **Driver** with many years of experience in making residential deliveries to customers.

A highly experienced **Driver** who holds all necessary and relevant qualifications including full UK D1 driving licence, HGV1, HGV2, Current Digi-card and Current Driver's Certificate of Professional Competence (DCPC). Driven commercially for 8 years whilst remaining accident free.

A **Dry Lining Specialist**. 15 years' experience of plaster boarding and dry lining to first fix stage.

An **Electrician** qualified to BS7671 17th Edition, Part P, experienced at working on domestic and commercial properties and alongside other trades.

An **Event Coordinator**, able to organise small and large public events. Familiar with promotion of ticket sales, licensing and management agreements, health and safety considerations, staffing levels and security.

A **Farmer** and Farm Labourer experienced in tractor and combine harvester driving, ploughing, bailing, herding, milking, managing livestock and maintaining machinery including welding and gas cutting.

A **Fire-Proofing Specialist**, highly experienced in the installation of fire safety equipment, qualified to fit fire suppression boxes and holding a CSCS card.
A **Fitness Instructor**/ Gym Instructor qualified to Levels 1 and 2. Able to facilitate a range of classes and also motivate and support people to live a healthier lifestyle both nutritionally and through consistent, suitable exercise.
FA qualified **Football Coach** and Referee with a wide range of additional sports and gym-based qualifications.
A qualified and skilled **Fork Lift Truck Driver** (counterbalance). Able to pick up heavy loads and manoeuvre in tight warehouse environments. Very aware of health and safety obligations, surroundings and location of other workers.
A **Fundraiser** and face-to-face promoter, able to generate support for worthy causes and sell by positively influencing other people.
A **Groundworker/ Pipeline Labourer**. Able to dig trenches to lay pipelines, disconnect and reconnect water meters, backfill, lay base and tarmac.
A general **Handyman**, able to call on numerous property maintenance skills and respond to emergency call outs. Experienced in a wide range of power tools, hand tools and materials.
A **Health Trainer** qualified to Level 3 (City and Guilds) with a passion for helping people to live fit and healthy lives.
A skilled and qualified **Highway Maintenance (street-works) Operative** with a current NRSWA Operator's Card. 15 years of experience and able to perform regular maintenance as well as emergency call outs.
A **Hotel Receptionist** with professionalism and good organisational abilities.
An experienced and qualified **Industrial Cleaner.** Qualified to British Institute of Cleaning Sciences Bio-hazard Supervisor level.
An experienced **Insulation Installer** specialising in lagging and thermally insulating pipes and boiler houses as well as installing ducting and dry boards, in residential, commercial and industrial settings.
A qualified and experienced **Interior Designer.** Highly recommended for plans and 3D drawings. Skilled in vector works and other design software.
IT Engineer and **IT Security Specialist** with almost 20 years' experience in the private and public sectors. Competent in all known software applications, server build, networking and database technology.
A CISCO qualified **IT Technician** and Networking Engineer.
A qualified and experienced **Gas Engineer** with knowledge of domestic repairs, maintenance and installation of heating systems.
A **Groundworker**. Experienced in digging foundations, cutting and positioning blocks, setting steel rods into floors and screening.

A **Kitchen Porter**, with experience of working in commercial kitchens, preparing and serving food.
A general **Labourer** for all trades holding a current Construction Skills Certification Scheme (CSCS) card.
A general **Labourer** for all trades, experienced in plastering, plumbing, bricklaying, flooring, kitchen fitting, tiling, bathroom installation, landscaping, drain work, sign work and road maintenance.
An experienced hard and soft **Landscape Gardener**. Knowledgeable about pathways, street works as well as horticulture and grounds maintenance.
A talented **Landscape Gardener**. Knowledgeable about horticulture and experienced in planting, cultivating, mowing, landscaping, designing, trimming, weeding, edging, pruning and all aspects of grounds maintenance.
A highly commended **Loft Conversion Specialist** with decades of experience and numerous satisfied clients.
A **Medic** with a calm and professional approach to desperate and difficult situations (qualified to Level 3).
A **Motor Mechanic** with a suite of relevant qualifications and experience with a wide range of vehicle brands.
A qualified and experienced **Motorcycle Engineer** able to carry out maintenance and servicing of all types of bike and scooters.
A **Musician, Singer/ Songwriter**, able to produce popular music and deliver high quality performances to audiences of all sizes. A confident and enthusiastic performer who goes above and beyond in all roles.
An experienced **NHS worker** and carer with attention to detail and excellent patient support.
An experienced **Office Manager**. Familiar with professional organisation, record keeping, scheduling, compliance and numerous software packages.
A professional **Painter and Decorator** with a keen eye and attention to detail.
An experienced **Panel Beater and Paint Sprayer** specialising in accident repairs on a wide range of vehicles from mainstream to prestige, domestic cars to commercial vehicles.
A **Personal Trainer** qualified in Levels 1, 2 and 3. Able to motivate and support people to live a healthier lifestyle both nutritionally and through consistent and suitable exercise.
Personal Trainer and **Referral Fitness Instructor** with specialist knowledge of working with people who have a wide range of considerations such as Anorexia, Arthritis, Diabetes, Health Problems, Hypertension, Joint replacement, Lower back pain, Obesity, Osteoporosis, Rheumatism and Stress.

"I can now see in one place all the things I achieved whilst I have been in prison. Looking at my finished CV, I would want to hire me!" SC

A skilled heavy and small **Plant Operator** in-house experienced at operating 360°excavators, counterbalance forklift, rough terrain forklift, telescopic forklift, scissor lift, side-shift reach forklift, dumper trucks, road rollers, whacker plates, strimmer, generator and chainsaw.

A skilled **Plasterer** who produces a neat and tidy, smooth finish. I see plastering as art and take great pride in my finished results.

A qualified and experienced specialist in **Plaster Boarding** and dry lining. Experienced in partitioning rooms in residential and commercial properties.

A qualified and experienced **Plumber** with knowledge of domestic and commercial repairs and installations.

A **Project Manager** in the Construction Industry, experienced in negotiating contracts, liaising with customers, coordinating trades and compliance.

A **Property Adaptations Specialist.** Designing and installing special needs bathing solutions for ease of access and continued personal independence.

A **Property Developer** with substantial experience of land finding, site planning, achieving planning permission, delivering multiple unit sites and completing onward sales.

An experienced residential and commercial **Property Manager** and **Lettings Agent.** Able to host viewings, negotiate, draft contracts, take inventories and organise maintenance.

Experienced in **property refurbishment**, construction of single storey and double storey extensions and loft conversions.

Pub Manager and **Landlord.** Experienced in problem solving, financial improvement and turnaround in the pub industry.

A highly skilled and qualified **Quantity Surveyor**, Estimator, Project Manager and Commercial Arbitrator.

A **Railway Worker** - qualified in Railway Engineering and Personal Track Safety, particularly seeking a signalling role.

An experienced **Records Management Officer.** Knowledgeable in professional filing systems, information retrieval and destruction of past expiry documents. Familiar with Data Protection legislation and best practise.

A highly experienced **Retail Store Manager** and department manager.

A highly experienced **Roofer**. Skilled in slating and tiling, lead-work, cement work, fascia, soffits, guttering, re-pointing and leak discovery.

A high achieving **Sales Person**, with a strong track record in the retail and home improvement sectors.

An experienced **Sales and Marketing** professional, able to conduct and coordinate campaigns and successfully liaise with customers, both over the telephone and face to face.

Work Skills A - Z	A **Scaffold Labourer** working with qualified scaffolders to fetch and carry scaffold tubes and boards whilst learning the scaffold trade.
	An experienced private **Security Officer** experienced in handling enquiries and concerns from customers, searching people, bag checks (using x-ray machines), document checking (passports and tickets) perimeter checks, CCTV monitoring and vehicle checks.
	An experienced **Shift Supervisor** and **Factory Worker**, able to motivate teams of people, organise rotas and ensure production targets are met.
	A **Social Media Manager** experienced in account management and running promotional campaigns across multiple platforms including Facebook, Instagram, Snapchat and Twitter. Able to build and optimise websites.
	A **Sport and Fitness Professional** and qualified nutritionist, able to supervise personal trainers and fitness instructors.
	A skilled **Steel Fixer.** Working with structural engineers and welders to ensure that steels installed fulfil all of the site requirements. Operates cherry pickers, forklift trucks and works in confined spaces.
	A qualified and experienced **Street Works** operative with a current **NRSWA** Operator's Card.
	A **Support Worker** for drugs and alcohol addiction, able to assist people through detox and help them with relapse prevention strategies such as understanding their personal triggers.
	An enthusiastic and confident **Teacher** able to present and engage audiences in a wide range of subjects.
	A skilled **Telephone Call Handler** able to handle high call volumes, coupled with a confident telephone manner and a customer service focus.
	An experienced **Telephone Engineer.** BT trained, qualified as a Telecoms Professional, able to work on all types of telephone systems, install telephone and internet lines and work with fibre optics.
	A Qualified and experienced Floor and Wall **Tiler**, able to work with varied tiling materials in a wide range of commercial and residential settings.
	A General **Tradesman** competent in bathroom and wet room installation, carpentry, dry lining, flat roof work, timber frame work, flooring, painting and decorating, tiling and general property maintenance and refurbishment.
	A **Transport Manager** experienced in operating a fleet of passenger coaches, coordinating drivers, overseeing maintenance and depot management.
	A trusted **Upholsterer** with superb attention to detail and a high quality of workmanship.
	Vehicle Inspector and Tester. Worked for prestigious clients including RAC and GM on new vehicles as well as pre-owned and Motability leases.

Work Skills A - Z	A qualified, skilled and experienced **Vehicle Maintenance and Recovery** specialist.
	A **Warehouse Operative** experienced in unloading deliveries and checking manifests as well as picking and packing goods for despatch.
	A **Welder** and Fabricator experienced in Manual Metal Arc Welding, Metal Inert Gas (MIG) Welding, Tungsten Inert Gas (TIG) Welding and Gas Cutting (Oxyacetylene) for cutting through steel. Able to weld steel and aluminium, manufacture and repair a wide range of products and heavy industrial goods.
	An experienced **Yard-man** able to organise deliveries, guide vehicles, load and unload whilst also maintaining a safe working environment.
	An experienced and qualified **Yoga teacher**. Able to write and facilitate courses for people from all different age groups, genders and health levels.
	A caring **Youth Worker** with 12 years' experience of supervising and working with children and young adults.

"I sent my CV, disclosure letter and application letter to an exclusive hotel. They wrote back asking me to attend for an interview. I like cooking and have lots of experience in prison kitchens, so I got the job. I now have a full-time job working in the kitchen of this top hotel." GW

Preferred Role (Optional)

Optional - This section is useful if you are targeting a specific job or certain industries.

If you are open-minded and flexible about your next role, then you do not need to include it.

This section is a good opportunity to explain what your ideal job is.

It does work particularly well when you are appointing recruitment agencies to find employment on your behalf.

Examples of Preferred Roles	*Seeking a hands-on role with pets and wildlife.*
	Seeking a customer facing role in the property industry.
	Seeking a sales conversion role in the home improvement industry.
	Seeking a permanently employed position in highway maintenance.
	Seeking a teaching or support role in the resettlement of ex-offenders.
	Seeking an employed position within a successful shop fitting company.
	Seeking an employed position, or sub-contractor role, in the plumbing industry.
	Seeking an employed driving position or a supervisory role in the transport and logistics industries.

"We believe in equal opportunities for all persons. If someone has the skills required for the job, their past is irrelevant."

Paul Farrelly - Director, Farrelly Construction

Employment Experience (with 300 pre-written templates)

This essential section is your opportunity to list the job roles which you have held.

It is your choice whether you call this section 'Experience', 'Work Experience' or 'Employment Experience'.

I recommend calling it 'Employment Experience' as this the most suitable for all CVs.

DO:

☑ List your jobs chronologically beginning with the current year and moving backwards to 15 - 20 years.

☑ List years instead of months to eliminate short term career gaps.

☑ Write about your achievements and the skills you gained in each job role.

☑ Only include the company name if they will give you a good reference.

☑ Make sure that everything you say is honest and that you are prepared to confidently answer questions about your experience.

☑ Include all of the following 3 things:

1) Prison jobs and experiences (one hundred examples from page 150).

2) Employed positions you have held (two hundred examples from page 167).

3) Full details of long-term career breaks, when you were out of work/ not working (examples on pages 197 and 198).

Example wording follows for each of these.

☑ If you are estimating dates, then at the bottom write the phrase:

Please note: dates listed, and the timeline are approximate.

☑ If you have a lot more experience going back further than the jobs, you have listed then add a short sentence underneath:

- *Previous work experience includes earlier years of providing tech support in the IT sector.*

- *Previous work experience includes 20 earlier years of labouring for construction companies, landscaping and roofing.*

- *Previous work experience includes client liaison, issuing of legal documentation (probate certificates), and resource management.*

148

Prison Jobs

Prison jobs improve a CV.

It is important to include prison jobs within your **Employment Experience** section because:

- You may have gained additional qualifications in these prison jobs.

- You can list the skills, knowledge and experience gained in these roles.

- These jobs show that you have an uninterrupted and consistent work habit.

- Prison jobs demonstrate determination and resilience to work in challenging environments, difficult situations and whilst enduring personal hardship.

You must be honest when you write about responsibilities, skills gained and achievements as you will be asked questions about your work experience at interview.

Skills needed to work in prison are transferable outside the prison walls and indicate stability and achievement.
(Source: Ellen Gardner, 'how prison facilitates or threatens achievement of desired self')

If you are reluctant to include your prison jobs, then you can account for any gaps in your CV with wording similar to the following:

*2012 - 2020 **Full Time Worker** within secure residential establishment. Worked in a wide range of roles, gaining skills and qualifications whilst meeting or exceeding all professional expectations. Please see accompanying Personal Disclosure Statement for further information.*

If, **as recommended**, you are happy to list your prison jobs then the following pre-written templates will help you to understand the knowledge and skills you gained and all the things that you achieved.

The examples are organised alphabetically, please edit them and use as much or as little wording from them as you wish.

149

Prison Job CV Templates A - Z	**Activities Coordinator**. Organised meaningful activities for residents of a secure custodial establishment including competitions, fitness sessions, charity fundraising, and community events aimed at breaking down barriers, building relationships and fostering a community atmosphere. Gained excellent people skills and organisation skills. Received praise and appreciation from residents and staff for the hard work and dedication which I showed in this role.
	Appliance Repairer. DHL. Working in a busy restoration department I repaired and restored white goods including tumble driers, washing machines, fridges, freezers and dishwashers. Became competent in identifying and resolving electrical faults and ensured compliance with health and safety.
	Art Teacher. Established and facilitated my own Art classes in a secure residential establishment. Facilitated informative training sessions and provided meaningful feedback to students. These classes helped people to improve their mental health and to express themselves emotionally when they were often experiencing extreme personal stress. This role required the ability to remain organised when helping multiple students, a positive attitude and good communication skills.
	Baker (Bad Boys Bakery). Started as a kitchen porter and progressed on merit and skill to bread and cake maker, utilising a wide range of ingredients. Gained skills in the use of electric mixers, industrial ovens as well as all hand tools including whisks and icing pipes. Met production targets through hard work.
	Barber Shop Mentor. Developed barbering skills and gained qualifications such that I was able to teach barbering to residents of a secure residential establishment. I maintained the salon diary and helped with various administration tasks. Facilitated training sessions and provided meaningful feedback to students as they cut residents' hair. Taught and supported mentees to progress from absolute beginners to formally qualified skilled barbers. Displayed good communication and organisation skills
	BICS Biohazard Responder. British Institute of Cleaning Sciences qualified responder. Responsible for securing areas, when and where, biohazard incidents have occurred. Duties included health and safety risk assessments, wearing of Personal Protective Equipment (PPE), cleaning of blood and bodily fluids and making safe all surrounding areas. Logged incidents and provided regular reports. Organisation, hard work and health and safety were essential.

"Getting ex-offenders back into work is a top priority if we want to see national crime rates fall. We all make mistakes in life, some bigger than others, but we believe those who fall hardest need the greatest amount of help." Charlie Bradshaw, Managing Director Matrix APA Product Design

B.I.C.S. Industrial Cleaning Operative. Cleaned office, residential and warehouse environments. Trusted in the highest security environments including Officer's mess in prison. Achieved proficiency in machine buffing and polishing. Developed chemical competency and knowledge of COSHH, HASSAS, MHOR, RIDDOR, HASAWA and PUWER regulations. Familiar with health and safety and PPE.

B.I.C.S. Industrial Cleaning Supervisor. Responsible for a team of cleaners in a secure residential environment. Maintained cleaning logs, ensured that high standards of cleaning were met, ordered products, unloaded deliveries and stored cleaning chemicals safely and recorded a product inventory.

B.I.C.S. Trainer and Assessor. Facilitated workshops for people new to BICS, trained and assessed them. Also trained trainers in a group setting and assessed assessors on a one to one basis. Gained qualifications to highest BICS levels. Taught people to progress from beginners to formally qualified skilled Industrial Cleaners. Organisation and communication skills were essential.

Bicycle Repair and Maintenance. Worked in a dedicated factory unit on behalf of a children's charity. Disassembled, refurbished and rebuilt high volumes of bicycles each week. Bicycles were donated by police recovery and by generous members of the public. Each bike would be repaired and given a full service. High value bikes were sent to auction for fundraising and low value ones were donated to families in difficulty. The team cared deeply about what they were doing. Worked quickly to a high standard whilst meeting targets and maintaining a clean and safe work station.

Braille Studio. Programmed and created indentations in paper, card and packaging for blind people to be able to read. Particularly focussed on the creation of materials to introduce the braille language and teach it. This role was on behalf of a blind persons' charity and the management and staff cared very much about producing high quality materials. I dedicated more time and energy than that which was required or expected.

Bricklayer. Completed City and guilds Levels 1 and 2 Diploma in Bricklaying within a secure residential establishment. Received praise and commendations for the high standard of brickwork. Developed a portfolio of fireplaces, garden walls, cavity walls, piers and window frames. Developed my skills so much that I was trusted to mentor and help other students on their bricklaying journey too. Fully complied with Health and Safety and PPE at all times.

Call Centre Trainer. Census data. I started with the company as a call centre operative (agent), progressed to team leader and then on to a trainer. As a trainer, working on behalf of a market research and telesales company, I taught new employees to call customers to solicit their opinions on products and services and to save them money on utilities. I ensured that employees followed scripts and procedures and professionally handled conversations.

"A good idea is not to have any unnecessary barriers to recruiting talent and for ex-offenders trying to re-enter the workforce."
John O'Brien, Destria Management Consultants

Careers Adviser. National Careers Service. Provided personalised consultations to residents of a secure residential establishment. Helped people to produce CVs and Personal Disclosure Statements, provided guidance on job application processes, careers advice and interview coaching. Treated people at all levels of academic achievement and careers success with decency, respect and professionalism. Maintained records in compliance with the General Data Protection Regulations.
Carpenter. Full-time carpenter within the works department of a secure residential community holding 300 people. Worked in a busy manufacturing unit, producing pre-built furniture units ready for permanent installation. Performed independently and on own initiative, fixing and installing benches, integral cupboards, kitchen units, worktops and frames, hanging and repairing doors, flat-pack assembly and staircase work. Made permanent play equipment, environmentally friendly bug houses and signs. Skilled in tooling, health and safety, quality control and manual handling.
Car Wash Manager. Operated a busy industrial car wash facility within a secure custodial setting. Duties included driving minibuses, staff cars and other vehicles to the facility, pre-wash preparation, jet washing, polishing, internal vacuuming and valeting. Followed Health and safety, COSHH and PPE.
Chapel and Mosque Orderly. Managed multi-faith chaplaincy provision in a secure residential establishment. Maintained Chapel diary and calendars, organised and catered for special events. Cleaned and maintained the chapel, halls and rooms. Welcomed attendees and served them refreshments. Assisted Chaplains, Imams and other faith leaders in various duties as required.
Charity Advisor. Responsible for liaison between residents of a secure residential establishment and a charity called St Giles Trust which helped prepare them for housing in the community. Provided additional information, advice and guidance to help reduce re-offending and helping clients to build a stable life. Trust, confidentiality and empathy were essential in this role.
Charity Co-ordinator. Maintained connections with charities to support adults in difficult situations. Liaised with a range of voluntary sector organisations including St Giles Trust, MIND, RAPT (Drugs and Alcohol), BASS Housing Trust, Family Matters, Citizens Advice and the Job Centre, amongst others. Made referrals and sign-posted prisoners to the most appropriate agencies for help. Organised resettlement such as assisting with jobs, housing, bank accounts, restorative justice and relationships problems; all with a view to reduce re-offending and assist resettlement. Maintained confidentiality and complied with General Data Protection Regulations.

"I was about to apply for a job when someone showed me this book. He explained that my CV had many years of gaps and it was not comprehensive enough. I had left out my good achievements and trusted roles in prison. Now, after redoing my CV to include my most trusted prison jobs and also the volunteer work, I had done, I was able to send my application confidently knowing I am more likely to get an interview." DC

Charity Project Leader. YOT Youth Offenders Team. As part of Keep Out - crime diversion scheme I worked with deprived young people who were identified as being at high risk of engaging in crime. I developed an understanding of the unique mind-set of young people who are engaged in anti-social behaviour and how to discourage this and to turn their energies into more productive behaviours. I gained experience in teaching, motivating and encouraging people. Gained qualifications whilst in post and job satisfaction through making a real difference to people's lives. Communication skills, organisation, positivity, professionalism, record keeping, and safeguarding were essential. I was praised for my honesty, empathy and compassion.

Charity Shop Worker. Sue Ryder Care. Worked as part of a team within a busy charity shop. Gratefully received donations of stock including books, pictures, clothing and general bric-a-brac. Organised, cleaned and displayed items for retail sale. Ironed clothes and packed unsaleable items for despatch to recycling facilities. Built rapport with regular customers and volunteers.

Charity Support Worker. Turning Point. Facilitated group therapy sessions, made appointments for people to see case-workers, gave out clean user kits and encouraged users to come off drugs. Provided additional information, advice and guidance with a view to reducing re-offending and helping clients to build a stable life. Displayed trust, confidentiality and empathy. I know that people don't change until and unless they are ready, so I made sure that I was there for them when they were ready. Gained success stories of people who turned their lives around from my time in this role.

Classroom Assistant/ Peer Mentor. Business Enterprise Class. Taught business skills and compliance to small classes of adults to level 2 (GCSE). Encouraged reluctant learners and gave personal attention to people who struggled. Marked papers and gave feedback. Helped people with business and financial planning. Showed a great deal of empathy, encouragement for others and personal motivation in this role.

Classroom Assistant/ Peer Mentor. Carpentry course. Facilitated workshops for new carpentry students. Taught and supported classes of 20 students at a time to progress from absolute beginners to formally qualified skilled carpenters. Detailed knowledge, organisation skills, communication skills and enthusiasm for the subject were essential in this role.

Classroom Assistant/ Peer Mentor. Catering Course. Taught and assisted on an accredited catering course within a secure residential establishment. Facilitated informative training sessions, marked papers, provided meaningful feedback to students and mediated between teachers and students in conflict situations. Achieved a 100% pass rate for the duration of my time in post. This role required the ability to remain organised, maintain a positive attitude and display good communication skills.

"I came to prison at a young age and have spent a long time inside. I hadn't completed a CV before. I felt that I hadn't really achieved anything worthwhile work wise in my life. HOWEVER, this book explained that a lot of the prison jobs I have done have taught me real skills which I can use. I now see my potential in a completely different way and believe that I have a value to an employer." PA

Classroom Assistant/ Peer Mentor. Graphic Design Class. Taught Graphic Design software and general PC skills to small classes of adults. Demonstrated Adobe suite, facilitated classroom training sessions and worked one-to-one with students. Encouraged reluctant learners and gave personal attention to people who struggled. Marked work produced by students and gave feedback. Showed motivation to help people move forwards and also introduced careers pathways after qualifying.
Classroom Assistant/ Peer Mentor. IT Academy. Taught MS Office and general PC skills to small classes of adults. Demonstrated software, facilitated training sessions and worked one-to-one with students. Encouraged reluctant learners and gave personal attention to people who struggled. Marked papers and gave feedback. Inspired people by explaining future career pathways.
Classroom Assistant/ Peer Mentor. Numeracy and Literacy. Taught functional skills (Maths and English) to adults to level 2 (GCSE). Encouraged reluctant learners and gave personal attention to people who struggled. Marked papers and gave feedback, made referrals to Additional Learning Support departments (ALS), mediated between teachers and students in conflict situations. Showed a great deal of empathy and motivation in this role.
Classroom Assistant/ Peer Mentor. "Resolve" Violence Reduction programme within a secure residential establishment. Facilitated informative training sessions within an anger management programme lasting several months. Provided advice and signposting. Developed understanding of a wide range of mental health issues, a positive attitude, good communication and organisation skills.
Classroom Assistant/ Peer Mentor. Street works (NRSWA). Taught principles of City and Guilds **Street-works** Road Maintenance, Excavation and Reinstatement to small classes of adults. Facilitated classroom training sessions and worked one-to-one with students. Personally, helped more than 25 men in custody to pass and gain valuable vocational qualifications that will lead to full time employment, reduce their risk of reoffending and lead to the creation of fewer victims of crime.
Cleaner. Independently cleaned office, residential and warehouse environments. Trusted to clean high security environments including Officers' Mess and Healthcare departments in prison. Achieved proficiency in machine buffing and polishing. Developed chemical competency and knowledge of COSHH. Familiar with health and safety and PPE.
Clothing Manufacturer. Worked as part of a productive team in a work-wear clothing factory. Manufactured jeans, shirts, sports clothes, towels, blankets, quilts, sheets, bags and underwear. Met pressing deadlines in a target driven environment. Duties included cutting fabric, sewing, stitching, packing and quality control as well as carrying out health and safety risk assessments (safe systems of work).

"I would encourage more UK businesses to hire ex-prisoners."
Diego Fuentes, Virgin Trains

Community Shop Assistant. *Example charity.* Worked as part of a team within a busy community warehouse. Duties included gratefully receiving donations of furniture and white goods from the public, displaying them for resale (primarily to low income households) and delivering them. Interacted with customers daily and built rapport with regular customers. Safe manual handling, PPE, good timekeeping and team work were essential.

Concrete Manufacturer. Making precast concrete blocks for road and street use. Primarily manufactured bollards for protecting pedestrian areas. Added sand and stones to cement to make the concrete, used an industrial concrete mixing machine, barrowed wet concrete into block moulds, unloosened bolts and de-moulded finished products. Followed health and safety procedures including safe use of machines, manual handling, clean work areas and PPE.

Drug and Alcohol Support Worker (Peer Supporter). Helped people in a secure residential establishment with advice and signposting whilst they were at their most distressed and vulnerable. Offered personal support to rehabilitate from drug use, detox from drug addiction, identify personal triggers and resist temptation to relapse. Undertook drug and alcohol awareness training including relapse prevention and the 12-step programme. Identified any related mental health issues. This role required empathy and organisational skills.

Employment Orderly/ Recruitment Consultant. Managed a busy employment department within a secure residential establishment. Interviewed candidates to assess their skills and personal goals, identified opportunities to fill roles with the right people, at the right time, to ensure a good fit with each placement. Guided people with interview techniques and helped them with future life planning. Verified documentation, maintained records and processed data in accordance with the General Data Protection Regulations. Gained excellent interpersonal skills and remained calm and focused in high pressure situations.

Equalities Orderly. Responsible for developing procedures with all stakeholders to ensure that all nine protected characteristics of the Equalities Act (Namely Age, Disability, Gender, Marriage and Civil Partnership, Pregnancy and Maternity, Race, Religion, Sexual Orientation and Gender Reassignment) were complied with across a secure residential establishment. Assisted with complaints and arbitrated in disputes. Showed attention to detail, empathy and objectivity when solving problems.

Fabric and Material Recycling. Converted high volumes of healthcare clothing, bedding and fabrics into multi-use cloths. Used cutting, pressing and baling machines following all health and safety procedures. Responsible for sorting, cutting, weighing, pressing, bailing and despatching orders by the pallet load. Managed time pressure, used machinery safely and co-ordinated a team of junior workers.

Floor Laying. Working as part of a team (and often in a supervisory role) which was in demand across a large custodial setting. My role included laying hard wearing linoleum in residential units. I conducted Health and Safety risk assessments, lifted furniture following manual handling procedures and was responsible for measuring, cutting, fitting, gluing and snagging.

Foreign National Representative. Responsible for liaising between staff and international residents of a secure residential establishment. Helped people to prepare for seeing Home Office Representatives by explaining procedures, completing paperwork and arranged translation services. Offered guidance, direction and personal attention to people in distress, coping with mental health challenges or preparing for deportation. Displayed good communication and organisational skills.

Gym - Cardio-Vascular (CV) Training Orderly. Explained the safe use of gym equipment. Looked after training area including cleaning and tidying. Gave advice on work-outs and fitness regimes. Managed training diary and kept register of attendance schedules. Gained health and first aid qualifications.

Gym Course Mentor. Organised, facilitated and assisted on structured gym courses. Courses included Fitness Instructor Level 2, Circuit Instructor Level 2, Volleyball Leaders Level 2 and Badminton for Beginners, as well as warm up and cardiovascular exercises for lasting health. Gained a full range of gym qualifications and developed an awareness of personal health and safety considerations.

Gym Instructor (Remedial). Provided remedial gym classes and coaching sessions for people who have been physically injured in car accidents, recovering from operations or addiction, needed to lose weight for medical reasons or who were losing their independence. Showed patience, understanding and compassion. Received positive references and became a GP Referral Fitness Instructor which is a prestigious accolade in recognition of the consistent results which I helped clients to achieve.

Gym Orderly. Responsible for ensuring the smooth running of a men's gym in a secure residential establishment. Assisted on structured gym courses and co-ordinated support roles, including cleaners and referees. Other duties included product ordering, taking register of attendance schedules, kit washing and kit management. I worked hard to achieve this post after gaining personal health and first aid qualifications.

Healthcare Orderly. Distributed documents and appointment letters. Maintained cleanliness and displayed promotional material in the practise. Monitored care provided to elderly people in a secure custodial setting. Liaised between healthcare staff and service recipients. Developed strong relationships and offered guidance and personal attention. Improved communication and organisational skills.

Health Trainer. Taught and coached gym members on nutrition and health & fitness, as well as making necessary lifestyle changes. Facilitated classes such as circuit training; as well as games and routines for overall improvement and wellbeing.

Health and Wellbeing Champion (HAWCS). Working in a secure residential establishment, residents came to me with healthcare complaints or concerns. Made referrals to mental health teams and drug rehabilitation agencies, attended NHS and Governor level meetings to design healthcare programme. I personally contributed to stop self-harming initiatives.

Hearing Aid Refurbishment. Sight and Sound Charity. Cleaned, repaired and refurbished hearing aids and glasses to be sent to third world countries. Individually packed and bulk boxed shipments ready for despatch. The staff and management cared deeply about what they were doing, and I was a valued member of the team. Worked quickly to meet targets but maintained a high standard and ensured compliance with health and safety.

Induction Orderly. Welcomed, registered and interviewed people as they arrived at a secure residential establishment. Offered a high level of guidance, direction and personal attention to people who were often in distress or coping with mental health challenges. Excellent communication and organisational skills as well as professional administration (including reporting and record keeping), were essential.

Job Centre Orderly. Helped serving prisoners to prepare for release into the community by signposting them to their local job centre. Organised job centre events and resettlement fairs and displayed posters. Helped people to complete forms and paperwork, wrote letters and provided information, advice and guidance related to employment and benefit claims.

Kitchen Porter. Responsible for food preparation and bulk cooking to cater for residents in a secure residential establishment. The kitchens provided two meals each day for 700 residents. Ensured that special dietary requirements for allergy sufferers were accommodated and religious requirements were followed. Duties also included general cleaning, loading and unloading deliveries, monitoring storage temperatures, labelling and stock rotation and safe handling to avoid cross-contamination.

Kitchen Servery Worker. Responsible for serving meals to residents in a secure residential establishment. The servery provided two meals each day for 120 residents. I ensured compliance (through separation of serving trays and utensils) with religious requirements and special dietary needs for allergy sufferers. Served people with a positive and professional attitude whilst confidently adhering to portion control.

Kitchen Supervisor. Progressed from general kitchen porter to overseeing and co-ordinating a team of twelve workers. Monitored food safety and hygiene, resolved short notice challenges, attended management meetings, mediated in disputes caused by the high-pressure environment and organised catering for special events such as group visit days and religious festivals.

Landscape Gardener. Worked independently with a wide range of maintenance responsibilities across a multi-acre site. Duties included planting, mowing, landscaping, designing, trimming, weeding, edging and pruning. Numerous other tasks were carried out to keep the sites clean, tidy, attractive and displaying to their full potential, both practically and aesthetically.

"With this book, I took a good look at my skills, I don't want to waste my life and hurt other people. I want to work and prove that I have a value. I will keep working through this book, thank you." NM

Laser machinery operator (Lasers Workshop). Used CAD to programme laser machines and safely operated them to make finished shapes out of wood for jewellery, toys and early years' puzzles. Packaged finished items for despatch to the manufacturer and created signs for custodial establishments and external government clients. Adhered to health and safety and maintained a safe working environment.

Laundry Operative. Worked in an industrial laundry department using large driers, washing machines and presses (ironing). Fulfilled time-sensitive orders by managing a workload of washing, drying, folding, packing cleaned items and hosting collections. Consistently met targets and deadlines through hard work and dedication.

Laundry Orderly. Performed service-washes for residents of a secure residential facility. Worked in an orderly fashion to wash, dry and fold clothing and bedding efficiently and to a high standard. Maintained a waiting list and managed urgent loads. Maintained a clean and tidy working environment and followed health and safety.

Lawnmower repair and maintenance. Worked in a dedicated factory unit, reconditioning lawnmowers and garden machinery. Disassembled, refurbished, serviced and rebuilt strimmers, hand mowers and ride-on lawnmowers. Met targets, maintained a high standard of work and followed health and safety.

Library Orderly. Responsible for the smooth management of a busy prison library. I issued reminder slips to residents, indexed and rotated stock and carried out after hours cleaning. When the library was open I greeted residents and processed book and media withdrawals and returns. Displayed professionalism and organisational skills.

Life Skills Orderly. In this role I worked alongside a Prison Governor and developed courses to help prisoners to gain employment and live more meaningful lives upon release. Subjects covered included employability, CV writing, cookery and catering environmentally beneficial farming such as Bee Keeping, learning additional languages. In this role I developed a wide range of skills (organisational skills and enhanced people skills) and gained additional knowledge on a wide range of subjects.

Mental Health Supporter and Peer Mentor. Helped people in a secure residential establishment who were in distress and struggling to cope with mental health challenges, by providing distraction packs, talking therapy and personal support. Signposted and made referrals to relevant agencies, completed paperwork and provided information, advice and guidance. This role required empathy, good communication and organisational skills. Gained relevant qualifications whilst in post.

Minibus Driver. Transferred residents from an open prison to hospital appointments and work placements in the community. Worked independently planning alternatives to set routes as required. Adhered to strict time schedules, drove safely and considerately (accident free) and was on call for short notice emergency journeys.

Motorbike and Scooter Repairer. Worked in a dedicated factory unit on behalf of a homeless and distressed children's charity. Motorbikes were primarily donated by police having been lost or recovered after theft. Each motorbike would be disassembled, refurbished, repaired and rebuilt, given a full service and then then testing and checked before the charity put them up for sale to raise income. Worked quickly to meet targets but maintained a high standard and ensured H&S compliance.

Music Orderly. Responsible for the smooth running of a music department in a secure residential community. Managed diary, sound engineering, held and promoted events and maintained a clean and safe studio environment. Helped people at all levels of musical ability. Provided vocal coaching and song writing guidance.

Offender Management Unit (OMU) Orderly. Responsible for liaising between case managers and residents of a secure residential establishment. Organised the safe storage of confidential and official documents, registered people and helped them to complete forms. Offered guidance, direction and personal attention to people in distress or coping with mental health challenges. Displayed good communication skills, organisational skills, professional reporting and record keeping.

Office Administrator/ Education Champion. Worked in a busy education office enrolling adult learners onto a wide range of courses. Persuaded reluctant learners to enrol or complete courses that would help them to progress. Organised registers and timetables, distributed enrolment confirmations and certificates, carried out filing and general office administration tasks. Adhered to Data Protection Regulations.

Officer's Mess. In this trusted Customer Service role, I served staff of a secure residential establishment hot drinks, hot food and snacks. Displayed a full range of skills including creation of different coffee types, equipment care, health, safety and hygiene. Created high quality fresh sandwiches, rolls and paninis as well as hot food. Gained customer service skills, as well as an understanding of payment processing and till operation. Built long term relationships with staff and regular customers.

Open University Orderly. Enrolled students in secure environments onto access modules and degree courses; such courses give people in custodial settings a purpose and direction. Guided students on the most relevant courses for their future life plans. Helped applicants to complete student loan forms. Provided general information, advice and guidance on Tutor Marked Assessments (TMA's), deadlines and the submissions process. Reviewed tutor feedback with students and discussed areas of improvement. This role required good communication and organisational skills as well as the ability to motivate other people when they feel low or deflated.

Painter and Decorator. Worked across a large site as part of a small team refurbishing vacant residential units and providing consistent internal and external maintenance. Solid application, time management, problem solving and health and safety considerations were all essential in this role.

Prison Job CV Templates A - Z	**Paint-line operative (Powder-coating)**. Worked in a busy industrial engineering workshop. Powder-coated doors, windows, large gates, secure metal shutters and grills and then conveyed them into a high temperature oven. Packed, palletised and despatched securely. Followed health and safety and wore all necessary PPE.
	Pallet Manufacture. Working in a busy carpentry workshop I manufactured pallets for heavy use industrial and logistics purposes. Gained experience in safe and efficient use of nail guns as well as other machinery and hand tools. Stacked pallets ready for despatch and ensured that the team met or exceeded targets set by our employer. Complied with health and safety and maintained a safe working environment.
	PC Refurbishment. Skills for Africa charity. Trained and qualified as a Cisco networking engineering and joined the team working on behalf of this worthwhile charity. Disassembled, repaired, cleaned and refurbished computers, wiped hard drives and reinstalled software ready for the computers to be sent to schools and villages in Africa.
	Peace and Community Engagement Representative (PACE). A peer-led mediation role. Facilitated discussions to prevent confrontation. Resolved conflicts, mediated disputes, supported and signposted people to agencies for help. I personally helped people break gang affiliations. Gained mentoring and leadership skills. I was highly praised for my work ethic, good communication skills and positive attitude.
	Plastic Manufacturing. Worked in a plastic goods manufacturing facility. Created tens of thousands of high impact multi-use and recyclable knives, forks, spoons, cups, bowls, plates, jugs and trays. Designed consumer goods using Computer Aided Design. Manufactured items from coloured and clear plastic beads. Managed logs of orders and their fulfilment, ensured timely packing and despatch and trouble-shooted problems. Oversaw quality control and maintained a safe working environment.
	Print-shop Operative. Worked in a busy printing warehouse, setting up machines and printing a wide range of literature and signs. The company were main contractors for prisons and government departments. Correctly operated printing, cutting and folding machines. Assembled training literature into professional portfolios, packed and despatched securely, met production targets and maintained quality control.
	Prisoner Information Desk (PID) worker AND Information, Advice and Guidance Provider. Helped hundreds of residents in a secure residential environment with letter writing, applications, information, advice and guidance. Helped people with advice and sign posting whilst they were at their most distressed and vulnerable or suffering from mental health challenges. Collected meals for ill people and provided basic social care. This role required empathy, good communication and organisational skills.

"Employment reduces offending by up to 50%, so it's in every community's interest to reduce the barriers to work for people with criminal convictions." Gemma Hughes, Chwarae Teg (Equality Charity)

Radio Production. Set up interviews and radio shows for a national radio network. Experience gained in adobe audition and other software packages. Trained other people in interview techniques, audience engagement how to use software and studio equipment (hardware). Helped people with business and financial planning and showed them career pathways into broadcasting. Showed a great deal of empathy, encouragement for others and personal motivation in this role.

Reception Orderly. Welcomed, registered and photographed people as they arrived at a secure, residential community. Offered guidance, support and personal attention to people who were often in distress, confused or struggling to adapt to change. Good communication skills, organisational skills and professional administration were essential in this trusted role. Processed people's property and paperwork prior to their leaving. Carried out cleaning duties to maintain a decent environment. Considered Health and Safety and security at all times.

Recycling and Waste Management Operative. Worked in a busy industrial recycling facility, sorting large volumes of residential and commercial waste. Supervised and trained a small team responsible for sorting, crushing, baling and despatching. Worked independently to meet pressing deadlines. Became familiar with health and safety considerations, including PPE and COSHH.

Recycling Operative (Plastics). Working in an industrial recycling plant, I opened and disassembled VHS videos and shredded CDs and DVDs, and other small plastic items to create plastic chips that were easily recyclable. Used a grinding machine. Bagged plastic chippings into 1 tonne bags and secured them to pallets ready for despatch to regional facilities. Gained experience in manual handling, PPE and meeting production targets.

Rehabilitative Culture Representative. Whilst in this post, I developed efficient processes and meaningful relationships between residents of a secure custodial facility, Officers and Civilian Staff. Assisted with complaints and professionally interceded in disputes in a fair and impartial, objective manner. Developed understanding of a wide range of mental health issues and emotional challenges. A positive attitude, attention to detail, good communication skills, organisation skills (including reporting and record keeping) and empathy towards others were essential.

Resettlement Representative. Helped serving prisoners to prepare for release into the community. I ensured that they had practical help in the 7 pathways of resettlement (accommodation, drugs and alcohol, attitudes, thinking and behaviour, education, training and employment, finance, benefit and debt, mental and physical health, children and family ties). Made referrals to housing charities, helped people to complete forms and paperwork, wrote letters and provided information, advice and guidance. Maintained client confidentiality and complied with Data Protection.

"I am very impressed with the ready-made inputs and the formats that are set up in this book. It relieves the pressure of producing a quality CV and makes creating your own professional documents a lot easier. It flows fluidly, no nonsense." CB

Restorative Justice Facilitator. Using mediation qualifications, I held Restorative Justice Conferences between residents of a secure residential establishment when they were at loggerheads or angry and upset with each other. Trained additional facilitators and mediators. Paid due consideration to security and Health and Safety and displayed a positive attitude, good communication and organisational skills.

Segregation Orderly. Responsible for cleaning and general maintenance of a Care and Separation Unit (CSU - aka Segregation) within a secure residential establishment. The role was a trusted position, often working in difficult and distressing situations. Many residents who were in the CSU suffered mental illness and required a lot of understanding as well as practical help. Duties included the serving of meals, provision of laundry services, cleaning, general minor property maintenance and provision of a small library service. Strictly followed Health and Safety protocols, reported minor and major incidents and carried out risk assessments.

Segregation Support Worker - Project Unite. Responsible for providing additional pastoral and practical support to people held in a Care and Separation Unit (CSU - aka Segregation) within a secure residential establishment. The role was a trusted position, often working in distressing and difficult situations. Many residents suffered mental illness and required a lot of understanding as well as practical help. Duties included borrowing books from the library on their behalf and delivering them, mediating in disputes, checked on their general well-being, documented safety concerns and listened to their grievances and causes of upset.

Sign Manufacturer. Supervised a small team of workers who manufactured signs for motorways and secure residential establishments. Used computer aided design (CAD) to design templates that ran through the printing and manufacturing machines. Managed logs of orders and their fulfilment, ensured timely packing and despatch and trouble-shooting of problems that arose. Oversaw quality control, health & safety and maintained a safe and clean working environment.

Social-care orderly (Prison Carer). Helped people with autism and mental health challenges to cope with challenges in a secure residential establishment. Provided personal care support and cared for elderly residents with dementia and disabilities. Welcomed, registered and interviewed people as they arrived for the first time. Offered a high level of guidance, direction and personal attention to people who were often in distress or coping with mental health challenges. Signposted and made referrals to relevant agencies, completed paperwork and provided information, advice and guidance. This role required empathy and good communication skills.

Stores Manager. Responsible for the smooth running of a busy stores department and warehouse serving a secure residential site and accommodating in excess of 1000 adults. Distributed furniture, personal care products, electrical items and clothing and also maintained logs. Conducted stock takes and placed orders with management.

Teacher/ Learning mentor. Shannon Trust Charity. Taught basic literacy (reading and writing) one-on-one to adults with educational deficits or who require additional learning support. Monitored individual progress and enabled them to reach breakthroughs in their reading abilities. Provided encouragement to reluctant learner. Developed a great deal of empathy and patience for other people in this role. Provided English as a Second Language (ESOL) support and helped people to write letters home to their children and families.

Tool Repairman and Stores Manager. Speedy-hire workshop. Responsible for the smooth running of a busy stores department and repair workshop. Repaired, cleaned and maintained power tools and plant hire equipment including heaters, de-humidifiers, portable lighting rigs, paint strippers, power saws, angle grinders, magnetic drills, hammer drills and all hand tools. Conducted stock takes and placed stock orders. I was responsible, flexible and organised and consistently met targets.

Translator. Provided reading, writing and spoken translation for Romanian and Polish residents in a secure residential establishment. Accompanied people to important meetings with Healthcare and offender management. Helped people with general administration, advice and sign posting when they were distressed and/ or vulnerable. This role required empathy, good communication and organisation.

Transport Co-ordinator. Managed a small fleet of vehicles operating from a D-Category residential establishment. Plotted efficient routes onto route planner and time schedule. Generated driver instructions, managed routine maintenance and emergency repairs, ensured vehicle compliance including insurance, MOT's and road tax. Produced monthly management reports including fuels and mileage logs. Showed excellent communication skills and good attention to detail.

Hand **Upholsterer**. Working in a secure residential environment, I hand upholstered heavy use chairs and sofas. I received pre-built wooden frames and stapled and stitched material and padding to each chair. I would manage health and safety through risk assessments and conduct quality control checks.

Vacuum Cleaner Refurbishment. Repaired and reconditioned Dyson vacuum cleaners for resale by charities. Used a wide range of hand tools and testing equipment. Individually and bulk packed cleaners ready for despatch. Followed health and safety procedures, met targets and maintained a clean and tidy work environment.

Violence Reduction Co-ordinator. Developed violence reduction initiatives within a secure, residential establishment. Acted as a mediator between officers and prisoners and liaised between prisoner groups to de-escalate tensions. Gained experience in mediation and conflict resolution, as well as a formal qualification in Peer Mentoring. Prevented many serious incidents and gained commendations by senior prison staff on multiple occasions. Offered guidance, direction and personal attention to people who were often in distress or coping with mental health challenges. Displayed a positive attitude, good communication and organisation skills (including record keeping).

Visitor Centre Orderly (Customer Service Assistant). Ensured that the overall experience for visitors to a secure residential establishment was pleasant. Helped to organise family days in the visitor's centre; decorated the hall, helped residents to apply and took family photos. Cleaned and prepared the room, tables and chairs before visits started. Served customers hot drinks, food and snacks. Developed positive interpersonal skills and made nervous visitors feel comfortable and welcome.

Waiter (Clink restaurant). Ensured that the overall experience for visitors to a café/restaurant was pleasant. Greeted customers, waited on tables, served a wide range of different coffees (including latte, espresso, cappuccino, macchiato, flat white, mocha, Americano) and other hot drinks, cleaned tables, chairs, floors and food services. Developed customer service skills and built positive relationships.

Warehouse Operative. DHL Working as part of a busy team picking, sealing and packing client orders. Worked to deadlines, maintained manual handling procedures and a safe working environment.

Warehouse Supervisor. DHL. Worked as a supervisor to a busy team. Responsible for logging incoming client orders, picking, sealing, packing, checking and despatching, as well as managing high value orders. Resolved client complaints, solved picking errors and maintained quality control.

Welder and Fabricator. Engineering Workshop. Worked in a busy industrial factory. Fabricated high security locks, doors, windows, large gates, secure metal shutters and grills. Programmed dimensions into a CAD system. Repaired heavy metal products on behalf of national commercial clients and government contractors. Packed and despatched securely, was trusted with quality control and met production targets.

Welder and Fabricator. Recycling Lives. Worked in a busy industrial engineering workshop manufacturing money safes, cages for security vehicles and skips. Read plans, cut sheet metal and manufactured finished products. Despatched securely, was trusted with quality control and met production targets. Trained and mentored new team members on standard and speed.

Wheelchair Maintenance. Worked in a dedicated factory unit on behalf of a charity for disabled and disadvantaged people. Disassembled, refurbished and rebuilt high volumes of wheelchairs each week. Each wheelchair would be repaired and given a full service. The staff and management cared deeply about what they were doing, and I was a valued member of the team. Worked quickly to meet targets but maintained a high standard of work and ensured compliance with health and safety.

Woodworker. Full-time woodworker in a busy manufacturing unit. Manufactured items for the restaurant trade. Generally worked independently and on own initiative making chopping boards, open fronted display crates, environmentally friendly bird boxes, pencil boxes and picture frames. Skilled in safe use of tools including circular saws and band saws, chisels, routers, hand held and belt sanders. Packed items ready for despatch and followed health and safety, quality control and manual handling.

Works Department/ Estates Maintenance. Full-time works operative within a secure residential establishment. Responsible for 2 labourers with myself as the skilled tradesman. Deployed a wide range of construction skills to keep the sites in general good order. Carried out routine maintenance and responded to emergency call outs to issues such as pipe leaks, broken fences and dangerous paving. Used a wide range of power tools, hand tools and materials. Adhered to health and safety, PPE and security requirements.

Workshop Manager. Plumbing Production Line. Subcontracted to Wickes home improvement, I coordinated and supervised a team of forty-three workers who assembled complex component parts into finished plumbing assemblages and guttering parts for retail sale. The team packaged the finished products and bulk packed them ready for despatch. Helped to train workers in all assembly line roles including heat sealing, pressure testing, weighing, quality control and health and safety. Met targets, deadlines and KPIs and provided regular reports.

Workshop Operative. Camouflage Netting. Manufactured large quantities of camouflage netting on behalf of the Ministry of Defence. Despite the repetitiveness of the role I often worked overtime and motivated my small team to keep hitting or exceeding targets. Unpacked deliveries and packed items securely for despatch.

Workshop Operative. **Doors and Windows.** Assembled UPVC windows and doors from component parts. Carried out quality control of finished items, ensured integrity of rubber seals, tested functionality of handles and locks and packed items securely for despatch. Met performance targets and worked well within a busy team.

Workshop Operative. Electronics Workshop. Working as part of a busy target driven team, I assembled complex wiring looms for use in the automotive industry. Bulk packed finished products ready for despatch. Experience gained in electronics testing, quality control and health and safety in challenging environments.

Workshop Operative. Fixings Workshop. Manufactured large quantities of plasterboard rawlplugs, nuts, bolts, nails, screws and other fixings on behalf of Grippit, B&Q and other prestigious brands. Personally motivated my team to achieve targets. Unpacked deliveries and packed items securely for despatch. Experienced gained in meeting targets, quality control and health and safety.

Workshop Operative. Fragrance workshop. Manufactured room air fresheners on behalf of Matalan, Asda and other household names. Despite the repetitiveness of the role I often worked overtime and motivated my own team. Conducted quality control checks and retrained workers where necessary to ensure high quality production was maintained. Unpacked deliveries and packed items securely for despatch**.**

Workshop Operative. Headphones. Refurbished and repackaged headphones and small consumer items on behalf of Virgin Airlines. Maintained a good work ethic and motivated other workers despite the repetitive nature of the work. Set and monitored performance targets for teams of workers to achieve. Supervised health and safety and carried out workplace risk assessments.

	Workshop Operative. Lighting Assembly. Worked for a fluorescent light manufacturer. Assembled complex parts into finished light tubes, tested and packed the finished lights securely, ready for despatch. Experience gained in electrical safety, quality control and personal health and safety in challenging environments.
	Workshop Operative. Plumbing Workshop. Subcontracted to Wickes home improvement, I assembled complex component parts into finished plumbing assemblages and guttering parts for retail sale. Packaged the finished products and bulk packed them ready for despatch. Experience gained in heat sealing, pressure testing, weighing, quality control and health and safety. Met targets and deadlines.
	Workshop Operative. Radiator Valve Workshop. Assembled and dissembled radiator valves and replaced the washers with high quality UK specification parts. Packaged the finished products and bulk packed them ready for despatch. Experience gained in heat sealing, quality control, meeting targets and complying with H&S.
	Workshop Operative. Tea Pack Workshop. Packaged tea, coffee, milk, sugar, cereals and sundries into hotel sized portion packs for residents of a secure residential establishment. Processed and fulfilled incoming orders by packing large quantities ready for despatch. Worked with enthusiasm which motivated other team members. Met or exceeded all targets and followed health and safety and PPE requirements.
	Yoga teacher. Gained qualifications to Level 4 and established my own Yoga classes in a secure residential establishment. Created and facilitated a 10-week Yoga and mindfulness course. These classes helped people to improve their physical wellbeing and to find balance and peace. Carried out Health and Safety risk assessments and maintained professional records.

"We accept that individuals may have made mistakes, however they should be entitled to a period of rehabilitation and should not be discriminated against because of this."

Duncan Jones, Director - Hortech Landscape Management

Conventional Jobs

It is important to include job roles you have held outside of prison.

If you came to prison before you gained full-time employment, then mention any experience that you gained in family businesses, apprentice roles or work experience.

Start with the current year and list backwards up to 20 years, listing years instead of months (to remove short term careers gaps).

You must be honest when you write about responsibilities, skills gained and achievements; you will often be asked questions about your work experience at interview.

The following pre-written templates will help you to think about what you achieved within each role and how your skills will be valuable to employers. The examples are organised alphabetically, please edit them to suit your own work experience.

Pre-Written Templates for Conventional Jobs

Conventional Job CV Templates A - Z	
	Accountant. Partner in Chartered Accountants practice. Acting for personal and corporate clients in the private and third (charity and not-for-profit) sectors across a wide range of industries. Provided advice and planning on all aspects of business including cost efficiency and income generation. Prepared business plans, cash-flow forecasts, budgets and financial statements. Worked with clients at all stages of business from new start-ups to well established firms with substantial turnover. Recruited, trained and managed staff and conducted performance appraisals. Sourced and secured new clients. Managed marketing and also secured recommendations and referrals. Represented the firm in a professional and positive light, face to face, over the telephone and via email.
	Accountant's Assistant. *Example firm.* Verified client identities, produced and filed accounts and tax returns, compiled records and drafted reports. Documented processes and procedures, created letter templates, established new filing systems and associated databases. Performed 'know your client' (KYC) and all general office administration tasks. Liaised directly with clients and adhered to the new General Data Protection Regulations (GDPRs).
	Advertising Executive. *Example firm.* Worked on behalf of prestigious and diverse clients performing media and marketing planning. Designed communications strategies for existing customers and subscribers and gained market share. Carried out market analysis and planned expenditure. Troubleshooted and comprehensively managed campaigns. Professionalism, multitasking and motivation were essential. Developed greater insights into consumer purchasing decisions and built on existing sales and marketing skills.

167

Advertising Installer. *Example firm*. Pasted large adverts onto hoardings and fitted posters into installed street frames on behalf of national companies. Primarily film based, our adverts appeared in areas of high footfall and busy road traffic areas. Sites included bus stops, building sides, site hoardings etc. Followed all health and safety procedures for working at heights or in high risk areas such as the sides of busy roads. Displayed excellent time keeping skills and exceeded all targets.

Advertising Salesperson. *Example firm*. Responsible for selling advertising space on buses and commercial vehicles. Primarily home-based, I displayed a high level of professionalism, personal motivation and time management. Researched potential clients for suitability of the service and canvassed decision makers by telephone and email. Followed up on historic leads and former customers. Created detailed advertising proposals as well as contracts for completion by the client.

Aerospace Engineer. (Assistant). *Example firm*. Performed repairs to emergency equipment including fixing landing gears, emergency door opening systems and fire extinguishers. Worked in clean room (pure oxygen) to mix chemicals for extinguishing systems. Tested oxygen tanks under water (hydro-sinking) to ensure they could withstand pressure. Fitted seamlessly within the existing team and gained a wide range of professional skills.

Air-Con Installation Draftsman. *Example firm*. Created drawings to scale with plan, elevation and 3D views for the installation of air conditioning units for both commercial and residential establishments. Liaised with clients to clarify and meet their specifications, maintained a high level of professionalism with demanding clients and met pressing deadlines.

Aircraft Engineer (trainee). British Airways. Carried out routine maintenance on aircraft, including 747, 767, 787, A319, A320, A380 and Dreamliner's. I performed safety checks, repaired seats, changed aircraft tyres, topped up engine oil and carried out basic electrical work such as inflight entertainment.

Alloy Wheel Refurbishment. Proprietary Business. Offered a mobile wheel refurbishment service which attended to people's vehicles at their workplaces and homes. Refurbished wheels on prestige cars as well as everyday vehicles where wheels may have been damaged by kerb impact and similar events. Used a compressor, sanding machine, spray gun and heat lights. Complied with H&S. Managed marketing and also secured recommendations and referrals.

Asbestos Removal Supervisor. *Example firm*. Managed a team of highly trained site operatives, making sure that all rules and regulations of the HSE regarding safe handling and disposal of Asbestos were complied with. Precautions taken and which I supervised included PPE, safe transportation, manual handling, site security and creation of air tight environments, site set up and clean-up. Worked in commercial and domestic premises as well as within the London Underground. Sealed existing asbestos in situ and applied precautionary stickers. Completed paperwork and record keeping. Completed site surveying 402 course for building work and asbestos.

Bank Manager. *Example Bank.* This was primarily a customer focussed role with a strong sales element. Modern banking is product based; branches and individuals are target driven to achieve expected sales volumes of each product e.g. mortgages, loans, credit cards etc. Motivated staff in groups and within one to one meetings; encouraged and supported them to monitor and achieve the Key Performance Indicators (KPIs). Managed cash-flow within the branch. Followed security and H&S protocols and carried out risk assessments.

Barber. *Example Barber's shop.* Delivered a high-quality personal hair cutting experience to individual clients. Gained familiarity and experience in a wide range of common styles. Gained a reputation for really listening to the client and meeting their needs. Maintained the salon diary and helped with various administration tasks. Displayed good communication and organisation skills.

Barista. *Example Café.* Greeted customers and served them hot drinks and food. Displayed a full range of coffee processing skills including brewing, creation of all coffee types (latte, espresso, cappuccino, macchiato, flat white, mocha, Americano), equipment care, health, safety and hygiene. Made fresh sandwiches, rolls and paninis. Gained customer service skills, built long term relationships and processed payments.

Bartender. *Example bar.* Ensured that the overall experience for visitors to a pub/restaurant was pleasant. Greeted customers, served drinks, cleaned tables, chairs, floors and food services. Provided for special dietary requirements for allergy sufferers. Duties also included general cleaning, loading and unloading of deliveries, monitoring of food storage temperatures, labelling and stock rotation, as well as safe handling to avoid cross-contamination. Processed and reconciled payments.

Bicycle Mechanic, experienced in manufacture, repair and recovery of Barclays Cycle Hire Bikes ("Boris bikes") in the City of London. Maintained and cleaned docking stations and performed customer demonstrations. Worked independently travelling around the City, consistently met targets and complied with reporting requirements placed on me by my employer. I was responsible, flexible and organised.

Biohazard waste disposal and hygiene specialist. *Example Hygiene Solutions Firm.* Emptied personal hygiene bins on behalf of airports, hospitals and schools. Gained experience of machine washing bins and of the use of personal protective equipment. Displayed excellent team work, time management and problem solving skills.

Bookkeeper. *Example firm.* Responsible for day to day aspects of accounts, financial planning and business forecasting. I was a key part of the management team accountable to the MD. Duties included preparing and filing company returns, credit control, debt management, payments, reconciliation, invoicing, purchase ledger management, CIS, VAT and tax returns.

"We strongly believe in rehabilitation and individual's capacity for change." Kate Gilbert, Head of Business Development - Genius Within CIC

General **Builder.** Proprietary Business. Skilled builder catering to domestic clients on a wide range of projects. Carried out full refurbishment of run down properties and fulfilled all maintenance and home improvement needs. Constructed both single storey and double storey extensions. Liaised with customers, calmly resolving their problems, concerns or complaints. Conducted health and safety risk assessments as well as site cleaning and securing. Significant experience gained of working in properties and on construction sites. Gained practical knowledge of health and safety protocols, managing teams, trades and sub-contractors.

Builder's Mate/ Contractor's Assistant. Agency work. General home improvement and property maintenance including painting and decorating, bathroom and kitchen refurbishment, repair and replacement. Gained experience in kitchen fitting and bathroom installation, as well as health and safety procedures.

Bus Driver. Transport for London. Gained PSV licence and drove single decker buses, double decker buses and bendy buses. Managed many challenging driving situations on London roads. Interacted with thousands of customers and showed great customer service skills. On evening shifts I deescalated conflicts between intoxicated passengers, managed bus evacuations and returned to depot after bio hazard incidents.

Butcher. Based within a local convenience store, I managed a general butchery providing a wide range of meats to the general public. I gained experience and skill in all forms of butchery and meat processing including cutting, cooking, curing, boning, and cleaning. Familiar with health and safety, hygiene and safe handling of food.

Cable Jointer's Mate. *Example firm.* Made up joint kits and generally assisted the jointer. Logged all paperwork required for record keeping and compliance, as well as forward planning jobs. Removed and replaced cut outs within lampposts and street furniture. Worked with electrical testing kits to ensure safety and certification.

Cable Puller. *Example firm.* Working as part of a regional team, I travelled to predominantly new-build sites where I installed dormant low voltage cables inside buildings and dormant high voltage cabling to the outside.

Call Centre Team-Leader. *Example firm.* Working on behalf of an insurance and services company, I called existing customers to sell and renew warranty policies. Professionally and positively handled conversations and developed excellent telephone skills which encouraged cooperation from others. Managed and motivated a team of 7-15 telesales people, helped them to naturally work through scripts and taught them to think on their feet and handle questions.

"Until I worked through the list of qualifications, I had forgotten most of my achievements. Now as I sit back, I am surprised at how many qualifications I have got. Thanks for the memory joggers - now my CV looks great!" JE

Car Delivery Manager. *Example car hire*. Worked in a customer service role face to face and over the telephone. Arranged collection and delivery of cars. Chauffeured customers back to their homes or workplaces after delivery of their cars. Provided reassurance when customers were concerned about time delays or unexpected costs. Liaised between customers and various department staff to troubleshoot and ensure smooth progression of cars through the system.

Carpenter. Sole Trader and Sub-Contractor. Commercial and Domestic carpenter. Worked on various roof types, loft conversions, staircases, built walls, door frames, floors, ceiling joists, skirting boards. Fitted windows, kitchen units, vanity units in bathrooms, flooring, skirting boards, architraves and fixed stud work. Liaised with other trades. Consolidated carpentry and refurbishment skills during this period and became a valued member of a highly commended team. Carried our Health and Safety risk assessments and ensured adherence to building regulations.

Carpenter (Technical woodworking machinist). Sole Trader. Machine operator skilled in the use of heavy machinery, milling down fresh sawn timber to finished product. Operates lathe, circular saw, planer fitnesser, band saw and spindle moulder as well as a wide range of hand tools. Able to work from drawings and descriptions and also provide scale drawings, specification and design plans and 3D mock ups.

Carpet Fitter and Floor Layer. *Example firm*. Working as part of a team (and often in a supervisory role) which was in demand across multiple regions. My role included fitting carpets, laminate flooring and carpet tiles in residential and commercial properties. I conducted risk assessments and was responsible for customer liaison, measuring, ordering, fitting and snagging.

Car Sales Person. Proprietary business. Achieved and maintained a high sales volume as a self-employed car sales person. Pro-actively followed up on old enquires and re-canvassed previous clients of sales and service departments, maintaining a full diary of client appointments. Sourced stock and developed supplier relationships. Gained confidence and interpersonal skills. Resolved client care issues, arranged collection or delivery of vehicles and ensured after sales satisfaction. Represented my firm in a professional and positive light, face to face and over the telephone. Maintained thorough records and systemised processes as the sales levels grew.

Car Valeter. Proprietary Business. Cosmetically enhanced tired vehicles and gave them a new lease of life through a highly focussed valeting service. Carried out interior cleaning, engine cleaning, paint renovation, exterior cleaning, polishing and waxing, hot water extraction, pressure washing, and upholstery cleaning and stain removal. Complied with health and safety. Managed marketing and gained referrals.

"As an equal opportunities employer, Gleeds believes that all applicants should be treated fairly regardless of their background and history. All candidates should be assessed on the merits of their application and aptitude for the role, not by their past." Richard Steer, Chairman, Gleeds Worldwide (Surveyors)

Car Wash Manager. Family business. Responsible for a busy car wash. Duties included driving vehicles through the facility as well as pre-wash preparation, jet washing, polishing, internal vacuuming and valeting. Health and safety, COSHH and PPE were important considerations in this role. Progressed to regional manager responsible for the operation of multiple sites and recruitment of employees.

Catering Manager. Family business. Managed a team of chefs, porters, and serving staff to facilitate the professional and successful catering of prestigious events and films. Many catering contracts lasted for 6 - 8 weeks and were repeat bookings with Paramount, Columbia and the British Film Industry. I personally conducted sales and marketing campaigns to gain new customers, ensured client satisfaction and solicited testimonials and referrals. Gained customer service, business and management skills.

Charity Fundraiser. *Example charity*. Canvassed door to door to attract financial support for a range of charities. Worked within a motivated team and progressed quickly to team leader, organised and motivated others and consistently hit or exceeded targets. Became very organised and developed excellent interpersonal and sales skills.

Charity Fundraiser. Various charities. Working on behalf of a 'commercial participator' which held contracts to generate income for a number of registered charities, I organised and conducted clothing collections. Worked within a motivated team which consistently hit or exceeded targets. Became a dedicated driver and developed good people skills and the ability to influence and inspire other people.

Chef. *Example Pub*. Worked in a pair of busy public houses as second chef (sous chef) responsible for ensuring the smooth running of the kitchen and that all food orders are completed to a high standard. Placed all food orders ensuring that stock levels were maintained of key menu items such as fresh vegetables, fish and high-quality meats. Gained experience in supervising and motivating staff as well as resolving problems with customer orders.

Chimney Sweep. Proprietary business. Cleaned and performed maintenance on chimneys, stoves and flues. Repointed chimney stacks, fitted roof tiles and installed bird stoppers. Loaded and unloaded equipment following all health and safety procedures. Contained soot and waste and maintained a clean and safe working environment. Treated customers with politeness and respect throughout the process.

Classroom Assistant/ Learning Mentor. *Example School*. Provided Additional Learning Support to children in a classroom setting. Taught functional skills, developed knowledge and understanding of special needs, supervised, and supported pupils. Managed children's emotional states with empathy, compassion and leadership. Escorted, supervised clubs and accompanied day trips. Safeguarding always took priority. Worked with management and external agencies to provide objectives and action plans for individual children and to aid their development. Helped children in difficulty to improve low self-esteem and academic results.

Cleaning Supervisor. *Example firm* working on behalf of The London Underground. Responsible for a team of cleaners, cleaning trains and platforms. I held a trusted access role and achieved proficiency in machine buffing and polishing. Worked to deadlines, maintained cleaning logs and ensured that high standards of cleaning were met. Developed knowledge of cleaning regulations, health and safety and PPE.

Clothing Sales Person. Worked in a proprietary business buying clothing and personal products items wholesale and selling them retail. Primarily internet based with some face to face customer interactions. Gained experience in business management, organisational skills, marketing, negotiation, customer service, problem solving, distribution, packing and despatch.

Coach Driver. (School). *Example firm.* Contracted to several independent schools I collected children from local drop off points, delivered them safely to school and returned them when their school days finished. Developed excellent route planning and timekeeping skills. Showed patience and managed challenging behaviour.

Coach Driver. (Tours). *Example firm.* Developed excellent route planning and timekeeping skills whilst driving across the UK and Europe. Interacted with thousands of customers from a diverse range of ages and backgrounds and consistently showed great customer service skills. Familiar with drivers' hours' legislation and use of Tachograph. Managed intoxicated, abusive and challenging customers assertively and positively whilst maintaining a high degree of professionalism.

Commodities Dealer. Proprietary business. Purchased wholesale gold, diamonds, emeralds and other precious stones from Africa and South America, near to their point of origin and sold them with a margin in Europe (primarily Belgium). Operated as a successful sole-trader for almost 10 years, during which time I gained experience in business management, organisation, marketing, negotiation and customer service. Sourced stock and developed supplier relationships. Ensured client satisfaction and solicited testimonials and recommendations. Maintained books and records.

Core Driller. Masonry Solutions Co. Working in New Orleans in the aftermath of Hurricane Katrina strengthening the pump stations. Concrete cutting/ diamond drilling bolt holes freehand or with a rig and motor, removing drill cores using suction, roughen hole edges and then injecting chemical resin to provide reinforcement for the bolts. After resin is hardened I tightened bolts using ratchet, carried out pull tests. Any failures were over cored/ re-drilled prior to the insertion of steel bars in the walls.

Customer Service Adviser. *Example Claims Management Company.* Worked in a customer service role keeping customers updated on the progress of their claims, as well as professionally handling their concerns and complaints. Liaised with the sales team, solicitors and the customers to ensure that any hurdles were swiftly overcome and that all parties provide the information required on a timely basis. Developed excellent telephone and face to face skills which encouraged cooperation from others.

Conventional Job CV Templates A - Z	**Customer Service Agent**. British Airways. I would greet customers, register them for their flights, security swipe passports, weigh and tag their baggage, hand them their boarding passes. I attended an intensive customer service course (totalling around 50 hours) which included overcoming challenges, dealing with different personality types and moods, whilst representing this prestigious company politely and professionally.
	Customer Service Assistant. *Example Fast Food Outlet*. Worked on behalf of a national chain of fast food outlets. Prepared food following set times and processes, served customers, encouraged up-sales and cross-promotional sales. Gained customer service skills as well as an understanding of payment processing, till operation, fraud and theft prevention. Gained knowledge of industry legislation including Health and Safety, Fire Regulations Act, Data Protection and food standards, health, hygiene and good practices. Built long term relationships with staff and regular customers.
	Customer Service Assistant. *Example Food Store*. Worked on behalf of a national chain of food stores. Helped customers to efficiently check out their purchases, process their payments and pack their shopping. Carried out stock audits and replenished both ambient and fresh shop displays. Gained customer service skills as well as an understanding of payment processing, till operation, financial reconciliation, fraud and theft prevention. Built long-term relationships with staff and customers and consistently exceeded targets.
	Delivery Driver. *Example Courier firm*. Carried out multi-drop deliveries and collections. Delivered time-sensitive cargo, loaded and unloaded following all health and safety procedures, and met pressing deadlines. Managed challenging driving situations in predominantly residential areas and maintained an accident free, flawless driving record. Personally, carried out sales and marketing to gain new customers, managed contracts to ensure a high level of client satisfaction and to gain recommendations.
	Delivery Driver. *Example Greengrocer's Food Co*. Drove a temperature-controlled van to deliver pre-ordered fruit and vegetables to clients regionally. Daily deliveries were made starting from the small hours of the morning through to late afternoon. Time management was essential in this role to avoid spoilage. Effective manual handling and health and safety procedures were followed. I was praised for consistently exceeding targets.
	Delivery Driver. *Example Home Improvement Stores*. Delivered DIY and building materials to homes, constructions sites and commercial premises. Used a tail lift and pallet truck. Time management was essential in this role to avoid causing delays to the clients' projects. Used a satnav to plan routes and ensure that the safest and quickest route is always taken. As the point of contact for each customer it was vital for me to ensure that the company was always represented in a professional manner. Effective manual handling and health and safety procedures were followed.

"Everyone deserves a chance to rebuild their life."
Joss Ronchetti, Managing Director, Pro-Driver Logistics

Demolition Engineer. *Example firm.* Responsible for the safe demolition of commercial and residential properties and subsequent removal of materials. Gained experience in the safe operation of 360° excavator and shears as well as explosives. Stripped out 22 story buildings and knocked down 8 story buildings. Able to co-ordinate teams of demolition workers and construction labourers. Carried out health and safety risk assessments and ensured site safety and security at all times.

Detainee Custody Officer. *Example security company.* Transported serving and un-convicted prisoners to court appearances and during transfer to other secure establishments. Performed control and restraint and carried out first-aid. Gained experience of mediating in volatile situations and hostage negotiation. Developed the ability to remain calm and professional and provide essential leadership in all situations and environments.

Document Shredding. *Example Shredding Company.* Collected sensitive and confidential documents from a range of clients with data confidentiality concerns. Used an industrial shredding machine located within the vehicle to immediately cross cut all documents prior to delivering them to a recycling centre. During my time in post I improved my customer service skills, team work, confidentiality and manual handling.

Dog Handler. Proprietary business. Trained German Shepherd and Rottweiler dogs for security purposes. Walked perimeters of important residential properties, commercial premises and building sites to maintain security, health and safety and to provide reassurance. Escorted people off site when required in a safe and controlled manner. Filed reports and documented incidents.

Domestic goods exporter. Proprietary business. Achieved and maintained a high sales volume as a self-employed reseller of second hand domestic goods. Primarily exported to Tanzania where the market for second hand goods was strong compared to the UK where the resale value of second hand domestic items was almost zero. Responsible for sourcing stock and developing supplier relationships. Gained additional experience in freight forwarding, including the movement of vehicles and the wider export market.

Door Supervisor. Agency work. SIA approved door supervisor subcontracted to work at multiple, high footfall, London sites. In this role I helped to control and monitor people entering and leaving premises and events. I developed excellent judgement of people and their intentions as well as the ability to manage and resolve difficult situations calmly. Developed an understanding of security systems including body scanners and CCTV. Recorded incidents to ensure informed handover to other staff.

Drainage Worker. *Example Drain Company.* Responsible for installing and maintaining drainage, concrete finishing, laying pipes and making and fixing manholes. Experienced gained of working in confined spaces and slinging (securing loads with chains and straps). Carried out workplace risk assessments, secured areas and followed health and safety procedures.

"Thanks to this structure, my CV shows the work skills I have gained." DT

Dry Cleaning. Proprietary business. Operated a collection and delivery based dry cleaning business. Gain experience of the safe use of industrial dry-cleaning machines and of cleaning chemicals. Built up a large volume of domestic clients who used the service regularly for the convenience and who recommended us to other people because of the excellent customer service experience. Represented my firm in a professional and positive light, both face to face and over the telephone. Maintained thorough records and systemised processes as the sales levels grew.

Dry Lining Specialist. Proprietary business. Read architect's working drawings, measured accurately and performed all works to preparation to first fix for electricians and plumbers. Created suspended ceilings and partitioned rooms in residential dwellings and commercial properties. Displayed excellent customer service skills, timekeeping, reliability and the ability to manage small teams of tradesmen. Personally, carried out sales and marketing to gain new customers, managed contracts to ensure a high level of client satisfaction and solicited testimonials and recommendations. Maintained books and records.

Ductwork Engineer. Multiple agencies both self-employed and employed. Familiar with maintenance, renewal and replacement of grease extraction units, air conditioning systems and carbon filters within residential and commercial properties, ships, restaurants, pubs, clubs, factories and high security sites such as hospitals police stations, air-bases and prisons. Liaised with clients to clarify and meet their specifications, maintained a high level of professionalism with demanding clients and met deadlines. Assessed sites for fire safety, health and safety and legal compliance.

Electrician. Proprietary business. Carried out electrical installation and maintenance work. Maintained and repaired electrical equipment. Connect wires to circuit breakers and transformers. Traced, diagnosed and remedied electrical faults. Upgraded fuse-boards, installed lighting circuits, power circuits, data cabling, trays work, trunking and conduit work. Used test equipment including oscilloscopes, amp-meters and test lamps as well as hand tools. Responded to customer enquiries, calculated cost of jobs and provided estimates for commercial and domestic work. Followed health and safety procedures and conducted risk assessments.

Estate Agent. *Example company*. Liaised with home owners to secure sales instructions and to update them on viewings and the sales process. Contacted and persuaded homeowners who were already on the market to instruct our agency. Carried out property research, gave informal valuations and produced property particulars. Managed buyer enquiries and hosted viewings. Ensured that solicitors were appointed, and buyers had mortgages in place. Consistently met sales targets.

Events Promoter. Agency work. Face to face promotions in the UK and abroad persuading and influencing people to purchase tickets and attend events. Experienced in Social Media management and running promotional campaigns across multiple platforms including Facebook, Instagram, Snapchat and Twitter. Developed sales skills, maintained personal motivation and consistently exceeded targets.

Facilities Manager. *Example council.* Managed a portfolio of council owned buildings and ensured that all facilities (IT, gas, electricity, water and phone) were in place and operating effectively. Worked to budgets and achieved costs savings where possible. Organised the letting of internal meeting rooms and the hire of council halls and community premises to generate income and serve the community.

Fencing Contractor. *Example firm.* Erected ready-made fence panels as well as overlap and ship-lap fencing. Installed concrete posts, mixed and used cement. Performed other landscaping work including turfing, slab laying, block paving and drainage digging as well as emergency call out repairs and storm damage repairs.

Financial Controller and later FD. *Example firm.* I accepted this role within a medium sized firm when they moved their accountancy in house. Managed a team of ledger clerks and ensured the smooth running of the company's finances. Prepared monthly accounts, managed payroll, Cash-flow forecasts, employment contracts and staff handbooks, filed returns. Carried out SWOT analysis and advised on compliance.

Fire and Flood Emergency Services. Assessment and Restoration. Proprietary Business. My team were deployed after accidents on behalf of insurance companies. I Itemised damage caused, remove damaged or contaminated items and also mitigated the risks of further harm by making good or safe any remaining effects, possessions and equipment. Gained experience of mould and fungus identification, damp testing (psychrometric), asbestos testing, Fire and water restoration and trauma cleaning.

Fire-proofing specialist. *Example company.* Installed fire safety equipment including dry riser pipe fitting, fire suppression boxes and sprinkler systems. Worked on commercial and residential properties primarily retrofitted in accordance with building regulations and architects' drawings. Carried out annual inspections and tests, provided test certificates, diagnosed and remedied faults. Followed all health and safety procedures and worked with conscientious attention to detail - understanding that ultimately people's lives could depend on the work I was doing.

Fitness Instructor. *Example Gym.* Qualified to Levels 1 and 2 I facilitated a range of classes, motivated and supported people to live a healthier lifestyle both nutritionally and through consistent, suitable exercise. Taught gym members how to use equipment, patiently guided and supported them and provided on-going motivation.

Forklift Truck Driver. *Example furniture stores.* Worked on behalf of a major furniture manufacturer and distributor. Gained my forklift truck licence in this role and proved my value to the employer by driving a counterbalance forklift truck without accident or incident during the full period of my employment. Responsible for loading and unloading deliveries and processing time-sensitive orders for multiple clients. Managed stock and despatch schedules and followed Health and Safety.

Conventional Job CV Templates A - Z	**Fresh Produce Manager**. *Example superstore*. Building on skills gained in the regional store, I successfully managed the fresh produce department in this smaller local store. Responsible for a team of 15 people I coordinated the work rota, carried out health and safety training, country of origin checks, date code checking, maintained wastage within budgetary operating limits primarily by timely price reductions of perishable items. Displayed a superb work ethic and complete professionalism at all times.
	Garage Owner. Provided car repair, maintenance and restoration services to the general public. Experienced in stripping down vehicles and repairing, servicing and carrying out all maintenance. Competent in the use of computer aided diagnostic equipment, multi-meters, power tools, diagnostic equipment, pneumatic wrenches and a wide range of hand tools. Restored classic cars and gained a reputation for high quality workmanship, even receiving rare cars from clients abroad for restoration. Responsible for managing, maintaining and motivating a team of 15 people.
	General Tradesman. A proprietary business providing an "odd job man" range of services to the public and as a sub-contractor to other tradesmen and small companies. Carried out external landscaping including digging, laying membrane, surfacing and internal works; as well as painting and decorating, wallpapering, installation of covings and skirting boards and provided general labouring services as required.
	Glass Cutter. *Named Glass Company*. An experienced glass cutter able to cut and process different thicknesses and types of glass to shape and size for a wide range of purposes. Experienced in cutting mirror glass and creating splash-backs for premium kitchens and table glass. Sandblasted glass, worked with pyrolite fire resistant glass and laminated glass. Loaded and unloaded deliveries and organised despatch to clients and sites. Maintained machinery and managed health and safety risks.
	Groundsman. *Example Golf Course*. Performed landscaping services to maintain the aesthetics of the site and also the suitability for golf. Experience gained in planting, mowing, landscaping, designing, trimming, weeding, edging and pruning. Carried out repairs to brickwork and fencing and building maintenance. Worked enthusiastically and efficiently to achieve a high-quality finish, a result that always met or exceeded my employer's needs. My reliability and my attitude were often praised.
	Ground Worker. Agency work. This role carried a wide range of responsibilities, including locating underground services using CAT and GENY, excavating identified areas and making holes for the jointer to access, as well as digging lamppost column holes. Experienced in general road working, slab laying, kerbing, concrete and timber edging, digging footings and all aspects of concreting. Worked in confined spaces, conducted risk assessments and ensured Health and Safety compliance.

Gym Receptionist and Administrator. *Named gym.* Responsible for ensuring the smooth running of a popular local gym. Welcomed new and existing members. Systemised the membership database and the billing process. Helped to develop and maintain the company website and online social media profiles. Designed leaflets and literature. Supported gym members with personal fitness plans and provided on going encouragement and motivation. Other duties included product ordering, followed up on expired memberships, chasing payments and gaining testimonials and referrals.
Hairdresser. Salon manager in a family business responsible for the day to day running of a busy high street hairdressing salon. Hired, trained and motivated staff and ensured that they really listened to clients and fully met their needs. Gained experience in business management, marketing, negotiation and customer service.
Hairdresser (Mobile). Proprietary Business. Visited clients at home and at work to deliver a high-quality personal hair cutting experience. Specialised in Afro Caribbean hair styles including corn rowing and dreading, as well as more mainstream hair cut styles. Gained a reputation for really listening to the client and meeting their needs.
Highways Maintenance and Street-works Operative (Ganger man). Agency Work. Supervisor of excavation teams tasked with digging up electrical cables when there were power cuts. Laid ducts for cabling. Backfilled, laid cold-lay bituminous materials and non-bituminous materials. Reinstated modular surfaces, concrete footways, signing, lighting and guarding. Experienced of using Cat and Genny. Able to read and follow 1-500 utility drawings for LV and HV cables.
Hod Carrier. *Example firm.* Laid out blocks and bricks and mixed mortar for bricklayers. Carried the blocks and bricks to the required places. Pointed up the brickwork using a pointing tool to ensure a good aesthetic appearance of the finished brickwork. Cleaned sites and performed regular site safety checks. Used a Long Reach (Telescopic) forklift and performed safe manual handling.
Hospitality. Media Agency. Met, escorted and accompanied celebrities and dignitaries to events. Managed schedules and organised fan meet ups for autographs signing and photographs. Catered for the delegates needs by organising food, refreshments and necessary sundries for example pet welfare. Stayed professional in challenging situations, gained customer service and management skills.
Hotel Receptionist. *Example firm.* Worked as part of a positive and professional team. Made reservations, welcomed guests (check in), arranged cancellations, processed payments, serve food and alcohol, resolved customer queries and complaints. Developed excellent telephone and face to face skills which encouraged cooperation from others. Gained professional problem-solving skills.

"Creating my CV using the templates was worth it. I could not have got into work without this. I wouldn't have known where to start." RM

Household Electrical Delivery. *Example firm*. Worked as part of a small team lifting goods manually and also with a tail lift. Delivered fridges, freezers, washing machines, tumble driers, dishwashers and other large household items to domestic customers. Carried out removals of unwanted items and installed the new purchase. Gained experience in manual handling, health and safety and PPE. Telephoned customers to arrange convenient delivery times and adhered to timekeeping schedules.

Household Removals. *Example firm*. As a Removal man, I helped to relocate families and businesses. I drove a 3.5-ton van and worked as part of a team lifting goods manually and also with a tail lift. Took care of clients' belongings and were sensitive to people's feelings during a stressful time for them.

Ice Cream Salesperson. Proprietary business. Operated an ice cream van in residential areas and at well attended public events. Gained licencing from the local authority and operated a fully compliant business. Gained skills in customer service, dealing with suppliers, business organisation and management, budgeting, record keeping, food safety and self-discipline. Maintained an accident free driving record.

Lagging **Insulation Installer.** *Example firm*. Lagging pipes and boiler houses primarily in hospitals, schools and banks. Lagging saves money and we demonstrated that the money saved through heat loss far exceeded the cost of insulating pipes. Installing insulation, ducting and dry boards and also gained supervisory experience by training new installers. Prioritised workflow and dealt with a wide range of different people in a positive and professional manner.

Loft and Cavity Wall **Insulation Installer.** Proprietary Business. Insulated to improve the thermal insulation ("U" value) of domestic and commercial properties. Maintained a high level of customer service and as little disruption as possible to people's homes. Respected health and safety and carried out risk assessments. Personally undertook sales and marketing to gain new customers, managed contracts to ensure client satisfaction and solicited testimonials and referrals. Gained customer service, organisation and management skills. Maintained books and records.

Interior designer. *Example firm*. Specialised in interior shop design. Produced plans, elevations and 3D drawings to scale for prestigious retail brands including high street name. Primarily office and studio based with occasional site visits. Utilised 'vector works' software and other 3D design packages. Explained and presented to clients and management. Made recommendations of service providers and delivery partners.

IT Network Support Technician. *Example firm*. Supported 300 users on a Windows server. Provided a full IT helpdesk service operating across 4 sites. Trained users on the use of bespoke software and all MS products. Liaised with third party service providers to troubleshoot and develop bespoke software to accommodate growth.

"I am about to start work and want to say THANKS for the guidance." BV

IT Systems Coordinator. NHS Trust. Developed and monitored the department's Unix based database. Created around 155 PCs, trained staff and provided support to 1500 users. Resolved hardware, software, networking and connectivity problems. Produced regular reports for the management team. Rolled out a new SQL database and carried out regular back-ups whilst ensuring security and integrity of data.

IT Systems Support Team Leader. *Example Housing Association.* Designed, developed and delivered corporate infrastructure and provided full technical support. Displayed full knowledge of all MS back office components. Determined upgrades and planned maintenance on all telecom links and devices. Build on existing team management experience, coordinated people at all different ability levels of ability.

IT Technician and Shop Manager. Family PC Repair shop. Operated a busy drop in PC repair centre. Gained familiarity with a wide range of IT software and hardware. Developed business administration skills such as work scheduling, invoicing, marketing and customer service. Additionally, gained online and telesales experience.

IT Technician. *Example Council.* Implemented a remote working scheme involving the deployment of laptops and PCs and the development of a Virtual Private Network. Configured blackberry, Nokia, HTC and PDA devices so that emails delivered to private mailboxes (via Remote Access Service tokens) and maintained security.

General **Labourer.** Agency work. Reliable labourer for construction workers supporting property developers, roofers, bricklayers, and scaffolders. Worked on properties and construction sites including bringing materials onto site (including bricks), demolishing buildings, removing tiles and fitting kitchens. Cleaned sites and performed fetching and carrying and maintained site safety.

Skilled **Labourer.** *Example firm.* Skilled labourer and site foreman, overseeing construction workers, roofers, bricklayers, and scaffolders. Worked on properties and construction sites including digging and laying foundations, bricklaying, plastering, flooring, kitchen fitting and bathroom installation, landscaping and snagging of new-build properties. Refurbished run-down properties, repaired damaged walls, replaced fascia boarding and fitted all UPVC products. Developed relationships with suppliers, carried out risk assessments and ensured compliance with building regulations.

Hard **Landscaper.** *Example Council.* Performed a wide range of hard landscaping services on behalf of the council. Experience gained of laying pathways, drop kerbs, running tracks, installing benches and other permanent fixtures. Followed site safety and security procedures including displaying signs, temporary bollards and cage fencing. Carried out remedial repairs and maintenance. Drove a 3.5 ton open back council vehicle without accident or incident. Displayed timekeeping and reliability.

*"After investing the time required creating a CV
I realised that I actually have a lot of potential."* RB

Landscape Gardener. Proprietary Business. Performed a wide range of landscaping services to occasional and regular, domestic and commercial, clients. Experience gained in garden design, planting, mowing, landscaping, designing, trimming, weeding, edging and pruning. Worked enthusiastically and efficiently to achieve a high-quality finish, a result that always met or exceeded each client's needs. My reliability and my attitude were often praised, and I received many recommendations. Gained excellent customer service skills, proved reliability and managed tradesmen.

Life Guard. North London Leisure Centres. Monitoring and supervising pool users. Gained my National Pool Lifeguard Qualification and first aid qualifications. Maintained a high level of personal fitness and passed my competency and fitness tests each month. Carried out health and safety risk assessments, completed reports and maintained records. Proved myself to be completely dependable to my employer.

Loft Conversion, Extension and Building Conversion Specialist Contractor. Worked with clients to produce base drawings. Liaised with architects to explain needs and problem solve. Liaised with scaffolders, opened roofs, installed staircases, fireproofed, built dormers. Worked beyond first fix to final finish, coordinated sub-contractors such as electricians, plasterers, plumbers and tilers. Remedied previous contractor's poor workmanship following all building regulations.

Lorry Driver (HGV1 Articulated). Agency work. Drove on behalf of major clients such as Sainsbury's and Baylis/ Culina distribution. Loaded and unloaded following all health and safety procedures as well as met pressing deadlines. Developed excellent route planning and timekeeping skills. Gained awareness of drivers' hours' laws and use of Tachograph. Received praise for consistently exceeding targets.

Magazine Circulation Manager. *Example Publishing House*. Entered as subscription sales manager and rapidly progressed on my own merit to circulation manager, tasked with expanding the subscriber database. By cross promoting titles, building a referral network and ensuring consistent quality of media, my team exceeded all targets and expectations. Managed and motivated five people through industry challenges.

Maintenance Manager. School maintenance operative responsible for reactive work and proactive upkeep of the school. Performed independently and on own initiative, fixing and installing benches, integral cupboards, kitchen units, worktops and frames, hanging and repairing doors, flat-pack assembly and staircase work. Performed many jobs including installing and bleeding radiators, hanging smart boards, tiling, filing holes, grounds maintenance. Organised and supervised other skilled tradesmen.

Marketing Manager. *Example firm*. Experienced in coordinating high profile product launches. Carried out direct marketing to distribution companies and developed appealing point of sale (POS) to ensure that the finished products displayed well, carried a uniform message and achieved high sales volume. Experienced in Social Media management and running promotional campaigns across multiple platforms. Developed sales skills and maintained motivation.

Vehicle **Mechanic.** Proprietary business. Disassembled engine parts and vehicles and carried out repairs, servicing and general maintenance. Gained knowledge and experience in using computer aided diagnostic equipment, multi-meters, power tools, diagnostic equipment, pneumatic wrenches and all hand tools.
Ordained **Minister**. Qualified as a Pentecostal Minister and practiced as a non-denominational pastor. I can interact effectively with a wide range of people and cultures within both happy and sad circumstances. Experience gained of conducting well-attended services as well as funerals, weddings, baptisms and blessings. Worked with youth, community leaders and the police.
Mobile Food Operator. Proprietary business. Managed a traditional burger van which regularly toured at major fairs, events and markets. Gained food safety and hygiene qualifications as well as customer service, business and management skills. Responsible for sourcing stock and developing supplier relationships. Ensured customer satisfaction and gained regular customers.
Mobile Phone Technician. Agency Work. Conducted function tests, radio frequency tests and fault diagnoses on returned mobile phones. Logged incoming parcels, traced missing phones, updated customers and packaged and despatched repaired phones. Demonstrated IT competence, good organisation and excellent customer service.
MOT Tester, vehicle service technician and tyre fitter. Example garage. As a DVSA/ VOSA MOT Nominated Tester I carried out full DVSA MOT tests on cars and commercial vehicles. Performed a wide range of servicing and maintenance, Including fitting tyres, exhausts and brakes. Familiar with diagnostic equipment, machinery and all tools. Developed health and safety awareness and customer service skills.
Multimedia Installation Specialist. *Example firm*. Installed audio and video technology and trained staff in use of the equipment. Troubleshooted and provided a support desk for after installation care. Professionalism, security and time keeping were important considerations in this role.
NHS Donor Carer (Blood and Transplant). I welcomed donors into a mobile blood donation unit and ensured that they felt comfortable. I carried out screenings with a suitability questionnaire and then ensured that paperwork was signed. Following all safety and sterile procedures, I then took blood. I monitored donors after donating to ensure their health and wellbeing. Assisted people who fainted or became light-headed by raising their legs and improving circulation and supported the duty nurse.

"I employ quite a number of ex-offenders in my own company. I'd say that 95% of the ex-offenders I employ will get on and be successful in not returning to a life of crime. Their past offenses are no problem to me as long as they are going to come in and channel their efforts into doing something with their lives. That's fantastic!" Michael Frazer - £6m turnover UK manufacturing company

NHS Theatre Assistant. Working within the orthopaedic department, I was present during operations and provided general assistance to surgeons, consultants and general staff. I would deep clean theatre before and after operations. I would ensure that patients' data is available and accurate, fetch necessary equipment, unwrap sterile items and pass them to avoid cross contamination. I would also input patient data under instruction from surgeons and Operating Department Practitioners (ODP).

Online Retail. Proprietary business. Established an internet business retailing baby clothes and wholesaling sportswear. Sourced stock from overseas (developed professionalism, communication and negotiation skills). Gained experience of marketing, business management skills and referrals.

Online Marketing Manager. *Example firm.* Provided online marketing services for a wide range of companies and brands. Services included website development and optimisation, PPC advertising and affiliate marketing. Experienced in Social Media management and running campaigns across multiple platforms. Supported business expansion and secured new clients for our online sales marketing and management services. Developed sales skills, maintained motivation and exceeded targets.

Online Sales Support Manager - Retail store. Converted sales, maximised upselling opportunities and managed the sales fulfilment process. Handled internal and external email communications as well as general administration and database management. Created leads and sales reports, built rapport with customers and resolved complaints.

Painting and Decorating. Proprietary business providing a range of services to the public and as a sub-contractor to other tradesmen and small companies. Worked to a high standard on residential and commercial decorating projects. Familiar with all aspects of internal decorating including all paint types and wall papers. Worked on external projects including painting render, sanding, priming and painting wooden windows and porches. Applied external texturing. Worked efficiently to achieve a high-quality finish that always exceeded each client's needs. Gained testimonials, maintained accurate records and carried out health and safety risk assessments.

Paint Sprayer. *Example firm.* Working as an industrial sprayer, my employer had contracts to spray Mini parts, BMW trim, Land Rover light lenses, Dyson home appliances (washing machines) JVC and Philips televisions. Gained experience in preparation, pre-clean, polish and paint.

Pallet Yard Workman. Working in a busy pallet yard, I bought, sold and repaired pallets for heavy use industrial and logistics purposes. Gained experience in safe and efficient use of nail guns as well as other machinery and hand tools. Operated a counterbalance fork-lift truck. Stacked pallets ready for despatch and ensured that the team met or exceeded targets set by our employer. Complied with H&S and maintained a clean working environment.

"The job descriptions helped me to explain my achievements and experience in a way that I could not on my own; clearly and accurately." JH

Paneller. *Example Mobile Home Co.* Fixing panels to new mobile homes, chalets and log cabins. Worked through all stages of a panel to meet the required standards including insulation, external and internal finishes. Took personal pride in meeting targets and maintaining quality of service.

Panel Maker. Working in a wood yard I manufactured fence panels and field gates. Competent in the safe operation of panel machines, nail guns, industrial Stena saws, plainer and rail machines. Managed time pressure, used machinery safely and co-ordinated a team of junior workers. Health and safety, COSHH and PPE were important considerations in this role.

Personal Trainer. *Example Health Club.* Supported gym members with personal fitness plans and provided on going encouragement and motivation. Specialised in strength and conditioning, often for competition preparation and exhibitions. Taylor-made plans to take into account existing levels of fitness and medical considerations. Showed a great deal of patience and understanding and also motivated members. Gained referrals from satisfied customers.

Personnel Coordinator. National Grid. Despatched maintenance operatives and engineers to sites where specialist plant and equipment was required. Selected the most suitable people for each job based on a range of criteria. Followed up to ensure that workers had arrived and that they could complete the task successfully. Organisation and communication skills were essential.

Plant Operator. Agency work. Qualified and experienced in driving diggers (awaiting ticket renewal) and dumpers, also confident with handheld tools such as disc cutters, jackhammers and winches etc. Proved myself to be reliable and efficient and had no accidents. Remained conscious of health and safety.

Plasterer. Sub-contractor. Progressed from plasterer's assistant to skilled plasterer and then on to team leader managing workflow and supervising other plasterers. Familiar with skimming ceilings (able to use Marshalltown stilts), walls, staircase alcoves, floor screeding and all internal plastering requirements. Externally rendered properties using a wide range of coatings. Familiar with Health and Safety requirements. Liaised with customers to receive keys, explain progress and treated them respectfully.

Apprentice to **Plumber and Heating Engineer.** Worked with a Corgi (now Gas Safe) registered firm to carry out boiler replacements and install central heating systems including all radiators, flues and pipework. Adhered to Health and Safety and regulatory compliance.

Plumber, Pipefitter and Heating Engineer. Proprietary business and sub-contractor. As a plumber, pipefitter and heating engineer I installed heating systems, maintaining existing systems and repairing faults. Gained customer service skills and the ability to reassure customers who were distressed on emergency call outs. My reliability and the positive attitude that I have with work were often praised and appreciated. Developed business skills including marketing, advertising, financial planning and organising workflow.

"After building my CV, I feel more confident; I have decided to go back to college, gain more qualifications and make something of myself." AS

Porter Manager. Based at Heathrow airport. Supervised a team of 10 people who carried luggage from forecourt to check in and from the baggage hall to the car park. I maintained staff rotas and ensured that health and safety procedures, particularly manual handling, were complied with. Gained experience of interacting with a wide range of people from all nations of the world and ensured a customer satisfaction both personally and within my team.

Post-person. Royal Mail. Sorted post and delivered mail whilst meeting pressing deadlines. Worked well as part of a dedicated team of people. Drove a company van, managed challenging driving situations in predominantly residential areas, maintaining an accident free, flawless driving record.

Postal Worker. Royal Mail. Operated automatic mail sorting machines, sorted mail manually, loaded and unloaded vehicles, recorded consignments in and out and ensured health and safety procedures were followed throughout. Worked in a dedicated team of people and met all targets and deadlines.

Printer. *Example firm*. Worked in a busy printing warehouse, setting up machines and making display products. The company were main contractors for shopping centres and superstores and provided many prestigious Point of Sale (POS) merchandise, window displays and gift bags. Experience gained in the safe use of printing, cutting and folding machines. Worked to targets and deadlines whilst maintaining quality control.

Product Distributor. Proprietary business. Primarily dealing in low cost and high turnover items such as inkjet cartridges and mobile phone accessories. During this time, I gained experience in business management, organisational skills, marketing, negotiation and customer service. Responsible for sourcing stock and developing supplier relationships. Liaised with a range of professionals including accountants, solicitors, shipping specialists and translators. Maintained books and records.

Production Manager. *Example chocolate manufacturers*. Machine operator and factory worker dedicated to moulding chocolate and ensuring quality control. My line processed around 12 tons of solid chocolate per 12-hour shift. I ensured cleanliness, metal and impurities detection, safe equipment and machine usage. With hard work and dedication in this role I consistently met or exceeded targets.

Production Manager. *School-wear Firm.* The company designed and embroidered high quality badges and logos onto a wide range of uniforms, gym kits, bags and other sundry items on behalf of over 500 schools. Planned production of more than 200,000 items each year. Organised staff rotas including overtime requirements, holidays and absences and ensured that staff performed according to targets based on several metrics. Monitored quality control and customer satisfaction and resolved problems.

Property Developer. Carried out full refurbishment of run-down properties in a proprietary business. Managed a team of employed tradesman and sub-contractors. Erected pre-fabricated buildings, repaired damaged walls and replaced fascia boarding. Experience gained in plastering, plumbing and boiler replacement, flooring, kitchen fitting, bathroom installation, landscaping and general labouring.

Property Development Consultant. Freelance. Advised major house builders such as Barratt London and St James. Carried out feasibility studies, advised on maximising Gross Development Value (GDV) of sites and strategic value of land, trouble-shooted when challenges arose at sites.

Property Maintenance Operative. Sole Trader. Operated a reactive maintenance service including emergency call outs. Carried out plumbing, carpentry (locks, sash windows, flooring, kitchen units/ doors), fencing, painting, patch plastering, tiling and kitchen/ bathroom installations and general repairs. Developed good customer service skills and the ability to reassure customers with empathy and professionalism.

Property Manager/ Letting Agent. Family business. Carried out tenant finds, hosted viewings, drafted tenancy agreements (AST's), conducted inventories, protected deposits, organised maintenance work, co-ordinated refurbishments and acted as a tenant helpline for emergencies (e.g. lost keys). Prioritised workflow and dealt with a wide range of different people in a positive and professional manner.

Pub Owner and Landlord. Multiple Sites. Responsible for operating local pubs in residential areas. Managed all aspects of the businesses including staff recruitment, stock ordering, bookkeeping and increasing sales volume through a wide range of initiatives. I developed excellent skills with people and the ability to diffuse conflicts and resolve problems. Good marketing skills, organisational skills and sheer hard work were all essential. Developed community ties and turned around struggling sites.

Quantity Surveyor. Range of prestigious companies. Worked on major building, civil engineering and high-end residential projects from inception to completion. Prepared and submitted tenders, valuations and reports on commercial aspects of projects. Sourced contractors and suppliers and arbitrated in disputes. Monitored final accounts to ensure accuracy and compliance and also provided valuations including source comparables and research links. Substantial experience gained of working on commercial and residential developments as well as complex sites including listed buildings.

Records Management Officer. *Example Council.* In this role I implemented a paperless office and a clear desk policy to prevent security breaches, reduce fire risk and save resources. Developed money saving processes by organising efficient retrieval systems. Scanned documents as PDF files, barcoded boxes of records and moved them off site to secure warehouses where they could be retrieved when required. Arranged for record deletion and destruction after storage requirement date has passed. Amended policies ready for the transition from the DPA to the GDPRs.

Recruitment Consultant. *Example firm.* Identified opportunities to fill roles with the right people, at the right time, to ensure a good fit with each placement. Responsible for writing job adverts, viewing applicants' CVs, liaising with employers, short-listing applicants and holding initial interviews. Primarily sales focussed I gained excellent interpersonal skills, remained focused in high pressure situations and consistently exceeded targets whilst growing the portfolio of clients.

187

Recruitment Officer. *Example Windows Ltd.* Progressed to recruitment officer after proving successful as a sales person and sales manager. Identified opportunities to fill roles with the right people, at the right time, to ensure continued success of the company. The company experienced unprecedented growth and new job roles needed filling daily. Responsible for writing job adverts, viewing applicants' CVs, liaising with recruitment agencies, short-listing applicants and holding initial interviews. Made recommendations to the directors and contributed to the final hiring decisions.

Renderer. *Example company.* Applied a variety of textured and weather resistant coatings to residential and commercial properties. Used a power wash and cleaning chemicals, hand mixed coatings, tapped for echoes and applied render. Repointed bricks and repaired stonework, repaired cracks and fitted UPVC including soffits, fascias and guttering. Carried out risk assessments including working from heights.

Retail Salesperson. Branded Clothing. Owned and operated a personally branded clothing line. Sourced sportswear and casual wear which I then branded with my logo and sold online (usually supported by personal delivery). Gained experience of marketing and identifying trends. Acquired many regular customers who appreciated the quality of the merchandise and the positive attitude that I had with each of them.

Retail Salesperson. *Example Furniture Stores.* Worked on behalf of a busy regional chain of furniture shops. Interacted directly with customers, hosted product demonstrations, closed sales, took orders and organised deliveries. Liaised with warehouse departments to ensure timely deliveries. Totalled up takings using PDQ machine. Dealt with customer complaints and provided aftercare service.

Retail Salesperson. Market Trader. Owned and operated a market stall and shop on a main road. Sourced lady's and children's clothing and footwear from wholesalers and sold them to retail customers. Gained experience of marketing and identifying trends. Acquired many regular customers who appreciated the quality of the merchandise and the positive attitude that I had with each of them. Developed many business management skills including hiring staff and organising workflow.

Road Haulier. Proprietary business. Owned and operated a fleet of 6 HGV1 lorries as well as 360° Excavator. Liaised with customers to gain contracts and calmly resolve problems, concerns or complaints. Conducted health and safety risk assessments and secured sites. Gained experience in business management, human resources, organisational skills, negotiation, customer service, problem solving, distribution, packing and despatch. Carried out sales and marketing to gain new customers, managed contracts to ensure a high level of client satisfaction and solicited testimonials and recommendations. Maintained books and records.

"Using the templates, I created a much better CV that I could ever have done on my own. I also did an application and Personal Disclosure Statement. These have helped me massively to progress and I now have a job ready to start in 6 days' time! Thank you." PI

Roofer. Proprietary Business. Worked on residential and commercial projects as a primary contractor and sub-contractor. Fitted lead flashing, burnt ash felt and installed onto flat roofs, hooked and nailed slate tiles and laid all types of tiles and zinc on commercial buildings. Undertook loft conversions, retro fitted insulation, carried out weather proofing and other building projects. Responsible for customer liaison, work scheduling and troubleshooting, health and safety and risk assessments.

Emergency **Rubbish Clearance** and Waste Management. *Example company.* Within a busy team of crisis clearance specialists, I helped to clear sites after major problems had occurred such as deaths in properties or building collapses. Experienced in emptying hoards; handling people's belongings with sensitivity and dignity, whilst also being mindful of the need to work quickly and effectively. Prepared properties for redecoration, sale or re-letting.

Sales Director. *Example company.* Progressed to Director level within this medium size company (60 employees). Managed marketing and advertising campaigns. Recruited, trained and motivated 6 regional sales representatives. Produced financial projections for the senior management team and contributed to business planning and strategy sessions. Established targets and set commission structures for the sales teams. Redeveloped the entire e-commerce strategy and platform resulting in a substantial increase in sales, a growth in our distribution network and a reduction in our quantity break points. Developed income from sales to consumers, small retailers and hotels.

Sales and Marketing Manager. *Example firm.* Responsible for a team of 8 experienced telemarketers selling fine wines to experienced investors and collectors. I focussed on bringing in experienced sales people, training and motivating them to achieve higher sales volumes. Achieved unprecedented sales figures, built a dedicated sales force and secured customer testimonials.

Sales Representative (door-to-door). *Example co.* Responsible for lead generation via managing door to door teams of cold callers. Designed recruitment campaigns and interviewed new sales people. Trained and motivated people to persevere even when faced with rejection. Researched areas, planned routes and organised drivers to ensure coverage of target areas.

Sales Representative (in-homes). *Example co.* Responsible for lead conversion of "warm leads" into completed sales and the initial stages of order fulfilment to ensure a smooth handover to the manufacture and installation departments. Experience gained of a wide range of products including windows, doors, conservatories, guttering and fascias. Gained excellent interpersonal skills and secured testimonials.

Sales Representative (regional clients). *Example company.* Headhunted into this role for my demonstrable sales skills, I swiftly proved my value to the company by meeting and exceeding all sales targets. Grew my customer base and progressed to sales supervisor with a team of 4 sales representatives that I had overall responsibility for. Co-ordinated target areas, distributed sales leads, followed up on historic enquiries and converted interests into signed contracts (sales). Made recommendations to directors including hiring decisions.

Conventional Job CV Templates A - Z

Scrap Metal Merchant and Recycling Operative. A proprietary business collecting and recycling scrap metal and other reusable materials. Ensured that suitable PPE was worn, that H and S procedures were followed at all times and that waste was handled and disposed of, or recycled appropriately. Drove a transit tipper truck in both residential and industrial areas and remained accident free. Managed customer expectations to ensure a high level of client satisfaction and gained recommendations.

Scuba Diving Instructor. Taught scuba diving to groups and individuals from beginners to advance, in open and closed water environments. Gained industry qualifications (HSE Level 3 Commercial Diver and BSAC Divemaster instructor) as well as Royal Yacht Association day and night skipper approval. Developed excellent interpersonal and problem-solving skills.

Security and Courier Driver. *Example firm.* Carried out high value collections and deliveries of cash, bank reconciliations and transactions. Drove a 7.5ton armoured vehicle to deliver time-sensitive cargo. Loaded and unloaded following all health and safety procedures and met pressing deadlines. Managed challenging driving situations in predominantly residential areas and maintained an accident free driving record.

Security Manager. Proprietary Business. Providing SIA approved door supervisors and security personnel to London sites. As owner of the company I developed excellent judgement of people and built relationships with clients from a wide range of backgrounds and industry sectors. Developed an understanding of security systems including body scanners and CCTV. Recorded incidents. Developed organisational skills and gained experience in the recruitment and retention of staff.

Security Officer (In Premises). *Example superstore.* Acted as the first point of contact for all visitors, staff and contractors and maintained a positive public image. Monitored staff and visitors to reduce loss of goods and ensure site security. Implemented theft reduction and fraud prevention initiatives. Dealt with incidents and emergencies in accordance with work manual, including escalating where necessary. Complied with Health & Safety and hazard reporting procedures. Mediated and resolved conflicts. Recorded incidents and concerns, provided reports to management and stored data in compliance with Data Protection. Operated security systems including body scanners and CCTV. Conducted patrols and out of hours receptions.

Shop Fitter. Agency work. Primarily focussed on a national Starbucks contract, I was part of a team that outfitted and refitted coffee shops. I worked to a very high standard and was frequently praised for my carpentry and property refurbishment skills.

Shop Manager. Managed a busy local convenience store and off-licence. Key holding with responsibility for opening and shutting premises and receiving deliveries. Presented stock and organised displays, designed and managed in store promotions, liaised with staff to organise staff rota, kept accounts, processed payments and banked takings. Used customer service skills and built long-term relationships.

Skip Yard Foreman. *Example firm.* Organised lorries, crushers, top soil sieves, hard core sifters, weigh bridges, JCB shovels, sweeper machines were located in the right places prior to them being required. Ensured that suitable PPE was worn, that H and S procedures were always followed, and that waste was handled, disposed of and recycled appropriately. Gave input into staff recruitment and managed staff rosters.

British Army Infantryman **Soldier.** I signed up for the army aged 19 and I stayed for 7 years because I enjoyed the camaraderie and personal development. I was part of a quick reaction/ rapid deployment force and served in Northern Ireland, Rwanda, Kosovo, Zaire (now DRC). In this role I grew up quickly and developed an uncommon maturity. I gained many skills; I am able to use a wide range of equipment and can interact with people of different ages, cultures and backgrounds.

British Army Avionics Engineer **Soldier.** I served within Royal Electrical Mechanical Engineers (REME) for 12 years. This role required maturity and excellent problem-solving skills alongside the ability to remain calm under pressure. I gained many skills, I am able to use a wide range of equipment and know how to interact with people of different ages, cultures and backgrounds. I am professional; I follow instructions, have a good work ethic, learn quickly and focus on the task at hand.

Sound Technician and Music Engineer. Example Music Studios. In this role I adjusted equipment to ensure optimum sound quality for recording. Maintained the studio diary and assisted recording artists with their sessions. Wired speakers and amplifiers, maintained equipment and oversaw all studio activities. Locked and unlocked the studio and monitored security, health and safety and cleanliness.

Sports Agent and Talent Scout. Example Agency. Attended football matches and networking events to secure new clients for representation. Advised the company on the most attractive and potentially lucrative clients and guided clients on their potential earnings through partnerships and sponsorship. Assisted in negotiations. Displayed excellent interpersonal skills.

Steel Fitter. *Example Truck Wash Company.* My duties included operating forklift trucks, cherry picker and working in confined spaces to fix steel supports and install corrugated steel fencing. The firm would build truck wash facilities around the UK. I was flexible and dedicated to my employer, travelling to every new site.

Store Manager. *Example Phone Company.* Working in a target driven high pressure and competitive sales environment, I was responsible for keeping a team motivated and highly trained to enable them to meet or exceed central and regional sales targets. I took over a struggling store and within 3 months of my management it moved from being one of the worst performing in the region to one of the best. I gained a reputation for professionalism and efficiency.

"Our business believes that every person deserves a second chance in life. We have living proof this can happen and assist candidates into a better life." Tom McLoughlin, CEO MACS Plasterboard Systems

Conventional Job CV Templates A - Z

Store Manager/ Department Manager. *Example Food Company*. Progressed from Shop Assistant to Department Manager following a clearly defined career pathway within this blue-chip company. I immersed myself in the company ethos and followed all rules and procedures whilst supporting my team to do the same. Gained a wide range of Customer Service skills that remain relevant and are transferable across the retail sector. With hard work and dedication in this role I consistently met targets.
Tailor and Clothes maker. Working in prestigious London and Birmingham based clothing factories, I designed clothes, created samples and manufactured clothing lines for high street names. Skilled in fine stitching, measuring, cutting and machinery.
Taxi Driver (Hackney Carriage). Owned and operated a black taxi cab. Achieved "The Knowledge" qualification (London roads, routes and places of interest). Developed excellent timekeeping, financial management and interpersonal skills.
Taxi Driver (Private Hire), worked as an independent contractor for Uber driving private clients typically to home and work addresses. Met and interacted positively with people from a diverse range of cultural backgrounds. Proved reliable and gained many regular customers. Maintained an accident free, flawless driving record and was praised by customers for my smooth driving and for how clean I kept my vehicle.
Taxi Driver (VIP). Freelance. Gained advanced driving and first aid qualifications. As a VIP driver I met and interacted with people from a diverse range of cultural backgrounds and from every level of society. Proved reliable and was trusted with private home addresses and secret film locations.
Teacher/ Learning mentor. PRU. Working in a Pupil Referral Unit, I supported and educated pupils who had been excluded or off-rolled from school. Primarily worked with Key Stage 3 pupils aged 11 - 14 but also provided ad-hoc cover for years 10 and 11. Taught literacy (reading and writing) and numeracy (maths) one-on-one to pupils with educational deficits or who require additional learning support. Monitored individual progress and enabled them to reach breakthroughs in their reading abilities. Provided encouragement to reluctant learners and managed challenging behaviour. Developed a great deal of empathy and patience in this role.
Teacher (supply)/ Cover Supervisor. Agency work. Provided short notice emergency cover for a wide range of subjects and age groups. Learnt how to build rapport quickly with unfamiliar groups of students and teachers. I ensured that I made a positive impact in the time available, even when I was only in a school for a short period of time. Gained a wide range of teaching skills and experiences such that I am rarely phased by any teaching environment. Additionally, provided private Maths and English tuition and grew a client base of students who achieved excellent results with the help of my teaching and coaching.

"This guide has shown me how to express my personality, qualifications and work history formally and to a professional standard." DG

192

Telephone Engineer. British Telecom. Worked in-between exchanges and customer's properties. Experienced in fault finding and remedying problems. Worked on own initiative to install routers, cabling, TV boxes and established communications networks. Gained experience in face to face customer service. Drove a company vehicle, adhered to timekeeping and maintained an accident free driving record.

Telesales Person. *Example firm.* Working on behalf of a busy promotional company I called existing customers to extend agreements, upgrade policies and recommend additional products. Professionally handled concerns and complaints. Liaised with the sales team to ensure that customers received the best possible service. Developed excellent telephone and face to face skills which encouraged cooperation from others. Gained problem solving skills and handled challenges professionally.

Tennis Coach. *Named Tennis Club.* Taught tennis fundamentals to beginners. Explained game rules and demonstrated basic shot skills and physical positioning. Hosted regular competitions for children and young adults. Gained a coaching qualification and guided and encouraged new players to progress.

Tiler. Sole-trader and sub-contractor. Fitting tiles in bathrooms and kitchens and on flooring within new-build houses and flats. Worked to a high standard and efficiently. Familiar with Health and Safety requirements. Liaised with customers to receive keys, explain progress and treated them respectfully.

Tool Hire Controller. *Example Hire Group.* In this customer service role, I served customers, resolved queries, issued invoices and processed payments. Made outgoing calls and received incoming calls and became skilled in successfully liaising with customers both over the telephone and face to face. Check out customer purchases and hires, help them to pack and process their payments. Carried out stock takes and replenished store displays. Followed fraud prevention and id verification procedures.

Tool Hire Driver. *Example Hire Group.* Delivered and collected plant to building sites and residential homes; scaffolding tubes and boards as well as towers. Driving a long, twin wheel base Iveco truck to deliver time-sensitive cargo. Loaded and unloaded in line with health and safety procedures and still met pressing deadlines. Managed challenging driving situations in predominantly residential areas and maintained a clean driving record.

Tool Hire Manager. *Example Hire Group.* Progressed to this supervisory role after 8 successful years within the company. Responsible for opening and locking the depot each day, daily bank reconciliation, purchase orders to buy plant and supplies, stock transfer to other branches, logistics of delivering plant, staff rotas and driver routes as well as training and motivation. Operated this busy depot with full autonomy.

Tool Hire Repairer. *Example Hire Group.* Tested, maintained and repaired equipment, plant and machinery and conducted safety checks. Worked on power tools and hire equipment including heaters, de-humidifiers, lighting rigs, paint strippers, power saws, angle grinders, magnetic and hammer drills. I was responsible, flexible and organised and met all targets. Adhered to H&S, PPE and security requirements. Conducted stock takes and placed orders.

Conventional Job CV Templates A - Z	
	Track Worker. Carillion contracted to Network Rail. Working under the supervision of Controller of Site Safety (COSS) and an Engineering Supervisor (ES) I was responsible for ensuring track infrastructure is safe for operation taking into account track component defects and the maintenance plan. Carried out mechanical and electrical checks following a work activity plan. Worked as part of a team at Oxford station laying geo-grids and new track. Performed track maintenance, built platform extensions and carried out structural repairs to bridges. Followed safe working practices at all times. Gained my Diploma in Engineering and Technology (RCF).
	Transport Manager. *Example Coach Firm.* Responsible for operational management of a fleet of 8 coaches and around 15 staff. Monitored maintenance schedules, managed defects and breakdowns, ensured legal compliance and health and safety adherence. Organisational skills and time management were essential in this role.
	Transport Manager. *Food Delivery Firm.* Organised the operation of a fleet of 7 vehicles and drivers delivering pre-ordered fruit and vegetables to commercial clients (restaurants, bars and hotels). Made daily time-sensitive deliveries, loaded and unloaded in full compliance with health and safety. Other duties included allocating loads, organising staff rotas, vehicle maintenance and fleet management.
	Tree Surgeon. Sole Trader and Sub-Contractor. Pruned and removed trees for safety, access and visual appeal. Used winches, wood-chipping machines and chainsaws. Worked enthusiastically and efficiently to meet or exceed each client's needs. Performed emergency call out repairs and reassured distressed customers after storms. My reliability was often praised, and I received many recommendations.
	Tyre Fitter. *Example firm.* Able to fit a wide range of tyres, balance wheels, fix punctures, tracking, fit exhausts and brakes to cars, van and lorries. Worked as a mobile fitter often called out to change tyres in all weather conditions and locations. Developed health and safety awareness and customer service skills.
	Upholsterer. *Example firm.* Worked at a prestigious sofa manufacturer, hand-upholstering specialist chairs for the elderly. Each item was carefully crafted to the client's specification, taking into account their personal preferences as well as their physical needs. Liaised with the sales team to ensure that client specifications were clear and with the despatch department to guarantee timely deliveries, whilst making certain that quality control was upheld.
	Vehicle Body Shop Repair. Proprietary business. Working as a panel beater and paint sprayer I gained skills in accident repairs on a wide range of vehicles from mainstream to prestige, domestic cars to commercial vehicles. Competent in the use of dolly and hammer, pin puller, slide hammer, grinder, drill, spray gun and sanding machine. Used jig and dozer to reverse chassis damage. Health and safety, COSHH and PPE were important considerations in this role.

"I have now been in my job for 6 weeks and it is going very well; it's a different life. Thanks for all the great advice!" RD

Vehicle Inspector and Tester. RAC. Road tested new car models at Millbrook proving ground, made recommendations and provided quality assurance. Carried out detailed assessed of pre-owned and Motability leased vehicles. Recorded damage, carried out mileage checks and generated valuation reports. Progressed to Regional Manager covering a large area from Southend-on-Sea to Birmingham, coordinating and responsible for 22 engineers. Left after redundancy when the RAC lost a contract.

Vehicle Recovery. *Example Recovery*. Drove HGV recovery trucks capable of recovering any type of vehicle. Responded to emergency call outs as well as planned movements for repossession of vehicles, corporate deliveries and plant and machinery. Gained a huge amount of experience in driving in difficult situations and recovering vehicles from challenging spaces and situations. Developed interpersonal skills to support people in distress with empathy as well as assertiveness when required.

Volunteer Co-ordinator. *Example charity*. Worked with a forward thinking and socially aware charity to organise crime-prevention initiatives and health awareness workshops. Provided information, advice and guidance on an individual basis as well as research programmes and information distribution to groups. Maintained confidentiality and complied with The Data Protection Act (more recently the General Data Protection Regulations).

Waiter and Kitchen Porter. Family Business. Ensured that the overall experience for visitors to a café/restaurant was pleasant. Greeted customers, waited on tables, served drinks, cleaned tables, chairs, floors and food services. Provided for special dietary requirements for allergy sufferers. Duties also included general cleaning, loading and unloading of deliveries, monitoring of food storage temperatures, labelling and stock rotation, as well as safe handling to avoid cross-contamination. Developed positive interpersonal skills and built relationships with staff and regular customers.

Warehouse Operative. Agency work. Responsible for loading and unloading deliveries and processing time- sensitive orders for multiple clients. Gained experience on the shop floor interacting directly with customers, demonstrating products, taking orders, completing sales and organising deliveries. Operated forklift trucks and scissor lifts. Met targets, followed health and safety, liaised with other departments, staff and management.

Warehouse Supervisor. *Example firm*. Progressed from warehouse operative to team leader. Responsible for processing and checking order sheets and despatch paperwork for incoming and outgoing goods. Carried out final quality control checks and reported failures or shortages. Supervised the loading and unloading of deliveries and the processing of time-sensitive orders for multiple clients. Produced staff rotas, facilitated staff training and provided input into recruitment decisions. Liaised with other departments, staff and management.

"My CV hadn't been working and I didn't know why. After reading through the pointers in this book, I made a few simple changes and began to get good responses. I was contacted through a CV website, met the team and I now have a trial period lined up with a local employer. Thanks!" VA

Waste Management Operative (Dustman). Agency work for multiple contractors. Emptied bins and collected recyclable materials and general refuse from domestic properties as part of a team. Good people skills, to assist team work and show courtesy to the public were important. Returned to depot and emptied vehicle ready for next round. Followed Health and Safety procedures, always wore PPE and ensured that waste was handled and disposed of, or recycled appropriately. Worked efficiently and to time schedules.

Waste Management Operative. (Refuse site). Used a waste baling machine to process, bale and wrap waste. Shrink wrapped bales ensuring they are safe for transport. Ensured that gas and temperature probes are installed and working effectively to ensure that flammable gases cannot ignite. Cleaned and ensured that health, safety and fire hazards are removed and appropriately dealt with.

Waste Management Operator. A proprietary business disposing of domestic and commercial / industrial waste as a licensed operator. Learnt about recruiting quality staff and all aspects of business organisation. Delivered the service personally and also retained additional drivers to ensure high service levels. Undertook sales and marketing to gain new customers, ensured client satisfaction and solicited testimonials and recommendations.

Welder. Welded on site and fitted steel raisers/ steel grids, balustrades, balconies and staircases in commercial and industrial premises. Skilled in working in confined spaces whilst complying with fire safety and hazard awareness. Prioritised workflow and dealt with a wide range of different people in a positive and professional manner. Drove a commercial work vehicle.

Window Cleaner. Worked in a proprietary business managing commercial and residential window cleaning contracts. Cleaned interior and exterior windows and provided a range of ancillary services such as blinds and tarpaulin, as well as gutter and carpet cleaning. Delivered the service personally and also retained assistant window cleaners to ensure high service levels. Undertook sales and marketing.

Window Installer. Family Business. Installed wooden windows, UPVC windows, doors, conservatories, guttering and drainage products. Used drills, hammers, chisels, silicon guns, electric saws and a wide range of other hand tools. Gained experience of customer service, safe working at heights, meeting deadlines and health and safety.

Window Manufacturer. *Named glass firm.* Fabricated windows, doors and conservatory panels for a medium sized national supplier. Used air drills, beading saws and a wide range of hand tools to make frames, insert glass and install beading. Prepared and packed windows for despatch. Gained experience in working under time pressure, quality control and health and safety.

Youth Worker with 5 years of experience working with children. Supervised, supported and educated ages 4 to 18 years. Collected children (a careful and accident free driver), supervised homework clubs and play schemes and facilitated trips to theme parks, cinemas, and residential activity accommodation. Developed knowledge and understanding of special needs. Managed children's emotional states with empathy and leadership. Safeguarding of children was always the priority.

Gaps in Employment

It is important to include details of how you spent your time when your CV has gaps in your employment history.

When these time periods are explained and worded positively, they can show character development and personal knowledge gained; they often showcase the soft skills that modern employers are looking for.

The following pre-written wording will help you to understand what you really achieved and how you developed personally during your gap years.

Feel free to edit these examples and use as much wording from them as you wish.

Gaps in Employment Examples A - Z	Full-time **Carer** to disabled father who is aged 88 and in poor health. In this intense personal time, I learnt a great deal of patience, compassion and understanding. I made a personal choice to dedicate my time and put my career on hold to pay my father back for the years he looked after me.
	Full-time **Carer** to wife who was in poor health with anxiety and depression, anaemia, pancreatitis and severe back problems. In this intense personal time, I learnt patience, compassion and understanding. I chose to dedicate my time to my wife of 21 years because I knew she would do the same for me if our positions were reversed. I took responsibility for our four children and immersed myself in the day to day routines of school runs, cooking and washing.
	Charity Co-Ordinator. I dedicated my time to a charity which supports elderly people in my local area. I used my professional skills to help raise awareness and also coordinated volunteers to organise fundraising events, support homeless people and care for the elderly. Loneliness has now become a clearly identified need and working to prevent loneliness is something I feel very strongly about.
	Charity Volunteering. I gave my time freely to a local food-bank charity. Unloaded deliveries of donated food and toiletries from local supermarkets including Morrison's, Tesco and Sainsbury's. Checked dates, sorted, cleaned and performed stock rotation. Packaged items ready into parcels for collection by families in need. Cleaned warehouse and maintained a safe working environment.
	Community Project Worker. I used my skills to landscape and clear an adventure playground for young people in my local area. The park had been misused and effectively abandoned for many years and I was proud to have improved the playground so much that it is now used every day by local people

"With the help of this system, I gained a fantastic job working in Estate Agency for a reputable company. It is possible for ex-offenders to get work and to do well, I'm proof of it!" WH

Gaps in Employment Examples A - Z	**Hospital.** Experienced hospitalisation for 6 months whilst my illness was monitored and eventually diagnosed prior to release with a treatment plan. During this time of forced rest, I read and studied and became a more balanced person. I discovered how many people really do care about me. I am determined to not let my illness hold me back in life but work hard and progress despite it.
	Long-term **ill health**. Suffered with Chronic Obstructory Pulmonary Disorder (COPD) and struggled to perform everyday tasks or maintain employment. During my time off of work I performed voluntary tasks and 'odd jobs' for local elderly or disabled people. This included gardening, painting and decorating and fixing shelves/ assembling flat pack furniture. After trialling many remedies, medications and professional opinions, I now have a new treatment which allows me to enjoy a greater amount of freedom, personal fitness and the ability to work again.
	Full-time **Parent**. I made a personal choice to care for my baby daughter until she reached the age of three. During this time, I really bonded with my child and learnt patience, compassion and hard work. I self-studied 13 books on professional skills, mind-set and positivity and undertook a lot of personal development.
	Studying. I took a year away from employment to focus on completing my University degree (BSc). I learnt dedication, focus and hard work and achieved a 2:2. I made myself and my family very proud and gaining my degree helped my confidence. I attended the University of West London (Thames Valley) and met such a diverse group of students that I can now comfortably and confidently interact with people from a wide range of countries, cultures and backgrounds.
	Therapy. Resident of a therapeutic community. Engaged in an intensive therapy programme which helped me to come to terms with my traumatic past, to deal with my thoughts and emotions and to communicate and manage relationships better. I read a lot, studied to improve myself and became a more balanced person.
	Spent a gap year **Travelling.** I toured Europe and gained a new understanding of cultural differences and developed a love of languages. I am now very comfortable with, and skilled in, interacting with people from a wide range of countries, cultures and backgrounds.
	Spent a gap year **Travelling.** I toured India with my family visiting temples and historic sites and spending time with distant relatives. I gained a new understanding of cultural differences and also of how similar people are despite the physical differences between us. I saw the poverty that many people endure and I am determined to help those worse off than ourselves. I improved my communication skills with people from different cultures and backgrounds.
	Youth Work. Dedicated time voluntarily to a local youth charity engaging with the young people and diverting them away from the allure of gang culture and crime. Refereed at football matches, trained young people in fitness, health and mind-set. I understand cultural differences between people and no longer prejudge. I also learnt compassion and empathy for disadvantaged people.

Professional Memberships (Optional)

This section is generally **optional** but becomes **essential** if the memberships are a requirement of the targeted job or industry.

Name those trade organisations that you are affiliated to or are a member of.

Memberships look very good on a CV because there are often minimum qualification requirements, adherence to a professional and recognised code of conduct and they also show commitment to your professional career.

Examples of Professional Memberships	Member of the Institute of Fundraising.
	Student member of the Institute of the Motor Industry.
	Member of the National Association of Estate Agents.
	Member of the National Association of Art Therapists.
	Member of the institution of Railway Signal Engineers.
	Qualified member of the British Institute of Verbatim Reporters.
	Full membership of the Recruitment and Employment Confederation.
	Associate Member of the Federation of Drug and Alcohol Practitioners.
	Membership of the Institute of Purchasing and Supply from St Helens School of Technology.
	Registered Health Play Specialist approved by the Healthcare Play Specialist Education Trust.

"I had a lot of help to work through this book, but there was a path to follow and templates to use. I could never have done this one my own, but my support worker worked through it all with me. I have got a complete document set which are great and because of all this, I have been invited for a job interview." SM

Qualifications

This section is an opportunity to list all your qualifications and awards.

Your qualifications demonstrate three important things to an employer:

1) That you care about your career.

2) That you are committed to self-development and are willing to learn.

3) They differentiate you from other candidates by showing specific knowledge and skills which are relevant to the job role being applied for.

DO:

☑ Begin this section with a positive introductory phrase, e.g.

> *I have gained many transferable skills over my working career, as well as formal qualifications, including the following:*

☑ List your School, College and University qualifications first as well as functional skills, followed by all the other qualifications you have gained.

☑ List all of your vocational qualifications, grouped together into related fields: e.g. Construction or IT. Leave a line space between each group.

☑ Include the grade achieved if it is impressive and unusual, e.g. Distinction.

☑ Mention the awarding body if they are widely known, e.g. City and Guilds.

☑ Include the qualification or the fact that you completed a course even if you do not have the certificate. You can request a copy of your certificate by writing a letter to the establishment where you completed the course.

☑ Include expired qualifications. For clarity, include the words "awaiting renewal" in brackets after the qualification. e.g.

> *First Aid certificate (awaiting renewal)*

☑ Include personal development courses that you have completed and highlight how these are relevant to employers by providing additional information in brackets, e.g.

> *Personal and Social Development course completed (including Body Language and People Skills)*

☑ Include social or compassionate courses that you may have completed e.g.

Trained by the Samaritans and qualified as a "Listener", providing support to other people in distress, or when they are struggling to cope.

☑ Include extra languages that you speak. Clarify whether you speak them fluently (perfect speaking and listening), or only passably (can understand others and can speak enough to be understood). e.g.

Fluent in English, Spanish and Urdu. I also speak passable French.

☑ State that you hold a full driving licence, if you do. e.g.

Holds full UK Driving Licence (including D1 entitlement).

☑ Include any current studies, e.g.

Currently studying to achieve a Construction Skills Certification Scheme (CSCS) card.

Currently studying for an Open University gateway qualification in Business and Management.

☑ Write the phrase "*Right to Work documentation in hand*" (You will need proof of your National Insurance Number (P45, P60 or Letter from HMRC) and proof of your Identification (Passport or Long Birth certificate).

☑ Finish the section with "*Relevant certificates can be provided upon request.*"

DO NOT:

☒ Do not include the dates of qualifications, unless recent.

☒ Do not include the names of schools and education establishments, unless they are local to the target employer or particularly prestigious or noteworthy.

☒ Do not mention low grades such as D or E, just write the qualification; e.g. 6 GCSE passes achieved in Maths, English, IT, German, Science and P.E.

"This book has a great knowledge of what the job market requires in an easy to follow package. I have now been able to skilfully craft the documents to a quality beyond my own abilities." JA

Work through this list of example qualifications and include your own in a similar order.

1	**UNIVERSITY qualifications**	BA (Hons) Business Computing Bournemouth University BA (Hons) 2:1 Accounting and Finance, University of Leeds BA (Hons) Humanities with Philosophy 2:1 {Hons} - OU Foundation Degree in Civil and Structural Engineering - Kings College BSc (Hons) Bio-Medical Science (University of Hertfordshire, Hatfield) Open University 60 Credits access module in Social Sciences (Distinction) BSc Foundation Extended Science degree (University of Herts, Stevenage) MSc Information Technology Security (Post-Grad) University of Westminster Open University 60 Credits gateway qualification in Business and Management
2	**SCHOOL and COLLEGE qualifications**	**(Insert How Many)___ A Level/ AS Level/ /O Level/ GCSE/CSE/ IB passes** Art, Biology, Business Studies, Chemistry, Design Technology, Drama, Dual Science/ Integrated Science, Economics, Electronics, Engineering, **English** Language, English Literature, French, Food Technology/ Home Economics, Geography, Geology, German, Graphic Design, History, Humanities, IT (Computer Science), Latin, Law, **Maths**, Media Studies, Metalwork and Woodwork, Music, Music Technology, Physics, Physical Education/ Sports Science, Psychology, Religious Studies, Sociology, Spanish, Technical Drawing and Textiles e.g. 7 GCSE passes including... 3 A Level passes including... If you achieved A or B grades, then include the grade in brackets after each subject. Do not include lower grades; the fact that you passed is enough for most purposes.

3	If you studied OVERSEAS include these qualifications	Albanian passes (GCSE equivalent) Business, Design Technology and Maths
		7 subjects studied to GCSE level in Cyprus including Art, English, Geography, History, Maths, Turkish and Physical Education
4	IT qualifications	BCS certificate in **IT security** Microsoft Certified **Office Specialist** GNVQ **Information Communication Technology** Gained ECDL **European Computer Driving Licence** BTEC Level 3 certificate in **ICT Systems** and Principles (Specialist Grade) BTEC **Business Information Technology** and Business Studies (4 A Stars) Advanced Level **IT Software, Web and Telecoms** Professional (e-skills UK)
5	Recognised INDUSTRY and VOCATIONAL qualifications	NVQ in **Animal Husbandry** and Care DVSA/ VOSA **MOT Nominated Tester** NPLQ National Pool **Lifeguard** Qualification PADI Scuba Diving - Level 2 **Divemaster Instructor** NCFE Level 2 certificate in **Sustainable Development** Study House Level 3 certificate in **Surveying Technologies** Participated in Continuous Professional Development (CPD) ACCA Chartered Association of **Certified Accountants** qualification EDI/ IQ Level 2 - **Security Officer** L/600/6705 EDI/IQ Level 2 - **Conflict Resolution** K/600/6310 EDI/IQ Level 2 Award - **Security Guarding** 500/7839/2 EDI/ IQ Level 2 - Working in **Private Security** M/600/5174 Highfield HABC Level 2 Award - **CCTV Ops** L3 **Teaching and Training** and Teaching Higher Education Higher National Diploma (HND) in **Heating and Ventilation** - Installing and Maintaining Domestic and Commercial Heating Systems **Diamond Drilling** - CSCS Skilled Worker Blue Card RMF/UKATA Cert. in Asbestos Awareness and Removal (awaiting renewal) GNVQ **Leisure and Tourism** incl. Sales, Customer Service and Management City and Guilds Hotel Management, Hospitality, Food Preparation and Customer Service (7061 and 7062)

6	**Example wording for ex-services personnel**	Army trained in **Motor Vehicle Maintenance** and Repair
		Completed 6 months of Combat Infantryman Vocational Training including the development of diverse skills and education on a wide range of subjects.
7	**FORK-LIFT, PLANT and MACHINERY experience, qualifications and licences**	Experienced in operating plant and machinery as follows:

Experienced in operating plant and machinery as follows:

Agricultural Tractor competent
Experienced **Tipper Truck** driver
Powered Pump Truck competent
Vehicle **Banksman** Safety Trained
Experienced **Whacker Plate** operator
Mini-digger competent (up to 4 tonne)
Trailer mounted **Concrete Pump** trained
Scissor lift operator's certificate, valid until
Hi-Ab crane operator proficiency, valid until
Slinger trained (chains and straps), valid until
CPCS/ NPQRS **Telescopic Handler Trained**
Straddle Carrier (container lifter) competent
Hopper forklift (under lorry) licence, valid until
8 wheel **Ro-Ro lorry** (20yd and 40 yd. bin lifting)
Piling Rig Trained, valid until / awaiting renewal
Ride on Roller licence, valid until / awaiting renewal
180° Excavator licence, valid until / awaiting renewal
360° Excavator licence, valid until / awaiting renewal
Loading shovels licence, valid until / awaiting renewal
Grab Lorry experienced, valid until / awaiting renewal
10 Ton dump truck licence, valid until / awaiting renewal
Experienced in using **Disc cutters** on bricks and concrete

Long reach telescopic forklift operator's licence
Order-Picker forklift operator's licence, valid until
Rough terrain forklift operator's licence, valid until
Side-shift reach forklift operator's licence, valid until
Flexible (bendy) forklift operator's licence, valid until
Counterbalance forklift operator's licence, valid until
Forklift licences incl. CTX, LLOP, OP, PPT, valid until

You may prefer to include a list in a sentence similar to this example:

*Experienced operator of **plant and machinery** including Agricultural Tractor, Tipper Truck, 180° Excavator and 360° Excavator, Grab Lorry as well as 8-wheel Ro-Ro lorry (20yd and 40 yd. bin lifting) please note: licences and tickets were in-house, and all require renewal.*

8	**Qualifications gained whilst in prison**	See examples from pages 207 - 215

9	**Currently studying or working towards**	Currently studying for an Open University gateway qualification in Business and Management.
		Working towards gaining a Level 3 qualification in Information, Advice and Guidance.
10	**Informal or less widely recognised qualifications**	*'High Volume Telesales'* training programme completed
		'Succeeding in sales and understanding buying decisions' training completed Nov 2019
		Daily Diplomacy award for studying **skills with people** and successfully completing a 30-point reflection diary.
		Many **personal development** courses completed including modules such as enhanced thinking, decision making and problem solving, emotional intelligence, equality and diversity, assertiveness, good communication and teamwork.
11	**DRIVING qualifications**	Current Digi-card Tracked vehicle licence Unrestricted motorcycle licence Public Service Vehicle (PSV) Licence ADR Dangerous goods by road qualified Full UK driving licence (Including D1 and D1E) 7.5 tonne vehicle licensed + trailer (C1 and C1E) Owning a fully insured van and comprehensive set of tools Driver's certificate of Professional Competence (DCPC) Heavy Goods Vehicle HGV1 Articulated Licence and HGV2 Rigid Licence
12	**LANGUAGES spoken**	e.g. **Fluent** in English and French and I also speak **passable** Spanish
		Afrikaans (South Africa), Albanian, Arabic, Farsi (Afghanistan), French, Greek, Hindi, Iranian/ Persian, Italian, Kurdish, Lingala (central African - DRC), Norwegian, Patwa (Jamaica), Russian, Somali, Spanish, Punjabi, Russian, Shona (Zimbabwe), Swahili (the language of East Africa), Turkish, Twi (the language of Ghana), Urdu, Welsh and Yoruba (Nigeria)
		Fluent means you can converse effectively and understand all words and phrases.
		Passable means you can hold basic conversations and understand the most common words and phrases.
		(If you only speak English then you do not need to include this section)

13	**'Right to work' documentation in hand**	You will need proof of your National Insurance Number (P45, P60 or Letter from HMRC) **and** proof of Identification (Passport, long birth certificate, biometric ID card or certificate of naturalisation)
14	**Relevant certificates can be provided upon request**	Insert this phrase **IF** you have your certificates and evidence. If you no longer have proof of your qualifications, then write to the awarding bodies to request them and leave this phrase out whilst awaiting replies.

"Ex-offenders have seen the harshest side of life and they don't want to go back there again. Once you've been to prison it's very rare that people want to go again, so most who come to us really want to make a difference. That's what I want - I want people who are passionate and are going to learn."

Simon Drake, Manager Conrad London St James Hotel

When you begin to list your qualifications, you will be surprised by how many you will have gained in your working career and during your time in prison.

Education is a strong feature of our prison system and most prisoners have numerous certificates and are more qualified than when they arrived.

Qualifications which you gained whilst in prison may include some of the following examples (taken from multiple CVs):

Examples of Qualifications obtained in Prison	**Functional Skills**	OCR Level 1 and Level 2 certificates in **Maths** (equivalent to high GCSE grade)
		OCR Level 1 and Level 2 certificates in **English** (equivalent to high GCSE grade)
		Awards in Numeracy (**Maths)** and Literacy (**English)** - equivalent to GCSE passes
	Alcohol Support/ Drug and Solvent Counselling	Drug and Alcohol Mentoring and support award
		St John's Ambulance Overdose Aid course completed
		NPS - Teaching drug effects, avoidance and relapse prevention through drama
		Stonebridge College Level 4 DIPLOMA in Drug, Solvent and Alcohol Abuse Counselling (letters S.A.C.Dip)
	Art, Design, Textiles	NOCN certificate in **creating ceramics**
		Certificate in **Upholstery Skills** Open Awards award in **Sewing Skills** NCFE Level 2 certificate in **Textile Manufacturing** Fine Cell Work award winner in **Stitching and Embroidery**
		BTEC Levels 1, 2 and 3 **Art and Design** Open Awards certification in exploring and producing **Art** City and Guilds/ Weston College Level 2 **Creative Writing**
		Gateway/ Aim Award - creative skills for working in **Art and Design** Industries
		City and Guilds/ AIM/ Way2Learn/ NCFE Level 1 and 2 certificates in **Creative Craft**, Art and Design
		OCR Level 2 award in **Professional Photography** (including professional photographic enhancement)

Examples of Qualifications obtained in Prison	**Barbering and Hairdressing**	City and Guilds Introduction to the **Hair and Beauty** Sector City and Guilds Level 2 and 3 awards in **Barbering** including Contact Dermatitis)
	Business, Finance and Sales	IOSH- **Managing Safely** award
		IAM - Level 2 Cert **Computerised Bookkeeping**
		City and Guilds Level 2 award in **Business Finance**
		NCFE L2 - Lean Organisational **Management Techniques**
		OCR Level 2 - **Bookkeeping** and Accounting incl. SAGE OCR 'Firm Start' - **Business ideas** and financial planning OCR Level 2 Cambridge Technical Certificate in **Business** OCR Level 2 - **Personal Finance** and Money Management OCR/ OCN/ Ascentis/ Weston Level 2 - **Business Enterprise**
		Institute of Sales and Marketing Management (ISMM) award in **Sales and Marketing**
		Skills First certificate - **Principles of Business** start-up Skills First Level 3 - Principles of **Human Resources** (HR)
		Institute of Leadership and Management L2 - **Team Leading** Stonebridge College Level 2 **Debt Management** (S.A.C.Cert)
	Cleaning and Laundering	City and Guilds - **Practical Cleaning** Skills City and Guilds/ Novus/ edexcel Level 2 - **Industrial Cleaning** and Support Services Skills
		British Institute Cleaning Sciences (B.I.C.Sc)/ Wamitab **Licence to Practice** - valid until February 2021
		British Institute Cleaning Sciences (B.I.C.Sc)/ Kay's Medical/ Wamitab/ RESPONSE Level 3 - **Bio-Hazard** management
		British Institute Cleaning Sciences (B.I.C.Sc)/ Kay's Medical/ Wamitab/ RESPONSE Level 2 - **Industrial Cleaning** including A1 - A13 and B1 - B13 modules.
		British Institute Cleaning Sciences (B.I.C.Sc) Level 2 - **Food Premises Cleaning** - incl AA1, AA3, K1, K6, L3, L4, L5, L10, L11, L13, L14, L17, M2, M5, M8, N1, N2, N6, N7, N8
		British Institute Cleaning Sciences (B.I.C.Sc) **Industrial Cleaning** Proficiency Levels 1, 2 and 3 incl. AA1, A1, A3, A5, A15, A2, A4, A6, A9, AA3, A7, A12, B1, B5, B2, B3, C2, C3, C4, C6, D1, D3, D4, D2, E3, E5, F1
		Guild of Cleaners and Launderers Level 2 - **Commercial Laundering** Technician including health and safety, processing different materials and machine operations

Examples of Qualifications obtained in Prison	**Construction**	City and Guilds Level 2 - **Block-paving** City and Guilds/ Cskills award L2 - **Site Carpentry** City and Guilds / CAA L2 - **Painting and Decorating** C&G L2 - **Dry Lining, Plastering and Ceiling Fixing** City and Guilds L2 - **Roofing Systems and Techniques** C&G/ Cskills L2 - **Wall and Floor Tiling and Splitting** City and Guilds/ CAA L2 - **Bricklaying and Brickworks** C&G L2 - Conducting **Risk Assessments** in Construction City and Guilds L2 - **Plumbing, Sanitation and drainage** City and Guilds L2 - **Heating and Ventilation Installation** City and Guilds L2 - **Skilled Carpentry and Bench Joinery** C&G L2 - **Plant and Machinery** (Lifting and Transferring) C&G/ Cskills L2 - **Fitted Interiors** - Bedrooms and Kitchens City and Guilds Levels 1 and 2 - **Plumbing** (Installing & maintaining Domestic, Industrial and Commercial Systems) City and Guilds/ CITB - **Construction Multi-Skills** including components, materials and finishing , flooring, tiling, painting and decorating, brickwork, pipework and plastering Woodwise certificate - Safe use of **Carpentry Machinery** NOCN Certificate in **Building Crafts** Occupations (Merit) Stonebridge College L2 Diploma - **Building Construction** GQA Level 1 certificate in **Window and Door Installation** CITB SSSTS - **Site Supervisor** Safety Training Scheme CITB/ BTEC/ OCN - **Health and Safety** in Construction **Construction Skills Certification Scheme** (CSCS) card, valid until May 2023
	Cookery, Catering and Customer Service	NCFE Level 2 - **Creative Cookery** City and Guilds - **Retail Knowledge** City and Guilds Level 2 - **Kitchen Services** City and Guilds Level 2 - **Food and Drink Service** C&G/ RSPH Level 2 - **Healthy Food** and Special Diets C&G / Redemption Roasters Level 2 - **Barista certified** C&G / NCFE/Pearson award Level 2 - **Customer Service** City and Guilds Level 3 - **Confectioners and Pastry Chef** C&G NVQ / Stonebridge/ OA - **Hospitality and Catering** C&G / NCFE/ Open Awards Level 2 - **Professional Cookery** City and Guilds / British Safety Awards/ RSPH/ W2L/ CIEH Highfield Level 2 - **Food Safety in Catering** (QCF) Highfield Level 3 - **Kitchen Management** (Supervising Food Safety in Catering)

Examples of Qualifications obtained in Prison	**Electrical**	**Portable Appliance Tester** (PAT) qualified Trade Skills 4U - **Domestic Electrical Installation** EAL Level 3 - Electrical Engineering Technology 501/1121/8 AIM L2 - Installation and repair of **Domestic Appliances** C&G - **Wiring** Circuits and Components (L/601/0124) C&G Level 3 - Part P Building Regs. Electrical (2393-10) C&G Level 1, 2 and 3 - **Electrical Installation** (2330-07) C&G L2 - **Inspection, Testing** and Verification (2392-10) C&G Level 2 - **Electro Technical Technology Installation** C&G L3 - **Solar Panels**, Environmental Technology Systems C&G L3 - **Requirements** Electrical Installations BS7671 (2382-12) (17th Edition -2011) 600/3046/X
	First Aid, Health and Social Care	NUCO Training - Good **Nutrition** NCFE Level 2 - **Preparing to work in Adult Social Care** NCFE / Cache L2 - Awareness of **Mental Health** Problems NUCO Training - **Emergency First Aid** at Work NUCO Training/ St John's Ambulance/ - Level 3 **First Aid** at work and **Resuscitation** (awaiting renewal) Open Awards Qualification in **Health and Wellbeing** including Interpersonal Skills, Healthy Lifestyles, Nutrition, Performance and Healthy Eating. **NHS** inclusion **Mental Health** (In reach) Training Package completed including Anxiety, Bereavement, Bi-Polar, Coping, Depression, Eating disorders, Mood Management, Paranoia Personality disorders, Schizophrenia and Trauma. Stonebridge College/ Aspirations Training - Certificate in **Health and Social Care Awareness** including knowledge of The Care Act, support plans, prompting medication, prompting nutrition, wheelchair assistance, infection control, personal dignity and safeguarding.
	Health and Safety (General)	**Fire Warden** Course completed **Industrial Lifting** courses completed ROSPA certificate in safe working at **heights** NUCO Training - Level 2 **Manual Handling** NUCO/ CIEH/ HABC/ British Safety Awards/ Highfield/ RSPH - **Health, Safety and Welfare** in the workplace (QCF) including Electrical, Fire, Manual Handling, Signs and PPE

"We believe we can access a broader talent pool by being open minded about people's pasts and giving them an opportunity to become a valued member of our team. We also want to give back to the communities in which we work and have a positive impact on local people." Lyn Rutherford, HR Director Carpetright

Examples of Qualifications obtained in Prison	**Horticulture, Landscape Gardening and machinery**	City and Guilds Levels 1 and 2 - **Practical Horticulture** City and Guilds Level 3 - **Horticulture** and Plant Science City and Guilds/ NPTC Level 2 - **Safe Use** of Handheld Hedge Cutters, Leaf Blowers, Vacuums, Manually Fed Wood-Chipper, Mowers and Strimmers.
	Information Technology (IT)	**Microsoft Certified** Office Specialist City and Guilds certificate in **video editing** Gained ECDL European Computer Driving Licence OCR CLAIT/ NOCN Levels 1, 2 and 3 - **Microsoft Office Suite** certification OCR/NCFE Level 2 - Interactive Media, **Graphic Design** (Adobe suite), Creative Media and web design City and Guilds (Pro-Coms) Award in **ICT Systems Support** - Networking, Installation and Diagnostics and PC Maintenance City & Guilds Levels 1 & 2 - **Desktop Publishing** incl. Adobe suite and Coral draw NCFE certificate in, Graphic Design (Adobe suite) and web design Diploma in ICT - **Customising software** (including databases such as Excel) **CISCO System's** Networking Academy - IT Essentials Books 1 - 3 CCNA OCR RSA Levels 2 and 3 - **IT and Computing** award (Integrated Business Technology) including Electronic communications, file management, data processing, automated presentations, publication production and software customisation.
	Manufacture, Warehousing and Logistics	City and Guilds award in **Workshop Management** C&G L1 & 2 **Printing** and safe use of printing machinery Pearson Edex L2 - **Performing Manufacturing Operations** City and Guilds/ Pearson/ Highfield / Open Awards/Edexcel NVQ Levels 2 and 3 **Warehousing, Storage and Logistics**

Examples of Qualifications obtained in Prison	**Music and Performing Arts**	BTEC Level 2 **Music** People Plus award in **Film Theory** NCFE certificate in **Interactive Media** NCFE Audio **Software Engineering** (multi-track loop sequencing) NCFE Level 2 certificate in **Music Technology** and Radio Production C&G Level 1 and 2 certificates in Sound Engineering and **Music Technology**
	Peer Mentoring and Teaching	NCFE / Cache Level 2 - **Understanding Autism** NCFE / Cache Level 2 - **Mental Health** Problems NCFE / Cache Level 2 - **Behaviour that Challenges** NCFE / Cache Level 2 - **Specific Learning Difficulties** NCFE/ C&G/ Ascentis/ Pearson - L2 **Learning Support** NCFE Level 2 - Preparing to work in **Adult Social Care** NCFE / Cache Level 2 - **Young People's Mental Health** NCFE/ C&G - L3 AET **Education, Teaching and Training** NCFE/ C&G/ AIM/ L3 **Information, Advice and Guidance** PTLLS qualification - Preparing to Teach in the **Lifelong learning** sector South London College Level 2 - **Teaching English** as Second Language (ESOL) OCR/ AIM/ NCFE Pearson BTEC - Levels 2 and 3 **Peer Mentoring** (Leadership, teaching and supporting students) Qualified as a **Shannon Trust** 'Toe by Toe'/ 'Turning Pages' mentor, teaching vulnerable adults, or adults with learning difficulties, to read
	Rail Work and Track Safety	**Holding a Sentinel Card**, Main sponsor Aspect/ Carillion NVQ Level 3 Diploma in Engineering and Technology (RCF) - Unit QETA / 099 **Railway Infrastructures** **Small plant qualified** including Rail Drill, Strimmer, Generator, Chainsaw, Cobra TT, Brush Cutter and Impact Wrench **Personal Track Safety PTS** AC including: TIC - Track Induction Course, ICI - Industry Competency Induction, DCCR - Direct Current Conductor Rail, Olec 1 - Overhead Line Equipment Construction

"I know that I made mistakes and I admit that. I am now taking a new path and I am going to stay on this path no matter what hurdles because it's best for me and best for my family." VG

Examples of Qualifications obtained in Prison	Sport, Gym and Fitness	City and Guilds Level 3 - **Health Trainer** award Active IQ/ REPS/ Focus - Level 2 **Spin Instructor** Active IQ - Level 3 **Nutrition** for Physical Activity Active IQ/ REPS/ Focus/ OCN/ C&G - L2 **Nutrition** Active IQ/ REPS/ Focus - Level 2 **Circuit Instructor** Active IQ - Level 2 **Smoking Awareness** and Cessation Active IQ/ REPS/ Focus - Level 2 **Kettlebells Instructor** Active IQ - Level 3 Instructing **Outdoor Fitness** Sessions Active IQ/ REPS/ Focus/ YMCA - **Lifestyle Management** Active IQ/ REPS/ Focus - Principles of **Health and Fitness** Active IQ/ REPS/ Focus - Level 2 **Minor Games Instructor** Active IQ/ REPS/ Focus - Active **Healthy Living** and Fitness Active IQ/ REPS/ Focus/ OCN/ YMCA/ C&G - Level 2 **Gym Instructor**/ Fitness Instructing including: anatomy and physiology, H&S and welfare, planning and instructing gym exercise, supporting clients, principles of fitness and health. Active IQ/ Stonebridge College/ City and Guilds - Level 3 **Personal Training** (QCF) Delivering personal training sessions, Principles of exercise, fitness and health, Programming personal training with clients, Anatomy and physiology for exercise and health, H&S and welfare, supporting clients, Applying principles of nutrition. Including Diploma in Personal Training S.A.C. Dip (Fitness Trainer) Active IQ/ REPS/ FOCUS - Level 3 **Exercise Referral** (QCF), 38 credits including: Instructing exercise, Anatomy and physiology for exercise and health, planning exercise referral programmes, professional practise, understanding medical conditions, applying the principles of nutrition. BWLA **Weight Training** Safety award QCA **Sports Leader** UK Level 2 award CSLA Community **Sports Leader** award FA 1ST 4 Sport award in **Coaching Football** BTEC Award in **Sport and Active Leisure** (QCF) Fitech - **Understanding Cholesterol and Diabetes** AQA - Basketball, Rugby, Table Tennis, Volleyball RFU Community Leader - **Coaching Youth Rugby** FA **Treatment and Management of injuries** certificate Northern Saints **Millennium Volunteer** award - 300 hours City and Guilds - **Sport**, Recreation and Allied Occupations NOCN Oxford Health - **Nutrition, Sport and Performance**

"Some of our very best people are currently employed whilst serving the remaining term of their prison sentence. We are committed to ensuring that our team is comprised of people from all different backgrounds. Once an individual's sentence is complete, they should be given equal opportunity to fully rehabilitate." Kelly Coombs CEO Census Data

Examples of Qualifications obtained in Prison	**Street-works**	City and Guilds - Confined Space Training completed
		Current **NRSWA** (New Roads and Street Works Training) 1 - 9 Operator's Card
		City and Guilds NVQ Level 2 - **Steel Fixing** (including 18 months in work training)
		National Electricity Registration Scheme authorised person for WPD System, SSE Networks, UKPN and Civils, Excavation and backfilling.
		Operator training certificate in M.E.W.P. **Mobile Elevating Working Platform** aka 'cherry picker' - now International Platform Access Federation (IPAF)
		C&G **Street-works** Road Maintenance, Excavation and Reinstatement including non-bituminous materials and cold-lay bituminous materials, signing, lighting and guarding, use of Cable Avoidance Tool (CAT) and Genny, backfill materials, modular surfaces and concrete footways.
	Vehicle Maintenance	NVQ Level 3 **Motor Vehicle Maintenance** and Repair City and Guilds Levels 1 and 2 - **Bicycle Maintenance** IMI Dip in Transport Maintenance - **Motorcycle** 601/8756/6
		C&G **Vehicle Valeting** incl interior and exterior cleaning knowledge and skill, working relationships, health and safety.
		C&G GNVQ L2 - **Vehicle Bodywork Repairs** to insurance standard - Panel Beating including metal inert gas (MIG) and tungsten inert gas (TIG) welding, brazing and soldering.
		Institute of the Motor Industry certificate in **Vehicle Maintenance** including braking and Exhaust Systems and Health and Safety.
		Skills and Education Group - **Motor Vehicle Studies** including ignition, transmission and braking systems, engineering equipment, Health and Safety and L2 - Specialist Tyre Fitting and Wheel Alignment.
		British Institute Cleaning Sciences (B.I.C.Sc) **Car Valeting** Certificate including interior and upholstery cleaning and stain removal, engine cleaning, paint renovation, exterior cleaning, pressure washing, polishing and waxing.
		City and Guilds L2 - **Vehicle Systems Maintenance** and Repair including Engines, Fuel and Exhaust, electrical, braking, transmission, steering, suspension, wheels, tyres, manufacturing and safe use of tools and machinery.

Examples of Qualifications obtained in Prison	**Waste Management and Recycling**	Wamitab **Waste and Recycling** accreditation
		Wamitab Level 2 Diploma in **Sustainable Recycling**
		CIWM certificate of **Waste Awareness** and recycling
		NCFE Certificate in **Environmental Awareness** and Sustainability (Developing Creative Sustainable Solutions)
	Welding and Engineering	Weldability certificate in **Brazing and Soldering** Weldability certificate in Manual Metal **Arc Welding** Weldability certificate in Metal Inert Gas - **MIG Welding** Weldability certificate in Tungsten Inert Gas - **TIG Welding**
		EAL - NVQ L2 - **Engineering Maintenance** EAL - NVQ - **Engineering Operations 500/1448/1** EAL - NVQ - **Engineering Operations 501/0274/6** EAL - NVQ - Working in an **Engineering** Environment EAL - NVQ L3 - **Fabrication and Welding Engineering** EAL - NVQ - **Engineering Operations 500/9836/6** including Metal Arc Welding, Manual TIG Welding, Plasma-Arc Welding, MIG, MAG and wire welding.
		Gas Cutting certificate (Oxyacetylene) for cutting steel
		Machine Setting and Operating Course (MSOC) - Lathes and milling machines
	Finish your qualifications list with Personal Development	**Problem Solving** Skills workshop completed
		AIM Level 2 Award in **Ethics and Social Change**
		Certificate in Effective **Decision Making and team work**
		Graduated from Chrysalis - **Leadership** and Personal Effectiveness Programme
		Gateway Level 2 - Understanding **Restorative Justice**
		Daily Diplomacy award for studying **skills with people** and completing a 30-point implementation and reflection diary.
		EDI/ Restorative Approaches/ Medway - certificate in communication, **conflict management** and **mediation**.
		Trained by the **Samaritans** and qualified as a "Listener", providing support to other people in distress, or when they are struggling to cope.
		Many **personal development** courses completed; including modules such as enhanced thinking, decision making and problem solving, emotional intelligence, equality and diversity, assertiveness, good communication and teamwork.

Other Achievements (Optional)

Optional - This section is your chance to talk about things that you have done in your life that you are deservedly proud of.

The achievements you list do not have to be directly related to work.

Examples of Additional Achievements	Recipient of Duke of Edinburgh Award for participation in Can-Do programme.
	Chaired a sub-committee for equality and received an award for **promoting equality.**
	I have volunteered in Ghana, supporting small villages and developing plumbing infrastructure. I now travel for one week each year to develop these initiatives further.
	Between the ages of fifteen and twenty-two, I helped elderly people in my community with groundwork and garden maintenance. I find this type of work so very rewarding. I often think about a lady I helped who struggled with multiple sclerosis. I will never forget the look of joy on her face each time her garden improved.
	I started a charity fundraising event called "Weights for Breaks". Along with 20 other men, we held a sponsored weightlifting event that raised £7,500 to send disabled children on holiday to Disney world. The event really took off and is now held every year in July. I felt so happy that I was able to co-ordinate and promote such a worthwhile event and I am very pleased that it has become an on-going project raising money for children's charities.
	During my property career I was involved in lobbying the Government for a change in legislation now called the 'Mortgage Repossession Protection of Tenants Act'. This now provides tenants with similar protections to homeowners in the event of repossession by the landlord's mortgage lender. Prior to me increasing public awareness around this issue, a large number of tenants were being evicted from rental properties with little or no notice period.

"We believe that people should have an opportunity based on desire, skill and a good fit with a current position, not on historical blemishes. Inclusion and rehabilitation is an on-going process brought about by acceptance, purpose and pride." Christian Hill, CEO Project Simply PR and Communications

Personal Interests

This section is your chance to show a more personal side and give the employer an insight into your life that they can to relate to; things that give them a better understanding of you.

Consider mentioning 3 or 4 of your favourite pastimes including a little bit about your family. Include the personal interests that you could happily talk about if asked. Share some details and avoid using one word generalisations like "film" or "music".

The following real life examples (in alphabetical order) may help you to come up with your own ideas and some of the pre-written wording may also work for you.

Example Personal Interests. A - Z	I enjoy **acting** and amateur dramatics; I have performed in a number of plays. My most recent was a part in a moving play called "rising in the sun" about an African American family in the time of racial segregation.
	I enjoy caring for **animals** and keeping pets. I am currently looking after three rabbits that are so pampered and domesticated that they enjoy coming in the house in wintertime. Animals are a great comfort to people. They also bring joy to children and teach them empathy, compassion and caring.
	I enjoy keeping **animals** and animal husbandry. I have looked after horses and ponies and dedicate a lot of my free time to volunteering at animal sanctuaries. I find working with animals very peaceful and I am currently exploring the idea of developing therapeutic initiatives based around animals for traumatised children and adults.
	Antiques fascinate me, probably as an extension to my love of history. I often browse charity shops and boot sales looking for lost or forgotten treasures and burn the midnight oil researching my discoveries.
	I enjoy **art**; I draw and illustrate to a standard that is appreciated by other people. I have created a number of works for friends and family and they have admired the quality and originality.
	I am a keen amateur **artist** and I like experimenting with hands on creative mediums such as illustrating, pottery and sculpture.
	I am a self-taught graphic **artist** and designer. I enjoy using adobe Photoshop and similar programmes to create logos, illustrations and leaflets for friends and charities. I am regularly growing my knowledge and skills in this area and find it a good outlet for my creativity.

I am currently self-studying a subject I am enthralled about, which is **Astrophysics**; understanding the natural rules and laws which govern our universe and within which we exist. The more I discover, the more I realise that there is still so much awaiting us to discover.

I take part in **banger racing**. I find interesting and cheap, old cars for sale, strip them out, install roll cages and harnesses for safety, place the battery and petrol tank inside the car, with cut out switches to prevent fire and then we race. Banger racing days are great events that are social and fun for all ages.

I like making and **baking** cakes and treats for guests and for special events. I provided a whole range of different flavour cheese cakes for Eid festivals which proved very popular.

I enjoy playing and watching **basketball**. I was once awarded 'best defensive player' at Millfield Sports Academy. My favourite element of the sport is team work and the high level of fitness that the best players achieve.

I enjoy **bible studies** as part of my commitment to being a Christian. I like attending church and appreciate the community atmosphere at regular events.

I have a strong personal interest in **body-building** and weight-lifting. In 2007 I was a British finalist for World's Strongest Man competition. I gain a great deal of personal satisfaction from achieving and challenging myself. More recently I started to coach other people and share my experiences of weight lifting at professional levels.

I really enjoy **Bollywood** movies. I get really engrossed in the atmosphere of these positive and colourful stories and find the rich culture and the background songs deeply immersive. I particularly like a decent movie when it first shows at the cinema so I can get the 'big screen' experience.

I am an amateur **boxer** who fights in medium weight and white-collar competitions. I train at my local sparring gym usually in a group and we then spar in pairs. For me boxing is a great way of getting fit and helps me to overcome fears or doubts.

I am really interested in **buses**. I like everything about them from the first historic vehicles to the modern, technologically advanced models we see on our streets today. I have enjoyed my career as a bus driver and the years of experience. I was involved in filming of buses for action films and have even been filmed as a bus driver in several roles, which was great fun too.

I am interested in **business** development. From a young age I have always been entrepreneurial and taken pride in spotting opportunities to improve things and make the world better. I also like to encourage others to start and develop their own projects and see them grow to be bigger that their original ideas.

I am really interested in **cars** and motoring. I am enthralled by car restoration programmes and have an ambition to restore my own classic car in the future, (hopefully a Morgan).

I am really interested in **cars** and motor racing, particularly the history of cars and the evolution of technology in racing cars. One of the highlights of my life was running my own prestige car restoration and modification garage.

I like performance **cars**. I enjoy modifying cars to enhance their performance and personalising them to make them unique. My last project was a BMW E46 M3, which became a real head turner when I had finished my customisation.

I enjoy playing **chess** and having played for many years I consider myself able to present most people with a challenge. Chess is a game with an almost infinite number of combinations, so it never gets boring or repetitive. It also helps people to learn the consequences of decisions and plan ahead.

I am an enthusiastic **collector** of rare Adidas trainers from all over the world. This started as an extension of my love of football and now I correspond with collectors from around the world and enjoy treasure hunting for new additions.

I am a **comedian** and get such an adrenaline rush from taking the mike and performing in front of an audience. The fear that grabs me before the event pales into insignificance with the joy that comes after delivering a successful performance. I have personally developed through thinking on my feet and overcoming my personal fears to follow my heart.

I like **cooking** for guests and seeing their delighted reactions as they taste my creations. I do experiment with different cuisines, usually taking ideas and inspiration from cookery programmes on TV.

I enjoy playing **cricket**; I am an all-rounder, equally at home as opening batsman or bowler. I have been a member of several local cricket teams and some of my best memories have been playing Sunday cricket in the sun.

I enjoy **cycling**, whether on my own or with my wife or friends. I enjoy taking long bike rides through the country and along canals. The feeling of peace in the open air and the health benefits are real attractions to me.

I am a trained **dancer** and since a young age I went through a number of dance academies. I can dance a range of styles but particularly break dance, street dance and contemporary. I haven't performed for a while but my times on stage are among my happiest memories.

I enjoy playing **darts**; it is a real passion of mine. I used to play for a local team and the weeks building up to tournaments were filled with practise and excitement. I have made many friends through dart competitions and I enjoy this social aspect of the sport.

I am a **DJ** in my spare time. I play a wide range of music, sometimes at clubs, but more often at weddings, christenings and birthday parties and I really enjoy the atmosphere of these celebratory events.

I enjoy **documentaries** and biographies, true stories of people's lives. I find it very interesting to understand how and why people make decisions and how different the stories look with the benefit of hindsight.

I enjoy **dog walking** with my partner. We often take our Terrier dog and Sprocker puppy along the beautiful, local, National Trust route walks.

I enjoy keeping **dogs**, training and understanding them. I have a Cavalier King Charles Spaniel cross. I am currently studying a Level 2 Introduction to Canine Psychology via distance learning and the insights into dog behaviour are very interesting indeed.

I enjoy **driving**. I don't just drive for work or to get somewhere; I actually enjoy the experience of driving and the feeling of freedom and control of being on the open road. For me it is nothing to do with speed, but is more about having time to see the scenery and gather my thoughts whilst driving.

I have a strong interest in **economics** and finance. It is really insightful to learn how the markets interact and how global politics and events impact on the value of money locally and internationally.

I feel very strongly about **equality**. My parents taught me that everyone should be treated the way that we would want to be treated, with politeness, respect and equality. I campaign for equality and support equality charities.

I am a committed **family** man, with a wife and four children. We particularly enjoy taking our German shepherd puppy on long family walks in the woods near our home.

I value **family** time, I am particularly mindful to spend as much time as possible with my mum, dad and my extended family. They have always been the guiding light in my life and I want to make sure that I take good care of them as they get older.

I treasure **family** time and making memories with my wife of 16 years and our three children. We also have a new bundle of joy - our first grandchild who is just 6 weeks old.

Family time with my three children is really important to me. We often go to the park, bowling, cinema, ice skating and swimming and spend as much time together as possible. It is a privilege being a positive influence in their lives.

I value **family** time; I am particularly mindful to spend as much time as possible with my two young sons. I am determined to be a positive and inspiring role model to them.

I enjoy **farming** and agriculture. I find animal husbandry to be an inspiring use of time and I sense a growing movement towards sustainable and ethical principles. Kindness to animals and to the environment is one of my passions.

I am very interested in youth **fashion** and have enjoyed branding my own clothing and marketing the range. I like discovering the psychology behind buying decisions and how fashions change.

I am an amateur **fisherman** and enjoy fly fishing for salmon, trout and grayling in rivers such as the River Tannet on the Welsh border.

I am an amateur **fisherman** and relish the challenges of coarse fishing for barbell, tench, chub, carp and match / competition fishing.

I am an amateur **fisherman** and enjoy the competition that comes from sea fishing on the Hampshire coast for bass and mackerel. My favourite fish to catch are flatfish such as rays because they present a bit more of a challenge.

I am keen on **fitness**; I love outdoor sports such as mountain climbing and rock climbing, abseiling and bunji jumping.

I am keen on **fitness**; I regularly attend the gym and primarily focus on working with weights, cardio workouts and cross fit training. I enjoy seeing myself progress, overcoming personal barriers and taking care of my personal health. I also play football and badminton.

I enjoy **fixing** mechanical things. I am often working with family or friends on cars and bikes and it is great when we as a team get them up and running again.

I **fly** as frequently as I can and I have a pilot's licence. I am confident and familiar in a wide range of light aircraft and often fly fixed wing Cessna 172 or 206. The best thing about flying for me the feeling of freedom and the exhilaration of seeing the earth from up high.

I am an FA qualified **football** coach (Levels 1 and 2) and enjoy coaching the youth in my local area because I can see the difference that football can make to the lives of children.

I enjoy supporting my local **football** team and have many happy memories of attending matches with friends. I also play frequently in my preferred position as striker. Football is a great way to learn team-work and cooperation.

I enjoy supporting my local **football** team and my son is a season ticket holder, so we have many happy memories of attending matches together. We train together at the local field (along with our dog who tries to play too!).

"Spending the time and working hard to create a good CV is well worth it, I have now got a full-time job in sales which is exactly what I wanted, good basic salary + commission so I can work hard, prove myself and also get well paid." LR

Example Personal Interests, A - Z	I am a keen **gamer**. I enjoy playing and progressing through a wide range of games. Technology has evolved so much in recent years and games are so immersive that they bring a great sense of achievement to the players. I find games entertaining and challenging and a relaxation aid.
	I love **gardening**, growing things and landscaping. I have horticultural qualifications and I am building on these as a current student of the Royal Horticultural Society. I cannot get enough of gardening and nature; there is nothing I enjoy more than a day spent working in the outdoor air.
	I am a keen **golfer** and have played for most of my life. I started as a junior pro and kept my interest. I play to a 7 handicap.
	I am currently learning to play the **guitar** and find this very rewarding. I can now play around thirty different popular songs.
	I enjoy **hairdressing**. It inspires me to see how cutting hair and improving someone's appearance can have such a transformational effect on their mood and confidence. I like being a part of something so positive that helps people.
	I am passionate about **health** and personal fitness; I really enjoy the gym, but more than that, I like inspiring others to improve their fitness. I am a keen rugby player and enjoy watching the sport too.
	I like to **help** and support people; I try to spread encouragement and positivity to others. I am particularly good at identifying when people are feeling lonely or depressed and would benefit from talking through their troubles.
	I have a keen interest in **herbal remedies** and holistic therapies. As an extension of this I am currently studying fertility therapy and stress consultancy via distance learning.
	I am an amateur **historian** with a particular interest in early 19th Century France (Revolutionary Period).
	I am interested in ancient **history**. I enjoy learning about the rise and fall of ancient civilisations and the lessons to be learnt. I do not think that modern people are that different to those ancient people, they had similar wants, needs and struggles; we just appear so different due to technology.
	I enjoy **interior design** and decoration and I have worked on a number of projects for families and friends decorating and staging properties and rooms.
	I am a **marathon runner** and a triathlete. Having run the London Marathon 19 times on behalf of disabled children, I now run a marathon in under 2.5 hours. I have run since the age of 11 for England in the European Championships and for local clubs. I have completed the Marathon Desable (MDS) this is 153 miles over the Sahara Desert in 6 days. Day 4 is 50 miles and the heat is up to 48-50° heat. I gain a massive sense of achievement from running and it really helps me to focus and clear my head.

I am a student of **martial arts**, currently training in Wing Chun. I enjoy the self-discipline and strength of mind required to excel at Kung Fu. I am also currently training in Muay Thai Boxing.

I enjoy **metal detecting**. I like the quietness of the hobby and also not knowing what I might be digging up; it really is treasure hunting. I have unearthed 5200 coins in total from a wide range of eras using a Mine-lab 'sovereign' detector.

As a hobby I build **model racing cars**. With my son I race electric and nitro fuel cars. We tinker with them and put new clutches on them, solder connections and change parts. We use a special fuel from USA which makes the cars even quicker and it is not unusual for them to reach road speeds. These cars are a great project which brings my son and I enjoy together.

I really like **motorbikes**. Although I no longer have a bike myself, I follow British Superbikes, World Superbikes and MOTO GP.

I like to ride my **motorbikes** as much as possible. I currently have a Harley Davidson Sportster and a Yamaha XSR 900 ABS. I find the culture and experience of bikes to be exhilarating and sometimes go to motorbike events.

I have a **motocross** bike (off road motorbike) and compete on tracks and fields with my friends who share the same interest. I really enjoy the thrill of riding these bikes and I like the way they look.

I enjoy **mountain biking**. My friends and I travel to various rugged trails and woodlands such as Cannock Chase which is purpose built and 16 miles long. This is a challenge and a thrill, as well as an opportunity to socialise with like-minded, driven people, who appreciate the great outdoors.

I particularly enjoy listening to classical **music** and guitar instrumentals.

I have a love of **music**; I like to attend concerts and festivals and make memories with friends at these events.

I have a love of **music.** I am a sound engineer with my own music label which brings artists and supporters together to make a diverse range of music.

I have a love of heavy metal **music**. I find that the music helps me to distress and relax. One of the highlights of my life was seeing Iron Maiden and Metallica live in concert at MK Bowl.

I have a love of **music**; I create my own music and often pay for sessions at my local studio. My taste is varied but I usually create hip hop at 90 beats per minute and grime at around 140 beats per minute.

I have a love of 1960s and 1970s **music**, I find the era very evocative and enjoy reminiscing. I also think that those decades were times of great political and global change and this is reflected in the music of the time.

I enjoy uplifting **music**; I am a drummer in a gospel group. We create and record original music and songs and also regularly perform. We are also known for putting our unique modern take on well-known classic songs and hymns.

I am very interested in **natural history**. I enjoy museums, books and documentaries about wildlife. My inspiration is David Attenborough who captivates his audiences with his unique insights into the natural world.

I am an amateur **ornithologist** and 'twitcher' (bird-watcher). Birds fascinate me; I photograph them and record their behaviour. I have had a number of my shots and research published in 'The Ostrich' scientific journal.

I am a skilled amateur **photographer** and specialise in capturing natural scenery in unusual, hard to reach places or at different times of the year. I particularly like it when my art can be used to capture the atmosphere of a place as if the viewer was actually there in person.

I enjoy writing and reading **poetry**. I find writing helps me to express my emotions and clarify my thoughts. I intend to publish my own collection of poems and verse in the future.

I enjoy **poker** and particularly the social aspect of the game as well as the ability to catch someone out when they are bluffing. It's not as much fun if they catch you bluffing of course!

I follow current affairs and **politics** and enjoy hearing the opinions of other people on the modern world.

I play **pool and snooker**. I enjoy these because I find them very sociable activities and they take a lot of concentration and skill. I feel that I can hold my own and give a good challenge.

I spend a lot of my spare time **programming** and coding. There is a whole new world of technology emerging with apps and increasingly powerful platforms. I have a fascination with computer connectivity and human interfacing.

I enjoy **rallying** cars. I regularly take Japanese turbo cars (such as Subaru Impreza, Nissan Skyline and Mitsubishi Evo) to track days at Silverstone and Santa Pod. Rally days are great events that are social and fun for all ages.

I enjoy property **refurbishment** and have worked on a number of projects, bringing neglected properties back to good condition. I have an ambition to develop my own property portfolio to perhaps 3 or 4 properties in the years ahead, to provide decent homes for tenants, as well as a pension for my future.

I **read** a lot of books; I have recently developed an interest in non-fiction philosophy and religious books. I enjoy discovering about different cultures, belief systems and how these have evolved over time.

Example Personal Interests, A - Z	I like to **read** and get lost in a good book. My preferred genres are horror, thrillers and science fiction. I like the way a great author will take you away from everyday life and give you a glimpse into their imaginary world.
	I **read** a great deal and enjoy classic fiction by authors such as George Orwell, HG Wells and John Steinbach. I appreciate how the English language was historically written and how these books have stood the test of time.
	I often **read** success and mind-set books; I am interested in personal development and have read most of the classic sales, mind-set and motivation books such as 'awaken the giant within' and 'think and grow rich'. I believe that we should always be learning and growing.
	I am an avid **reader** with a particular interest in non-fiction history books or biographies or a perfect combination of the two - a historic biography.
	I am an enthusiastic **reader** with a particular interest in non-fiction books such as "Sapiens" which chronicles the history of mankind's evolution and enhances understand of our species.
	I enjoy **reading** biographies of people who have overcome great challenges in their lives and come through the other side to help make the world better.
	I get a lot of pleasure from **reading.** My preferred genre is thrillers such as Dan Brown's 'Origins' and Joseph Heller's 'Catch 22' and authors such as James Patterson and Lee Child.
	I spend a lot of my free time **reading**. I enjoy getting lost in history, science fiction and comedy books. I am currently devouring Charlie Brooker's hilarious collection of scathing articles about current affairs and everyday life.
	I am a qualified **rugby coach** and a keen player. I really enjoy the team spirit and the excitement of the game. Friendships made on the field last for years, even off the field and I am pleased to have many long-term friends.
	I enjoy **running** and athletics and I attend a weekly park-run. There is an experience called a runner's high, which is a natural release of endorphins after about 15 minutes of running. This helps me think clearly and appreciate life.
	I am a keen **sailor** and I grew up around boats. I particularly enjoy a day or weekend yachting with family and friends. I am currently studying to complete a Royal Yachting Association Day Skipper course.
	My favourite past-time is **Scuba diving**. After diving in many tropical locations, I gained diving qualifications and an interest in marine conservation.
	I like to ride and owning **scooters**. I own 2 Lambrettas and a Vespa. I enjoy the community atmosphere at events and like seeing the classics on display.

"Getting ex-offenders back into work is a top priority if we want to see national crime rates fall. We all make mistakes in life, some bigger than others, but we believe those who fall hardest need the greatest amount of help." Charlie Bradshaw, Managing Director Matrix APA Product Design

I enjoy clay-pigeon/skeet **shooting** at weekends. I enjoy the challenge, competitiveness and the social element of shooting. It is a relaxing way to network and gives a real sense of achievement.

I am a people person. I really like **socialising** and networking whether for business or just to expand my circle of friends and broaden my horizons. I am interested in people from all cultural backgrounds and their life stories.

I am a keen **sportsman** with a particular interest in athletics (I attend a weekly park run), badminton, soft tennis, football and basketball.

I like all **sports** events whether I am taking part or in the audience; I get a lot from the atmosphere and from the positive environment.

I enjoy physical **sporting events** whether watching or participating. In my spare time I like to go carting, paintball or hurtling down indoor ski slopes, these kinds of fun and social teambuilding activities.

I like attending **sporting events** with friends in a small group. I enjoy football, rugby, cricket, tennis and F1. I keep the programmes, tickets and brochures and have collected hundreds of memories of my times as a spectator at these days.

I enjoy **Sudoku** puzzles and quizzes which really test my thinking and problem-solving skills.

I am a keen **swimmer**; I swim regularly and find it refreshing. It is good exercise and an excellent way to de-stress. I have also completed 2 five-kilometre swim-a-thons for Cancer Research charities.

I have a keen interest in body art and **tattoos**. I have tattoos myself and I have friends who are tattoo artists. I do feel that this art form has gained wider acceptance and recognition in recent years. I like the uniqueness of each design and how they reflect a person's individuality.

I have a deep interest in the field of software and **technology**. I enjoy researching information about gadgets (mainly including mobile phones and games consoles) and tech-related products.

I am very interested in **technology** and the mechanics behind it. It is exciting to see how fast technology changes and how it is easy to feel left behind if you don't keep up to date with it. I am keen on user-friendly, intuitive hardware and software which is accessible to people of all ages and backgrounds.

I enjoy the experience of the **theatre** and like being close to the actors. Theatre gives such a complete and immersive experience that is hard to replicate in any other setting and makes each trip memorable.

I enjoy **travelling** and have goals to visit other countries that I haven't been to yet including South Africa, Indonesia and New Zealand.

Example Personal Interests, A - Z	I enjoy **travelling** and experiencing different environments and cultures. I am fortunate to have visited Antigua, Cambodia, France, India, Italy, Jamaica, Kenya, Thailand and Vietnam as well as throughout the UK.
	I enjoy **volunteering** and helping charities. I regularly board guide dog puppies in training up to around 18 months old and before they are placed with their permanent owners.
	I enjoy **volunteering**, charity work and helping people. I help in the Sikh open kitchen which feeds disadvantaged members of society. I tour with the mobile kitchen to areas of economic hardship and enjoy personally serving.
	I enjoy **volunteering** and helping people. I have received many awards and recently organised a half marathon and a sponsored walk which raised several thousand pounds for children with special needs.
	I enjoy **volunteering** and helping people. I have worked with the Samaritans as a coordinator and my team received the prestigious Queen's Award for Voluntary Services 2018 for our dedication to helping people and saving lives. I also work with the Shannon Trust and have taught many adults to read for the first time. Being able to read makes a massive difference to their future lives.
	I enjoy **walking** and hiking in the wide-open outdoors. I often take long leisurely walks and where possible I will walk rather than using transport, even if it takes longer. Walking helps me to think clearly and appreciate the world.
	I like **woodworking**, carving and turning. I gain a lot of personal satisfaction from making personalised gifts for friends and family.
	I am a keen **writer**. I have written a lot of insights into psychology and I create poetry about the lives and thoughts of different people.
	I work with **local youth**; engaging with them to divert those young people most at risk away from the allure of gang culture and crime.
	I volunteer at a local **youth club** where I mentor and help young people when they are having a difficult time. I organise day trips and ensure that they had plenty of positive activities to do as well as healthy peer friendships.
	I practise **Yoga** most days. I find this helps me to keep fit, stay calm and centred and to experience everyday life more mindfully. I do encourage others to start Yoga classes because it is so fulfilling and really helps to improve breathing, stiff joints and back aches.

"Following CV-Builder enabled me to see clearly what I have achieved, and I feel proud. I struggled because I am not good with words, but the ready-made templates made it easy, almost as if someone was doing it alongside me." HW

Example CV 1

Charles Change
Hope Prison
Any town,
AB1 2CD

CV Updated - 31st July 2019

Profile, I am:

A very capable individual who works independently and also thrives as part of a team.

Very organised and reliable; people and companies who depend on me are never disappointed.

A hardworking person; I take pride in my work and enjoy the sense of satisfaction that comes from doing a good job.

Key Skills:

Good interpersonal skills and a natural way with people.

A superb problem solver, able to manage and resolve difficult situations calmly.

Highly skilled and qualified in **Street Lighting** and **Street Works**.

Experience:

2018 **Materials Recycling and Waste Management Operative**. Working in a busy industrial recycling facility, sorting large volumes of residential and commercial waste. Supervising a small team responsible for sorting, crushing, baling, despatching, as well as working independently to meet pressing deadlines. I am familiar with health and safety considerations including PPE, COSHH and safe working conditions.

2017 **Engineering Department.** Metalworking to manufacture metals into high security locks, doors and windows. Learnt how to programme dimensions into a CAD system and was personally responsible for quality control.

2016 **B.I.C.S. Industrial Cleaning Operative.** Duties included independent cleaning of office and warehouse environments. Familiar with machine buffing and polishing, chemical competency and COSHH, HASSAS and RIDDOR regulations.

2015 - 2016 **Cable Jointer's Mate.** Johnsons Cabling. Making up joint kits and generally assisting the jointer. Logging all paperwork required for record keeping and compliance, as well as forward planning jobs. Removing and replacing "cut outs" within lampposts and other street furniture. Working with electrical testing kits, to ensure safety and certification.

2012 - 2015 **Ground Worker.** Diggers UK. This role carried a wide range of responsibilities including locating underground services using CAT and GENY, excavating identified areas and making holes for the jointer to access as well as digging lamppost column holes.

Comprehensive record keeping and maintenance of accurate paperwork were essential. I personally carried out daily risk assessments and followed all relevant instructions and procedures to ensure health and safety compliance.

2011 **Courier Driver.** UK Mail. Carrying out multi-drop deliveries and collections. Driving a long twin wheel base Iveco truck to deliver time-sensitive cargo. Loading and unloading following all health and safety procedures, as well as meeting pressing deadlines. Managing challenging driving situations in predominantly residential areas whilst maintaining an accident free, flawless driving record.

2004 - 2011 **Household Removals.** Fletchers Fetchers Ltd. As a Removal man, I helped to relocate families and businesses. I drove a 3.5ton Luton van and worked as part of a small team lifting goods manually and also with a tail lift. Our team took great care of client's belongings and were sensitive to people's privacy during what was often a stressful time for them.

Qualifications:

I have gained many transferable skills over my working career, as well as formal qualifications, including the following:

8 GCSE passes including **Maths, English**, French, Geography, Physics Education, Religious Studies, Information Technology and History

First Aid at Work
Manual Handling certificate
Vehicle Banksman certificate
ROSPA certificate in **Working at Heights**
City and Guilds certificate in Basic **Construction** Skills
Qualified in use of Underground **Cable Avoidance Tool** (CAT) and Genny
Construction Skills Certification Scheme (CSCS) card, valid until May 2023
M.E.W.P. Mobile Elevating Working Platform (Cherry picker) operator's certificate
Forklift truck licence "counterbalance" and also "long reach" (both awaiting renewal)

National Electricity Registration Scheme Authorised person for WPD System, SSE Networks, UKPN and Civils. Excavation and Backfilling. (Expires 9/8/2020)

Certificate in Assertiveness and Decision Making (Body Language and People Skills)

Fluent in English, French and I also speak passable German

I hold a full driving licence (including D1)

Right to Work documentation in hand

Relevant certificates can be provided upon request

Personal Interests:

I enjoy spending quality time with my two children.

I am an amateur fisherman and enjoy the challenge that comes from carp fishing.

I am a keen sportsman with a particular interest in Swimming, Football and Snooker.

Example CV 2

John Smith
1 New Beginnings
Hope Avenue,
County

CV Updated - 8th June 2020

Profile, I am:

A positive and loyal person. I am looking for a new opportunity in which I can commit to an employer for the long term. I will work hard in my new role, work cooperatively within the team and I will be willing to learn any new skills required.

Fit and healthy, enthusiastic and open minded about my next job role.

Key Skills:

IT competent in MS Word, Excel, PowerPoint and Publisher.

Excellent at problem solving, with a proven ability to resolve difficult situations calmly.

A wide range of construction skills including erecting pre-fabricated buildings, plastering, plumbing and boiler replacement, flooring, kitchen fitting, bathroom installation, landscaping and general labouring.

Experience:

2018 **B.I.C.S. Industrial Cleaning Supervisor.** Responsible for a team of cleaners in a secure residential environment. Maintaining cleaning logs, ensured that high standards of cleaning were met, ordered products, unloaded deliveries and stored cleaning chemicals safely, securely and maintained a product inventory. Conducted regular Health and Safety risk assessments and documented these in a manual.

2017 **Induction Orderly.** Welcomed, registered and interviewed people as they arrived at a secure, residential establishment. Offered a high level of guidance, direction and personal attention to people who were often in distress or coping with mental health challenges. Good communication skills, organisational skills and professional administration (including reporting and record keeping) were essential in this role.

June - Dec 2016 **Recycling and Waste Management Operative.** Worked in a busy industrial recycling facility, sorting large volumes of residential and commercial waste. Supervised a small team responsible for sorting, crushing, baling and despatching. Worked independently to meet pressing deadlines and became familiar with health and safety considerations including PPE, COSHH and maintaining safe working conditions.

Jan - June 2016 **Lighting Assembly Workshop.** Worked for a fluorescent light manufacturer, assembled complex parts into finished light tubes, tested and packed the finished lights securely ready for despatch. Experience gained in electrical safety, quality control and personal health and safety in challenging environments.

2015 **B.I.C.S. Industrial Cleaning Operative.** Independent cleaning of office, residential and warehouse environments. Achieved proficiency in machine buffing and polishing. Developed chemical competency and knowledge of COSHH, HASSAS, MHOR, RIDDOR, HASAWA and PUWER regulations.

2014 **Laundry Operative.** Worked in a busy industrial laundry department using large tumble driers and washing machines. Order fulfilment including folding and packing of cleaned items and hosting collections.

2008 - 2012 **Property Developer.** Carried out full refurbishment of run-down properties in a proprietary business. Managed a team of employed tradesman and sub-contractors. Erected pre-fabricated buildings, repaired damaged walls and replaced fascia boarding. Experienced gained in plastering, plumbing, flooring, kitchen fitting, bathroom installation, landscaping and general labouring.

2005 - 2008 **Apprentice to Gas Engineer.** Worked with a Corgi (now Gas Safe) registered firm to carry out boiler replacements and install central heating systems, including all radiators, flues and pipe-work. Health and Safety considerations and regulatory compliance were essential in this role.

2000 - 2005 **Carpet Fitting.** Working as part of a team (and often in a supervisory role) which was in demand across multiple regions. My role included fitting carpets, laminate flooring and carpet tiles in residential and commercial properties. I was responsible for customer liaison, measuring, ordering and fitting as well as snagging to ensure customer satisfaction. I was responsible for Health and Safety risk assessments and ensured that all members of my team remained Health and Safety aware.

Dates listed and the timeline are approximate.

Qualifications:

OCR CLAIT certificates in Microsoft Word, Excel, Power-Point and Publisher

Numerous Personal Development Courses completed including modules such as Problem Solving, Assertiveness, Communication Skills and Decision Making, Organisational Skills, Money Management.

I have gained many transferable skills over my working career and expect to achieve CSCS by November 2018

Holding a full driving licence

Right to Work documentation in hand

Relevant certificates can be provided upon request.

Personal Interests:

I really enjoy spending time with my long-term partner and my two children, making memories.

I am a skilled amateur photographer and specialise in capturing natural scenery in unusual, hard to reach places or at different times of the year. I particularly like it when my art can be used to capture the atmosphere of a place as if the viewer was actually there in person.

I am a keen sportsman with an interest in football and boxing.

Example CV 3

John Smith
HMP Establishment
Any Location
Any Town
AB12 34CD

CV Updated - 28 November 2019

Profile - I am:

Dependable and trustworthy, able to work on own initiative and be relied on to deliver the results required.

A flexible worker with numerous vocational skills and qualifications and I am open minded about my next role/ challenge.

Reliable, loyal to my employer and hardworking; I take pride in my work and I enjoy the satisfaction that comes from completing a task well.

Key Skills:

Good communication, organisational and functional skills.

Competent in Microsoft Word, Excel, Publisher and PowerPoint.

A qualified **Barista** with a full range of skills including coffee processing, brewing, creation of all coffee types (latte, espresso, cappuccino, macchiato, flat white, mocha, Americano), equipment care, health, safety and hygiene.

An experienced and qualified **Industrial Cleaner**. Qualified to British Institute of Cleaning Sciences Bio-hazard Supervisor level.

Experience:

2019 **Kitchen Worker.** Responsible for food preparation and serving meals to residents in a secure residential establishment. The kitchens provided two meals each day for 350 residents. Helped with the provision of special dietary requirements for allergy sufferers and religious needs.

2017 - 2018 **Officer's Mess**. In this trusted Customer Service role, I served staff of a secure residential establishment hot drinks, hot food and snacks. Displayed a full range of skills including creation of different coffee types, equipment care, health, safety and hygiene. Created high quality fresh sandwiches, rolls and paninis as well as hot food. Gained customer service skills, as well as an understanding of payment processing and till operation. Built long term relationships with staff and regular customers.

2016 **Foreign National Representative**. Responsible for liaising between staff and international residents of a secure residential establishment. Helped people to prepare for seeing Home Office Representatives by explaining procedures, completing paperwork and arranged translation services. Offered guidance, direction and personal attention to people in distress, coping with mental health challenges or preparing for deportation. Displayed good communication skills, organisational skills, professional reporting and record keeping.

2015 **B.I.C.S. Industrial Cleaning Operative**. Cleaned office, residential and warehouse environments. Trusted in the highest security environments including Officer's mess in prison. Achieved proficiency in machine buffing and polishing. Developed chemical competency and knowledge of COSHH, HASSAS, MHOR, RIDDOR, HASAWA and PUWER regulations. Familiar with health and safety and PPE.

2011 - 2014 **Manager of Rehearsal and Recording Studios**. Managed booking diary of a suite of offices and a studio. Adjusted equipment to ensure optimum sound quality for recording and assisted recording artists with their sessions. Wired speakers and amplifiers, maintained equipment and oversaw all studio activities. Locked and unlocked the studio and monitored security, health and safety and cleanliness.

Previous work experience includes earlier years of painting and decorating, bricklaying and general labouring within the construction industry.

Please note: dates listed, and the timeline are approximate.

Qualifications:

I have gained many transferable skills over my working career, as well as formal qualifications, including the following:

OCR certificate in **English** (equivalent to GCSE pass)
OCR Level 1 and Level 2 certificates in **Maths** (equivalent to high GCSE grade)

OCR CLAIT **Microsoft Office Suite** certification

City and Guilds Level 2 - **Barista certified**
City and Guilds Level 2 - **Customer Service**
Highfield Level 2 - **Food Safety in Catering** (QCF)

British Institute Cleaning Sciences (B.I.C.Sc) Level 2 - **Industrial Cleaning**
British Institute Cleaning Sciences (B.I.C.Sc) Level 3 - **Bio-Hazard** management

NVQ City and Guilds Level 2 - **Bricklaying**
Working towards a **Construction Skills Certification Scheme** (CSCS) card

Active IQ - Principles of **Health and Fitness** and safe use of gym equipment

NCFE - **Peer Advisor** award - supporting and guiding students and team members with information, advice and guidance

Many personal development courses completed including modules such as enhanced thinking, decision making and problem solving, emotional intelligence, equality and diversity, assertiveness, good communication and teamwork.

Qualified as a Shannon Trust 'Toe by Toe'/ 'Turning Pages' mentor, teaching vulnerable adults, or adults with learning difficulties, to read

Fluent in English and I also speak passable Arabic

Holds full UK Driving Licence   Right to Work documentation in hand

Personal Interests:

Family time and making memories with my three children is really important to me. It is a privilege watching them grow and being a positive influence in their lives.

I like to ride and own scooters. I currently have two Lambrettas and a Vespa. I enjoy the community atmosphere at scooter events and like seeing the classics on display.

I enjoy running and athletics. I attend a weekly park-run and particularly. There is actually such a thing as a runner's high, which is a natural release of endorphins after about 15 minutes of running. I find that it helps me to think clearly and appreciate life more.

Example CV 4

Private Person
12 The Willows
Fresh End
Sea Town

CV Updated - 1st March 2019

Profile - I am:

A polite and respectful person; I treat everyone equally with patience and understanding.

A flexible worker with numerous vocational skills and qualifications and I am open minded about my next role/ challenge.

Loyal to my employer and hardworking. I take pride in my work and enjoy the satisfaction that comes from doing a good job.

Key Skills:

Excellent communication, organisational and functional skills.

Competent in MS Word, Excel, Publisher, PowerPoint and Functional Skills.

An experienced and professional **Delivery Driver**.

An experienced and qualified Industrial **Cleaner.** Qualified to British Institute of Cleaning Sciences Bio-hazard Supervisor level.

Experience:

2018 **BICS Biohazard Responder**. British Institute of Cleaning Sciences qualified responder. Responsible for securing areas, when and where, biohazard incidents have occurred. Duties included health and safety risk assessments, wearing of Personal Protective Equipment (PPE), cleaning of blood and bodily fluids and making safe all surrounding areas. Logged incidents and provided regular reports. Organisational skills, hard work and health and safety were essential in this role.

2018 **B.I.C.S. Industrial Cleaning Operative.** Independently cleaned office, residential and warehouse environments. Trusted to clean in the highest security environments including Officer's Mess in prison. Achieved proficiency in machine buffing and polishing. Developed chemical competency and knowledge of COSHH, HASSAS, MHOR, RIDDOR, HASAWA and PUWER regulations. Familiar with health and safety and PPE.

2017 **Health and Wellbeing Champion (HAWCS).** Working in a secure residential environment I was the person that residents to go to when they had healthcare complaints or concerns. Made referrals to mental health teams and drug rehabilitation agencies, attended NHS and Governor level meetings to design healthcare programmes and to explain the unintended consequences of decisions. Contributed to stop self-harming initiatives.

2014 - 2016 **Delivery Driver**. Family Business. Carried out multi drop deliveries and collections. Drove a VW Caddy van delivering time sensitive flowers and fragrances. Loaded and unloaded following all health and safety procedures and met pressing deadlines. Managed challenging driving situations in predominantly residential areas without accident or incident.

2013 **Warehouse Operative**. DHL. Worked as part of a busy team. Responsible for logging incoming client orders, picking, sealing, packing, checking and despatching as well as occasionally managing high value orders. Resolved client complaints, solved picking errors and maintained quality control. Worked to deadlines, maintained manual handling procedures and a safe working environment.

2012 **Laundry Operative**. Worked in an industrial laundry department using large driers, washing machines and presses (ironing). Fulfilled time sensitive orders by managing workload of washing, drying, folding, packing cleaned items and hosting collections.

2011 **Kitchen Worker.** Responsible for food preparation and serving of meals to residents in a secure residential establishment. The kitchens provided two meals each day for 800 residents. Helped with provision of special dietary requirements for allergy sufferers and religious needs. Duties also included general cleaning, loading and unloading of deliveries, monitoring of food storage temperatures, labelling, stock rotation and safe handling to avoid cross contamination.

2010 **Gym Orderly**. Responsible for ensuring the smooth running of a men's gym in a secure residential establishment. Assisted on structured gym courses and co-ordinated support roles including cleaners and referees. Other duties included product ordering, taking register of attendance schedules, kit washing and kit management. I worked hard to achieve this post after gaining personal health and first aid qualifications.

Please note: dates listed, and the timeline are approximate.

Qualifications:

I have gained many transferable skills over my working career, as well as formal qualifications, including the following:

7 GCSE passes Design Technology, Dual Science, English Language, History, IT (Computer Science), Maths and Physical Education

OCR Level 1 certificate in Maths and Level 2 in English

Forklift truck licence- counterbalance Valid until January 2023

NCFE Award in Business Enterprise
OCR Level 2 Award in Business Enterprise (including financial management)

NCFE Level 2 certificate in Music technology

Level 3 British Institute Cleaning Sciences (B.I.C.S) cleaning operator's proficiency certificate including the following modules: AA1, A1, A3, A5, A15, A2, A4, A6, A9, AA3, A7, A12, B1, B5, B2, B3, C2, C3, C4, C6, D1, D3, D4, D2, E3, E5, F1

Pearson BTEC Level 2 Peer Mentoring (Leadership, teaching and supporting students)

Open College Network (OCN) Level 3 Award in First Aid at Work (RQF) expires 19/10/2021

Numerous personal development courses completed including modules such as enhanced thinking skills, problem solving, emotional intelligence, assertiveness, equality and diversity, communication skills and decision making, organisational skills and teamwork.

Holds full UK Driving Licence.   'Right to work' documentation in hand.

Personal Interests:

Family time and making memories with my partner and our 5-year-old son is really important to me. We often go to the park, bowling, cinema and spend as much time together as possible. It is a privilege watching them grow and being a positive influence in their lives.

I am keen on fitness; I regularly attend the gym and primarily focus on working with weights, cardio workouts and cross fit training. I really enjoy seeing myself progress, overcoming personal barriers and taking care of my personal health. I also play rugby and basketball.

I have a love of music; I create my own music and often pay for sessions at my local studio. My taste is varied but I prefer Jazz, Hip Hop and RnB grooves.

"I would advise any potential employer not to employ ex-offenders out of charity. Do it because these guys are high-level problem solvers - and I've yet to meet any business owner who doesn't have a problem that needs solving. These guys have a brilliance to them that doesn't exist in any other sector. They have come through challenges that no one else has faced."

Judah Armani, founder, InHouse Records.

Chapter 5 -
Applying for Jobs

"While I was still in prison, I followed all of the instructions in this book. I created a really professional CV which included the extra vocational qualifications I gained on this sentence. I arranged for it to be uploaded to an online CV library. Within 9 days, I had 5 interview invitations! This system works!" LS

The Process of Applying for Jobs

The system in this book encourages you to send the following documents TOGETHER as a set to employers.

- ✓ Personal Disclosure Statement (chapter 4).
- ✓ Curriculum Vitae (CV) (chapter 5).
- ✓ Application Letter (this chapter).

On average, 50 carefully targeted applications, supported by well worded CVs and Personal Disclosure Statements, results in 3 interviews and at least one job offer.

Persistence is the key to success. Don't give up! A well-matched job will really change the quality of your life and it is worth working hard for.

Send lots of applications to multiple employers who might be a good match for you. Be organised and keep a record of the companies you write to and the dates. The template provided on page 244 can be used to record the letters that you send.

Your chances of successfully securing your ideal job increase when you contact a large number of the most suitable potential employers (taking into account your current experience and skill levels).

It is like looking for the 4 aces in a pack of 52 cards. Do not be disappointed if you get a similar response rate. The ace in the pack (i.e. the perfect job), could be the first contact you make or it could be the last; you just do not know until you start contacting employers.

Your document set can be:

1. Posted to potential employers and agencies.
2. Emailed electronically to potential employers and agencies.
3. Copied and pasted or retyped into online job application forms.
4. Uploaded to websites for potential employers and agencies to read.

The Benefits of Posting (or pasting into an online form) an Application Letter (AL)

The AL is also called a **Covering Letter** or **Introductory Letter**; it is your chance to personalise the contact with each prospective employer.

The purpose of the AL is not to get a job, or even to get an interview. It is simply to encourage the decision maker to read your CV and Personal Disclosure Statement.

Your AL is like the bait on the fishing line - the more appealing and relevant we make it; the more likely we are to 'get a bite'.

Applicants who included a covering letter with their CV were 10% more likely to get a positive reply. (Source: CV Doctor)

Joining Your Documents Together

To avoid employers only reading your CV it is important to send your three documents together as a set because if we send them separately then sometimes the employer will only read the CV.

When posting them, it is fine to keep them as separate documents with your Application Letter (AL) first, your CV behind it and your Personal Disclosure Statement (PDS) last.

When sending your documents electronically or uploading them to websites always:

1. Join them together as a single document set.
2. Select '*Save as PDF*' so that it keeps its format on any platform.
3. Save with the file name '*firstname lastname CV Document Set*'. This is important because employers receive lots of CV's and almost all of them are confusingly labelled as '*CV*'. Saving documents with your name makes it easier for employers to locate them.

Applying for Advertised Jobs

Job opportunities are advertised in many places including:

- Local social media pages and groups.
- Local newspapers and industry/ trade magazines.
- Job websites (e.g. Indeed, Monster, Find a job, Total jobs and others).

When you contact employers, send them your AL, PDS (chapter 3) and CV (chapter 4) and use the form that follows to record your responses.

Applying for Pre-Advertised Jobs (before they are advertised)

Some companies prefer to use Recruitment Agencies because these can save them a lot of time in the recruitment process. It is worth registering with several agencies, particularly for specialist/ skilled job roles.

Many others are now turning to online CV libraries where job hunters upload their CVs and invite companies to contact them directly. This saves money and time. Websites such as www.cvlibrary.co.uk should be part of your job-hunting campaign.

Applying for Unadvertised Jobs (one created just for you)

Contact those companies who you seem well-matched to, even if they are not currently advertising a job opportunity.

Carry out research to find employers who will value your skills, qualifications and experience. If you can't access the internet, ask family, friends, the library or your careers/resettlement department for help.

70% of available jobs are not advertised.

(Source: BBC Employable me 27/11/17)

Recommended Companies

We want companies to give us a chance and not prejudge us. We should hold ourselves to the same standard and not prejudge companies either; we should give them a chance too.

Contact all the companies that would most value your skills and that you would like to work for.

If you are not sure where to start and want to gain employment experience, then the following employers have already shown a willingness to publicly support ex-offenders and not unfairly pre-judge them. **This list is just a drop in the ocean** of the many thousands of employers that are open-minded to employing ex-offenders.

If you know of any company or organisation that would like to appear on this list or that deserves to be included, please contact the author.

Companies that consider and do not prejudge ex-offenders		
	Accenture	Accountants and Management Consultants
	Adnams	Ales, food and drink manufacturer
	Adventure Learning Charity	Residential activity provision for children
	Aldermans	Engineering and Industrial Manufacturing
	Amey	Utilities, Facilities, Waste and Infrastructure
	Aramark	Catering
	ASM	Metal recycling
	Balfour Beatty	Road works, Infrastructure, Construction
	Beefeater	Restaurants
	Bernard Matthews	Poultry Farmers and Food Producers
	Biffa	Waste, recycling and facilities management
	Boots the Chemist	Personal care, wellbeing, food and medicine
	Cambridge University Press	Media, Marketing and Public Relations
	Carbon 60	Technical recruitment
	Carpetright	Flooring retailer
	Census Data	Education and Employment support services
	City and Guilds	Skills development and education provider

Companies that consider and do not prejudge ex-offenders	**Compass Group**	Distribution and logistics
	Concept Design Solutions	Design and Marketing services
	Cook	Frozen ready meals
	Co-Op	Retail and service delivery
	Costa	Coffee shops and outlets
	Costain	Construction
	Currie and Brown	Construction, asset management and consultancy
	DHL	Distribution and logistics
	Enterprise	Car and van hire
	Evans	Cycle shops
	Everyone Active (EA)	Fitness, Sport and Leisure
	Farrelly Building Services	Construction
	First Direct	Banking
	Fujitsu	Technology
	Genius Within CIC	Education, Employment and Training
	Genuine Solutions Group	Technology Recycling
	Gleeds	Surveyors
	Greggs	Bakers and take away food
	Greene King	Pubs, Catering and Hospitality
	Greenzone	Cleaning and Support Services
	Halfords	Bike and car part retailer
	Heat Connection	Utility company
	Henley Homes PLC	Construction
	Hodgkinson	Bricklaying contractors
	Hortech Ltd	Landscape Management
	Iceland	Frozen food retailer

Companies that consider and do not prejudge ex-offenders	Icon Designs Ltd	Manufacturing
	Inderflame	Heating services
	Interserve	Construction and Facilities Management
	JP Concrete	Construction
	Jury's Inn	Hotels and Hospitality
	Keepmoat	New homes
	Keltbray	Information Technology
	Kinnerton	Food, drinks, confectionery manufacturer
	Land Securities	Real Estate management and consultancy
	Linklaters	Legal services
	Leo Burnett	Communications
	MACS	Plasterboard Systems
	Marriott	Hotels and Hospitality
	Marks and Spencer	Quality clothing and food retailer
	Matrix APA	Product design and procurement
	MVF	Technology
	National Express	Coach travel, Tourism and Hospitality
	NMC	Construction and Utilities
	Pets at Home	Pet supplies retailer
	Poundland	Specialist discount retailer
	Powerday	Construction
	Premier Inn	Hotels and Hospitality
	Pret A Manger	Take away food
	PRO-Driver	Logistics and Distribution
	Project Simply	PR and Communications
	Quesera (Q)	Utilities
	Rinkit	Home and Garden Products

Companies that consider and do not prejudge ex-offenders	Roast	Hospitality and Restaurants
	RMF Construction Ltd	Commercial and Residential Construction
	Sainsbury's	Grocery, distribution and logistics
	Screwfix	Electronic component and goods retailer
	SES GROUP	Events Recruitment
	Skanska	Road works and highway maintenance
	Sodexo	Food services, Housekeeping and Cleaning
	Speedy Hire	Tool and plant equipment hire
	St Giles Trust	Mentoring support for ex-offenders
	Styles and Wood	Architects
	Taylor Wimpey	National House Builders
	Tesco	Grocery, distribution and logistics
	Timpson	Shoe Repairs, key cutting and other services
	Total Ship Services	Shipping, Forwarding, Warehousing and Storage
	User voice	Support for people with criminal records
	Virgin Group	Predominantly transport and media
	Viridor	Utilities and Waste Management
	Wamitab	Industrial Cleaning and Supplies
	Wilmot Dixon	Highways Maintenance

"People offend for a variety of complex reasons. The most powerful thing that employers can do is help to create a second chance for offenders, help them enter employment and get their lives back on track." Marco Pagni - Boots the Chemist

Your Record of Applications Made to Potential Employers

No.	Company	Name and Contact Details	Application Date	Notes
1				
2				
3				
4				
5				

"Following this book meant that I now have a job; I can change my life for the better and not do criminal activities." JM

No.	Company	Name and Contact Details	Application Date	Notes
6				
7				
8				
9				
10				

"I got a really positive response when I emailed my document set to a potential employer. The Managing Director contacted me directly and praised me for making such an effort, said he was very impressed with my paperwork and asked when I could come for an interview." LR

'Application Builder' - Your Application Letter (AL) Framework

Following these 15 steps will lead to the creation of a professional Application/ Cover Letter which will be appreciated by the employer who receives it.

Your AL is formal letter, it should be laid out traditionally and similar to the examples included at the end of this chapter.

The first time you follow this 15-step process it should take around 20 - 30 minutes.

Each AL should be personalised to the employer and these amendments will usually take less than 5 - 10 minutes each time. Of course, any time that you invest in creating your employment documents is time well spent!

Step 1, Contact Details	Type your personal details in the top right corner. **If you are currently in prison** - then use your prison number, prison address and no telephone number or email address. **If you are at home, or shortly returning home** - then use your home address, home telephone number and an email address. There are many free services such as Outlook and Gmail that make it easy to set up an email address Ensure that your email address is clear and professional so that it makes a good impression such as firstname.lastname@serviceprovider.com.	*Name* *Address* *Postcode* *Telephone* *Email* *1st January 2020*
Step 2, Recipient	On the left-hand side and slightly lower than your address, insert the contact name and the address of the potential employer e.g. *John Smith* *Head of Recruitment* *Sensible Employer* *Nice Town* *Postcode*	

Step 3, Subject	Begin your letter with the most applicable of the following sentences:	
	If you responding to an advertisement	*Re: Application for _____ position.*
	If you are writing a general introduction	*Re: Possible employment with your company.*
	('Re:' is generally accepted as an abbreviation for 'reference' or 'regarding'.)	

Step 4, Contact Person (Addressee)	If possible, telephone the company and ask for the name of the most relevant person to write to e.g. Branch Manager, Director of Human Resources, (H.R) Manager.
	Try not to get into a long conversation over the telephone (unless it is a pre-booked appointment) because you will not have had time to prepare for this. At this stage you are merely asking for the relevant contact name.
	With a contact name, you can address the letter to:
	'Dear Mr Johnson,' or *'Dear Miss Faulkner,'*
	Personal approaches mean that someone takes personal responsibility and they have been proven to generate better response rates than just:
	'Dear Sir/ Madam,'
	Many companies have a jobs section on their website, and these often provide details of the relevant person to write to.

Step 5, Advertised or Not-Advertised Position	**If you are applying for a position that is advertised**	*Further to my recent telephone conversation with your colleague, I am writing this letter in the hope that you will consider me for an employed position within your company.*
	If you are applying to an employer with no advertised vacancies	*Further to my recent telephone conversation with your colleague, I am writing this letter in the hope that you will consider me for an employed position within your company.*
	If you have not yet spoken to anyone	*I am writing this letter in the hope that you will consider me for a full-time training place within your company.*

Step 6, Introducing your CV	Insert this sentence: *I enclose my CV and a comprehensive Personal Disclosure Statement. I genuinely feel that I would be an ideal candidate to interview who can offer real value to your company.*

Step 7, About you		Explain why you should be considered for the role or to work for their company. You could mention your experience, relevant qualifications and motivation, work ethic and track record. Your AL letter is just a brief taster, an introduction to your CV, so keep it short.
	Consider writing a paragraph which includes two or three points similar to these examples	*I am highly experienced in coding and customising software.*
		I have a suite of highly relevant qualifications and experience.
		I have a proven ability to add value in all professional environments.
		I have a keen interest in working in vehicle mechanics, maintenance and fault repair.
		I am hardworking, reliable and loyal. I take pride in my work and work to a high standard.
		I always offer full commitment to my employer and go above and beyond in any job role I hold.
		I have previously carried out ground works including laying tarmac and I have just renewed my CSCS card.
		I am professional, organised and hardworking, with excellent people skills, being an asset to any team.
		I am hard-working with pleasant communication skills and I would be an asset to your customer service team.
		I am experienced in the operation of a wide range of plant and machinery and I would quickly become a valuable member of your team.
		I do stand out as a highly praised employee, to me a job is never just a job, but is a responsibility I take a great deal of personal pride in fulfilling.

Step 7, About you, Continued	**Further Examples -** (For more ideas, read the CV Personal Attributes on pages 137 - 138)	*I have completed the Construction Industry Training Board (CITB) exam and I have recently upgraded and expanded on my qualifications. Additionally, I am qualified to conduct and document risk assessments.*
		I have experience of working in a servery and in kitchens. I have a Level 2 Award in Food Safety in Catering (QCF) and I am familiar with special dietary needs as well as religious requirements within the food industry.
		I have previously worked as a Barber and Barbering Trainer. I am formally qualified with City and Guilds in Barbering, in the skincare conditions which affect barbering, First-Aid and Health and Safety.
Step 8, Reason for Choosing this Employer		Give a reason why you have chosen to apply to this company (you may need to carry out some research to do this).
	Example Reasons	*Out of all the companies in my industry I believe that 'Example firm' are the best equipped to make the most of my skills and talents.*
		I am a technical woodworking machinist with a lifetime (25 years +) of carpentry experience so would be ideal to work for 'Example firm'.
		I was employed by 'Example firm' in the year 2000; I have nothing but good memories of my time and would like the opportunity to come back.
		I recently read about the Employee Advancement award that you received, and I would like the opportunity to be part of such a forward-thinking company.
		I have a friend who has progressed well within 'Example firm' and I would like the chance to prove myself within a similar, well-structured career pathway.
		I have heard great things about the help and the opportunities that 'Example firm' provides to people who have recently left prison or who are in the later stages of their prison sentence.
		I have excelled in my recent role as Education Administrator with a similar company to 'Example firm' and have put systems and processes in place since holding that role. I have proven myself to be organised, hardworking and dependable and I am only leaving due to redundancy.

Step 9, Willingness to Train		Mention that you would be willing to undertake any extra training	
	Example Wording	*I am willing to complete any courses to fill any possible knowledge or skills gaps.*	
		I will be pleased to do any extra studying necessary to bring myself up to date with current systems.	
		I am willing to undertake any additional training whether in work hours or in my own time to ensure that I am suitably qualified for the role; as well as Continuous Professional Development (CPD) when in post so that I can always perform my role effectively.	
Step 10, Interview		Insert a sentence similar to the following:	
		I would welcome the opportunity to attend an interview, or to answer any questions you may have.	
Step 11, Feedback	**If you are applying for a position that is advertised**	*If my application is unsuccessful, could I respectfully request that you provide me with some helpful feedback on how I could improve my approach and presentation.*	
	If you are applying with no advertised vacancies	*If you do not have any vacancies at the moment, please be kind enough to let me know and keep my application on file in case a suitable opportunity arises.*	
Step 12, Thank		Insert the following sentence:	
		Thank you for your kind consideration.	
Step 13, Goodbye	**If you are writing to a named person**	*'Yours sincerely,'*	
	If you are writing "Dear Sir/Madam"	*'Yours faithfully,'*	
Step 14, Your Name	Add your full name, letters and point the reader again to the documents you enclosed:	*John Smith BA (Hons)* *Enclosed: CV and Personal Disclosure Statement*	

Step 15, Sign	sign in-between Yours faithfully, *Sign Here* Your name

Some employers have a web-based application process,
in these cases, copy *(keyboard shortcut ctrl-c)* and paste *(ctrl-v)*
your AL, PDS and CV (or re-type the contents) into the online form.

Congratulations on working through this process!

Your own Application Letter
should now be comparable to the
examples on the following pages.

"I received an email back from an employer who specifically thanked me for taking the time to include a covering letter with my CV. Apparently many people skip this important step; it made a good first impression. I had a trial day which went well and a job offer followed. I have now started a 3-month probationary period which will hopefully lead to me being taken on full-time with this prestigious employer. Sometimes it is the little things that matter." AN

Example Application Letters

Example AL 1 (Unadvertised Job)

Mr Ralph Responsible
7 Interesting Road
Employment
Norwich.
NR1 2AB

Sally Supportive
HR Manager
Example Employer UK
NW1 2XY

24th July 2020

Re: Possible employment with *Example Employer UK.*

Dear Mrs Supportive,

Further to my recent telephone conversation with your colleague, I am writing this letter in the hope that you will consider me for an employed position within your company.

I enclose my CV and a comprehensive Personal Disclosure Statement. I do believe that I would be an ideal candidate to interview who can offer real value to your company.

I am willing to undertake any additional training whether in work hours or in my own time to ensure that I am sufficiently skilled and qualified to work at _____.

I would welcome the opportunity to attend an interview or to answer any questions you may have.

If you do not have any vacancies at this time, I would be grateful if you would keep my application on file in case a suitable opportunity arises.

If my application is of no interest to you, could I respectfully request that you provide me with some helpful feedback on how I could improve my presentation.

Thank you for your kind consideration.

Yours sincerely,

R Responsible

Ralph Responsible
Enclosed: CV and Personal Disclosure Statement

Example AL 2 (Advertised Job)

Mr Peter Positive
7 Interesting Road
Employment
Norwich.
NR1 2AB

For the Kind Attention of
Mr John Example
Managing Director
Trades Employer Ltd
MK1 1LM

24th July 2020

Dear Mr Example,

Re: Possible employment with Trades Employer Ltd.

I am writing this letter in the hope that you will consider me for the advertised position as Site Manager at Newtown.

I enclose my CV and a comprehensive Personal Disclosure Statement.

I honestly believe that I an ideal candidate for interview and who can be of real value.

I have many construction qualifications, a CSCS card and lots of experience.

I am professional, organised and hardworking, with excellent people skills and would be an asset to any team. I am willing to undertake any additional training whether in work hours or in my own time to ensure that I am suitably qualified for the role; as well as Continuous Professional Development (CPD) when in post so that I can always perform my role effectively.

I would welcome the opportunity to attend an interview or to answer any questions you may have.

If my application is unsuccessful, could I respectfully request that you provide me with some helpful feedback on how I could improve my approach and presentation.

Thank you for your kind consideration.

Yours sincerely,

P.Positive

Peter Positive

Enclosed: CV and Personal Disclosure Statement

Example AL 3
(To a company which are not known for employing ex-offenders)

Mr Steve Hope
HR Director
Admin Angels
New Road
Leeds
LS1 2TU

Mrs Ruby Redeemed
Uphill Street
New Horizons
Bingley
BD1 EF2

14th September 2019

Re: Possible employment with Admin Angels

Dear Mr Hope,

Further to meeting your team at the Career Champions event, I am writing this letter in the hope that you will consider me for an employed position within your company.

I enclose my CV and a comprehensive disclosure letter. I worked for several years with an office administration agency when I lived in Sheffield, so I have lots of relevant experience. I genuinely believe that I would be an ideal candidate who can offer real value to your company.

I understand that you might have some concerns about employing an ex-offender. According to a report called 'Bridging the Gap' by the Forward Trust; the four most frequent concerns are:

> 1) Whether the employer can afford to hire another staff member,
>
> 2) Whether the applicant can work well with the existing team,
>
> 3) Whether the applicant poses a risk to the company or to the public and
>
> 4) Whether the applicant can actually do the job required, reliably and to a high enough standard?

I would like to address these legitimate concerns by explaining that:

> 1) I am a very reasonable person and would be willing to start on a salary at the lower end of the scale, whilst I prove my value to the company.
>
> 2) I have good interpersonal and communication skills, I am comfortable adjusting my style to work well with other people and I enjoy being part of team.
>
> 3) I have proven worthy of trust, my conviction is not related to my employment and I do not pose a risk of problems in the workplace; in fact, employment is a proven stabilising factor which would form the solid foundation of my future life.
>
> 4) I do believe that I am capable of doing the job required; I have proven my reliability by working hard and consistently across several roles in recent years. I am willing to undertake any additional training whether in work hours, or in my own time to ensure that I am skilled and qualified enough for the position.

I would welcome the opportunity to attend an interview, or to answer any questions you may have.

Thank you for your kind consideration.

Yours sincerely,

RRedeemed

Ruby Redeemed
Enclosed: CV and Disclosure Letter

Working Outside of Prison on Release on Temporary Licence (ROTL)

In 2019 the national ROTL policy was expanded to allow those D-category prisoners, trusted in open conditions, to access full-time employment earlier in their sentence.

Although a 'victim support levy' of 40% is imposed on net earnings (after tax and national insurance deductions), the opportunity to work outside and earn money is a blessing to many prisoners. The money earned enables some people to save for release, so they are less likely to have accommodation challenges and money problems. The opportunity gives others the satisfaction of being able to contribute to the family budget after years of having to ask their family members to support them whilst they were earning prison wages of around £10 - £12 per week.

All open prisons have preferred and pre-approved employers but many of the jobs available will not reflect everyone's skills, qualifications and aspirations post-release. Some people make their own approaches to employers, have interviews in prison or outside on ROTL and successfully receive job offers.

It is possible to contact employers from open prison, to begin employment before your release and to stay in the same job after release. **This smooth transition and the resultant stability is the optimum result for anyone planning their resettlement.**

The following employer and employee checklists reflect the general HMPPS and police criteria before a serving prisoner can be approved to attend outside work.

"ROTL is a critical aspect of enabling a prisoner who has been incarcerated for many years to adjust to the normality of life in the community; and the opportunity to work for a wage which reflects the skill and effort invested in their work is an important element of restoring self-esteem."

His Honour John Samuels QC

Employers' Eligibility to Employ Serving Prisoners on ROTL

These are the general requirements that an organisation must meet before the police and prison can approve a serving prisoner to be employed by them.

		Tick
1	Registered company/charity.	
2	Three years of trading history.	
3	Clear DBS check of Director(s)/ Trustees.	
4	Up to date filing with company's house/ the charity commission.	
5	Currently solvent according to the accounts.	
6	Work located within 50-mile radius of prison.	
7	Commercial premises with a fixed address; no roaming.	
8	Public liability and employers' liability insurance in place.	

9	Employer provides details of the:
	    a) The nature of the work,
	    b) Salary or salary range, and
	    c) Health and Safety information.	

10	Employer confirms knowledge of:
	    a) Sentence length,
	    b) Full details of convictions, and
	    c) That the applicant is still a serving prisoner.	

11	Points 9 and 10 should be included in a formal job offer letter (similar to the offer letter template which follows).	
12	The employer should be prepared to wait around 8 weeks from the making of a formal employment offer to the first employee starting work on ROTL. Subsequent employees are cleared quicker once the employer has been approved.	

**NB: These requirements vary between
establishments and are subject to policy changes.**

"Working outside of the prison helped me to get into a routine and to pull out of the deep depression I had got stuck in whilst in closed conditions. I was able to earn money and save for release. Now I only have a few months left and I have agreed a tenancy with a letting agent recommended by my employer. I have hope again and a chance of success thanks to the company I work for who gave me a chance and because of the ROTL framework that allowed me to work and start contributing to society again for a year before release." FE

Example Job Offer Letter to a Serving Prisoner who will be Working on ROTL (to be issued on company headed paper)

Name
Title
Address line 1
Address line 2
Employee/ Prisoner name   Address line 3
Number   Email
HMP Address   Website
Telephone

Re: Offer of Employment

Date

Dear _____ ,

Further to our recent conversations I am writing to you to formally offer you the job of _____ (insert job title).

You have made me aware of your convictions for _____ (insert convictions), that you received a prison sentence of _____ (insert sentence length) and that you are still currently a serving prisoner.

Notwithstanding this, I have been impressed with your determination to improve yourself.

You would be required to work from _____ - _____ (insert hours) Monday to Friday at _____ (insert address).

The agreed salary is _____ (insert pay rate), paid _____ _____ (insert frequency of pay).

Health and Safety risk assessments are regularly carried out and you will be required to follow company health and safety procedures including _____ (insert specific H&S requirements).

I understand that the process of approving you to work at our company may take up to 8 weeks and I am keen for you to fill the role as soon as possible. In order to assist with the necessary checks, I am willing to provide any information required and any help necessary to your offender management and activities teams.

I confirm that I am happy for you to copy this letter to any relevant parties and for them to contact me directly.

Yours sincerely
(Insert name and position)

Prisoner Eligibility to Work Outside on ROTL

		Tick
1	Sentence plan and any required courses completed.	
2	Minimum level 1 in Maths, English and IT achieved.	
3	Community/ voluntary work completed as required by OMU.	
4	Successfully completed ROTL's (typically 2 - 3 unaccompanied RDR's).	
5	Satisfactory risk-assessment e.g. no recent adjudications or intelligence).	
6	Application to attend outside work completed. This is sometimes known as 'paper-chase' because other departments such as healthcare and education need to sign it too.	
7	Explain how the job opportunity was sourced; any prior relationship to the employer must be declared so that the work can be accurately and transparently risk-assessed/ boarded.	
8	CV and Personal Disclosure Statement to be attached to paper-chase.	
9	**'Right to work'** documents to be attached to paper-chase: a) National Insurance number - <u>evidence</u> e.g. one copy of P60, P45 or HMRC letter. (A letter confirming your NI Number can be ordered free from HMRC by telephone, post or internet). **AND** b) Identification - <u>evidence</u> e.g. one copy of passport, long birth certificate, biometric ID card or certificate of naturalisation.	
10	Formal offer letter received from employer and submitted to risk board - The 'offer letter' template (page 257) is ideal and some employers will find it helpful if you send it to them.	
11	There will be additional requirements if you are seeking permission to drive to, and from, a fixed place of employment, (11a - 11g).	
11a	Vehicle must have road tax.	
11b	Vehicle must have valid insurance.	
11c	Vehicle must have MOT test certificate.	
11d	Prisoner must have national breakdown cover.	
11e	Driving licence must be registered to the prison address.	
11f	The vehicle must be registered to the prison address on V5 log book.	
11g	Insurer must confirm in writing that they are aware the policy holder is a serving prisoner and that the car will be kept at the prison.	

NB: These requirements vary between establishments and are subject to policy changes.

Chapter 6 -
Job Interviews

"Preparing in advance for my interview
has greatly increased my confidence." BH

Preparing for an Interview

Well Done! So far you have:

- Set your employment goals.
- Developed your people skills.
- Assessed your top employability skills.
- Created your PDS, CV and AL.
- Researched currently advertised jobs.
- Uploaded your document-set to CV libraries and job-hunting websites.
- Researched the most suitable employers who may have unadvertised jobs.
- Posted or emailed multiple packs containing your AL, PDS and CV to employers.

Now your efforts have paid off and you have been invited to an interview.

Congratulations!

Getting a job interview is an important step on the road to permanent employment.

It is natural however to feel nervous and fearful in the run up to the interview.

Fear of the unknown and of the unfamiliar is to be expected. Do not berate yourself for this, human beings are designed to operate in 'Comfort Zones'; this is all the things that you are used to doing and that come naturally to you. Anything outside of this familiarity is outside of your comfort zone and by definition, uncomfortable.

**"Remind yourself of this simple acronym POW!
This stands for Planning Overcomes Worry."** PM

The more planning you can do in advance, the more confident you will be, because you will have eliminated most of the things that are unknown and unfamiliar.

There are 6 important steps to take before you attend a job interview.

I explain these using the coincidental acronym

P.R.O.P.E.R.

Plan, Research, Organise, Prepare, Enquire, Rehearse

I elaborate on each of these steps as follows:

P = Plan

Role-play the day in your head; imagine in advance how you see the day going.

Create a plan of the day itself and do not leave anything to chance.

Consider a range of issues that could affect you on the day	What will you eat in the morning?
	Do you need to arrange childcare?
	Do you need travel sickness tablets?
	Will you travel by public transport or by car?
	What time do you need to get up to avoid panicking in the morning?
	What can you do to make sure that you get a good night's sleep the night before?
	What will you wear? Do your clothes need ironing and/ or shoes need polishing?
	Do you need to inform probation about the interview or arrange a ROTL from prison?
	Are you depending on anyone else? Are they reliable? Do you have an alternative Plan B if something changes?

Your list will look different to this one because there will be other considerations that affect you personally.

The more that you plan, the smoother the interview day will go.

R = Research

Invest an hour or two researching the:

1) Industry sector, 2) Employer, 3) The job role and 4) Interviewer

Researching all 4 of these areas will give you lots of things to discuss at interview and will really show the potential employer that you have made an effort and are interested and professional.

If you are unable to access the internet, then ask a family member, supporter or friend to carry out research on your behalf and print it out for you. Study all the information until it becomes familiar to you.

O = Organise

Keep all your documents for this interview together in a folder.

Your folder should be clean, tidy and professional but understated/ not flashy.

Keep all these items in your 'interview folder'	Your AL, PDS and CV.
	Printed directions, public transport routes and times.
	Printed emails and all correspondence from this employer.
	Evidence of personal memberships, trade cards and certificates or Individual Learner Record.
	Personal testimonials and in-hand references, as well as portfolio of work/ images (if applicable).
	Documentary proof of your National Insurance Number along with your Passport, Long Birth certificate or UK Biometric ID card ('Right to Work' requirements).

The more organised you are, the less worried you will be in the days before your interview and the more confident you will feel at the interview itself.

The more confident you feel, the better you will come across at interview.

P = Prepare

Preparing in advance for the actual interview will help you to feel more confident and not to be caught off-guard by any questions you are asked.

Try not to answer questions with one-word answers - these are very frustrating for employers.

If you are asked "what are you like in the workplace?"	**Do not just say "good".**	ELABORATE with a smile in your voice and enthusiasm saying something like *"I am actually really good in the workplace, because I enjoy working and being productive. It makes me feel useful and like I am contributing."*
If you are asked "what are you like with customers?"	**Do not just say "great".**	EXPAND on your answer, by saying something like *"I am great with customers because I really care about making a good impression for the company and I genuinely like helping people."*

Employers expect you to make an effort when you communicate and to share some information with them.

Research has revealed that when employers are considering hiring ex-offenders, they are most interested in answering the following four questions:

1) Can I afford to hire this person?

2) Can this person work with my existing team?

3) Does this person pose a risk to my staff, my company or to the public?

4) Can this person do the job required, reliably and to a high enough standard?

(Source: The Forward trust; Bridging the Gap report)

The better we can reassure a potential employer of these 4 points, the more likely we are to succeed at interview and be offered the job.

Mentally prepare some answers to these four points before the interview. Bear in mind that they may not ask these actual questions, but they will nevertheless be looking for the answers to emerge during the interview.

The following are examples of good answers and points which have been given by people in a similar position to you - it will be helpful if you familiarise yourself with some of these answers. My preferred answers are **in bold**.

Employer Question 1 - Can I Afford to Hire this Person?		
Examples of good answers and points	*I have a track record of bringing in business and generating many times my salary in billable income to the company.*
	I am a very reasonable person and would be willing to start on a salary at the lower end of the scale, whilst I prove my value to the company.
	I am a loyal person and if I am given an opportunity I will stay with the company for a long time and save the company future recruitment costs.
Reminder - You must be honest with prospective employers; these answers will not all apply to you.	*In the past I have saved my employers a lot of money by improving processes and designing efficient systems. The money saved has actually been as much as my salary.*
	I represent good value for money because taking into account the time I have been away from the conventional job market I am not demanding a salary at the top of the scale.
	Usually my skills and experience would attract a much higher salary; it is only due to my time away from the workplace that I am available for a salary which is much less than I used to be on.

Employer Question 2 - Can this person work with my existing team?	**Examples of good answers and points** Reminder - You must be honest with prospective employers; these answers will not all apply to you.	*I am good at working alongside other people in a team.*
		I fit into teams easily and I get on well with new people.
		I communicate well; I am patient and respect other people.
		I am a helpful and supportive person and I can definitely work well as part of an existing team.
		I have no problem working with other people, I am easy going and relatable and I get on well with others.
		I am absolutely a team player. I support other people and always work so that the team wins, and everyone benefits.
		I have excellent people skills, I am not dominating but vary my approach to accommodate and work with other people.
		I have excellent interpersonal skills and people feel comfortable around me, I am used to working alongside other team members.
		Yes, I am good at working in a team and helping the team to move forward, I don't get distracted by side issues or make problems bigger than they are.
		I have good interpersonal and communication skills, I am comfortable adjusting my style to work well with other people and I enjoy being part of a team.
		Yes, definitely! I see the benefits of working well in a team; by using each person's skills to work in different tasks that they might be better at and supporting each other.
		I am very good at working with other people and interact brilliantly with people from different ages, backgrounds and ethnicity. I find people interesting, so I never prejudge but just seem to naturally get on with others.
		I have very good interpersonal skills; I recently completed an education programme called Daily Diplomacy; I gained a certificate for studying 30 different people skills and recording my practical results in a reflection diary.
		I have demonstrated that I can survive and thrive in a wide range of environments; from the most professional of workplaces to the most difficult and challenging environment that is prison. I am an adaptable person and I get along with all different types of other people.

| Employer Question 3 - Do I pose any kind of risk? | Examples of good answers and points

Reminder -

You must be honest with prospective employers; these answers will not all apply to you. | I have turned my life around and do not want to go back to crime; I do not consider myself to be a risk. |
|---|---|---|
| | | Not at all, I have served my time in prison, I have matured a lot and I take time to consider things more than I used to. |
| | | I do not believe that I pose any risk. I would like to explain that this was my first and only crime and I have learnt and matured a lot. |
| | | My disclosure statement confirms that my conviction(s) are not related to my employment and do not present a risk in the workplace. |
| | | **I have no intention of breaking the law ever again; I have learnt my lesson and demonstrated that I am determined to turn my life around.** |
| | | This was my first offence; it was a single event in my life which was completely out of character for me and which will definitely never be repeated. |
| | | I do not pose any risk, I am a very loyal person who would never betray someone, or an organisation, who was helping me and giving me a chance. |
| | | I have changed for the better and broken ties with past criminal associates. I am very choosy about who I associate with and how I spend my time. |
| | | I don't pose any risk because I have put a lot of hard work in to ensure that I don't make the same mistakes again. I have developed and matured personally. |
| | | I have been trusted to work with vulnerable people and to handle them with dignity and respect. I am always professional and have never let anyone down at work. |
| | | I have proven worthy of trust and do not pose a risk of problems in the workplace; in fact, employment is a proven stabilising factor which would form the solid foundation of my future life. |
| | | I completely regret my crime and I have no intention of ever breaking any rules or laws in future. I value my life in the community and with my family far too high to jeopardise my freedom ever again. |
| | | Not at all, I have seen the effects of the crime that I committed, and I will never impose my behaviour and issues on anyone else ever again. What I did was wrong, and I will never repeat those behaviours. |

Employer Question 4 - **Am I capable of doing the job and will I be reliable?**	**Examples of good answers and points** Reminder - You must be honest with prospective employers; these answers will not all apply to you.	*Yes, I am often praised for my reliability and job performance.*
		I am a very motivated individual and I have maintained my habit of work.
		I have proven my reliability by consistently working hard across a number of roles in recent years.
		I do work to a high standard and have a good track record of reliability. I would never let an employer down who gave me a chance.
		I am a very reliable and organised person; I am consistently prompt and hardworking and I would like the chance to prove myself again.
		I have always worked to a high standard and I am self-motivated. Throughout my career I have proven worthy of trust and have never let an employer down.
		I am reliable and professional; I enjoy new challenges and I don't give up. I work and perform to a high standard until the job is done and the mission is accomplished.
		I learn quickly and I am willing to undertake any additional training whether in work hours, or in my own time to ensure that I am skilled and qualified enough for the position.
		I am dependable in the workplace and give my job roles my best possible efforts. I have proven and demonstrated my work ethic in recent years and have nothing but praise and positive comments for every role I have held.
		I have proven my reliability and demonstrated my willingness to work hard in recent transitional employment. I also enjoy learning new things and am willing to undertake any additional training required.
		I am a conscientious worker. I believe that 'if a job is worth doing - it is worth doing well'. I like to stand back, see the work I have done knowing that it has been done to a high standard and see the satisfaction in a client's face.
		I always worked before I came to prison and I have also worked throughout my prisons sentence. I did not think that any job was too menial but instead I considered them to be 'transitional employment', which enabled me to continue to demonstrate my work ethic and to prove that I am in the habit of contributing through work.

Think about other questions that you may be asked specifically to do with this job or employer and also to do with your CV and disclosure.

Additionally, it will be helpful to prepare a list of questions to ask the employer and things to tell them. Do not rely on memory alone because when we are nervous things get forgotten; instead write everything down as you think of it. Carry a pen and paper with you and keep one next to your bed so that you can capture thoughts when they arrive.

A good investment of time will be to create a simple document called 'Things to Discuss at Interview'. This type of preparation is a sign of professionalism and shows that the interview is important to you.

The following template gives you an idea of how this can be a simple but effective document:

Things to Discuss at Interview		
Subjects to talk about	**Information to tell**	**Questions to ask**
e.g. I read about the award the company got.	*e.g. Pre booked holiday dates.*	*e.g. Will the employer support me to get my next qualification?*

"My prepared questions and answers were a life-saver in my interview. I felt so ready and oozed confidence. It really paid off thanks. I beat three other applicants to be offered a two-week trial in the company!" SO

267

E = Enquire

Contact the potential employer in advance to fill in any knowledge gaps that you may have e.g.

- Exact location.
- Nearest car park/ train station.
- Dress code for interview (if unsure).
- Asking whether you need to bring anything along with you.
- Whether you are expected to confirm your attendance in writing.
- Details of who will be interviewing you (so you can research their biography and job title etc.).

Give it some thought and add some more of your own questions to this list.

IMPORTANT NOTICE: If you are on licence, you must inform your Probation Officer before you undertake any paid or unpaid work. If you are not sure whether you are approved to work in a certain role or industry, enquire with them first. Employment is proven to reduce re-offending so it is likely that your Probation Officer will offer you a lot of support and encouragement before your interview.

R = Rehearse

Rehearse the day.

Get dressed in the clothes you are going to wear to the interview. If possible, go on a practise journey, using the same route and transport option that you intend to use on the interview day.

Rehearsing will massively help your confidence; your time keeping and will alert you to any potential problems e.g. if the office is hidden away somewhere and takes 15 minutes extra to find (Yes this does happen!).

Practise talking about your skills and experience and answering tricky interview questions with a partner or friends who play the role of the interviewer(s).

You would not dream of performing in a play without rehearsing first - well your interview day is your chance to perform at your best so rehearse for this important occasion too.

P.R.O.P.E.R. - Plan, Research, Organise, Prepare, Enquire, Rehearse

Plan the day, research the company and industry, organise your paperwork, prepare yourself for questions, make any necessary enquiries and rehearse.

"I read this chapter again before my job interview. It helped me in so many ways. It reminded me what to consider beforehand and it was good to know that I had covered everything. My interview actually went really well." AM

The Interview Day

All your work up to this point has led to this moment.

Do the best you can, try your best. Now is your chance to shine and to show your best angle. Today's mantra is *"if a job's worth doing, it is worth doing well"*.

Be proud of yourself for persisting and getting this far. Hold your head up high.

DO
Get rid of any chewing gum before you enter the building.
Arrive early but wait patiently even if the interviewers are running late.
If you have a cold or hay fever, take some tissues with you to avoid sniffing.
Get yourself in a good frame of mind and play your favourite music before arriving.
Smile even if you feel nervous, it will really help your confidence and improve your mood.
Leave any negative feelings of shame, sadness, resentment, or disappointment in the past now.
If you wear aftershave or perfume, then it should be used very sparingly, or you are taking a risk that the interviewer may find it overpowering.
Shave, clean your nails, brush your teeth, wear your hair tidily and carry out any other personal grooming required for you to look tidy and presentable.
Work on your attitude and self-talk; tell yourself "I am ideal for the job; the job is ideal for me. It's gonna be great! I deserve this chance."
Smoke your last cigarette before you get dressed in the clothes you are wearing for the interview; the smell lingers and can be off-putting to non-smokers.
If you are feeling a little nervous this is a good thing because you are taking the day seriously. Do not let your nerves turn into anxieties, there are lots of opportunities, your whole life does not hinge on this moment. Do your best and that is all that anyone can ever ask.
Dress appropriately, this is a formal meeting. Unless told differently, men will be expected to wear a suit, tie and shoes and ladies will be expected to wear formal 'court' attire with clothes that are not too revealing or distracting. Dress as smartly as you can, even if you need to borrow a suit or get it from a charity shop. Clothing should not make a statement; avoid wearing anything which is heavily branded or obviously expensive, and minimise jewellery. Where possible cover up any body art or tattoos that you feel no longer reflects the real you, if they distract or stop you from presenting the image you are aiming for. If you are happy with your tattoos and they are inoffensive, then do not worry about them, many people have tattoos and they are not a barrier to full-time employment.

During the Interview

Interviews are no longer intimidating events dominated by arrogant people wearing red ties, (as many used to be years ago).

Instead they are "getting to know you" meetings, where interviewers want to help you to feel comfortable so they can get to know you as a person.

This is a big day for the employer too.

Hiring people costs a lot of money and time, so they want to make the right decision and employ someone who will stay long-term.

The fact that you have been invited for an interview speaks volumes; your CV, PDS and AL have already worked their magic and you just need to support these in person.

Most people (including the employers themselves) believe that **hiring** decisions are made based on skills and qualifications but this is not the whole story.

In fact, it is only the decision to invite someone for **interview** which is made based on qualifications, experience, skills and on making a professional application.

Hiring decisions at the interview stage are based almost solely on likeability.

Professor Richard Wiseman (Psychologist) analysing statistical research explains that the biggest factor which affects why interviewers hire candidates is whether the candidate appeared to be a pleasant person. Candidates can literally charm their way to success by: smiling, making good eye contact, showing enthusiasm for the organisation and chatting about topics of mutual interest.

> **"In order to get your dream job, going out of your way to be pleasant is <u>more important</u> than qualifications or past work experience."** (Source: 59 Seconds by Professor Richard Wiseman)

Interviewers will ask you questions and may ask you to clarify points about your CV and PDS. Answer everything honestly and positively, in an open manner.

There are standard interview questions as well as recommended answers available online and in certain books; I do not think these are particularly helpful. Instead, I recommend that you answer questions on the day in a pleasant manner. Talk clearly and avoid using slang or swear words, smile frequently throughout.

After getting to know you, the interviewer will usually ask you whether you have any questions, and this is the perfect time to ask the questions which you prepared in advance.

> **"The most helpful way for you to view an interview is that it is a friendly discussion between you and a potential employer to assess whether you will be a good fit for each other."** PM

Maintaining Employment

I recommend treating every day at work as a Job Interview day. When you are working in a job, act and perform as if you are being interviewed for a job at the next level.

Getting a job is important, but keeping a job is essential. Imagine a game of snakes and ladders. The longer you keep your job the better it looks on your CV; the more chance you have for progression (climbing the ladders) within that company or another company. Losing a job is like sliding down a snake and having to go backwards.

This is where it will be a good idea to re-read chapter 2 'Improving Employability' and perhaps read it regularly. You may remember that we talked about viewing your employer as if they were a customer who is buying a service from you. The service that you are selling is that you will:

- Perform work at the expected standard (or better).
- Within the expected timescale (or even more efficiently).
- In accordance with the employer's rules and procedures.

We want our employer/customer to like the service that they are buying from us so much that they keep buying it and that they do not consider going to competitors instead (rival job applicants).

We should be willing to deliver more than expected so that our employer/customer is pleasantly surprised and so that you really earn your wages.

That is the reality of the modern job marketplace.

We discussed the importance of developing and showing your transferable skills.

The two most important transferable skills are:

- **your work ethic** (commitment, extra mile, rises to challenges, self-discipline, team player)
- **your communication skills** (friendly, listening, patient, talking clearly, positive body language, good manners)

In summary, this means <u>trying your best</u> and <u>treating other people well</u>.

If you keep working to develop yourself and you consistently offer good value to your employer, then you will have no problem maintaining employment and you will be able to progress onwards and upwards to better and better job opportunities.

"I have now been in the same job for 11 months. My employer appreciates me, and I definitely appreciate them! When you are at work, give it 100%; when you are with your family, give them 100% - That works for me." RE

"One of the biggest barriers, if not the biggest barrier to successful rehabilitation of ex-offenders, is being unable to obtain meaningful employment, aligned with their hopes and goals. Employment is a strong protective factor against poverty, poor mental and physical health, substance abuse and reoffending. This in turn fosters less reliance on the welfare state, health care and other services."

Sarah Taylor, ACAS Trainer and former Probation Officer

Chapter 7 -
Self-Employment

"Every aspect of my new self-employed business makes me want to do it. I love it; it's my dream, my own, not someone else's. I always knew that I had an independent streak and now I can express it through my work. Wanting to do it every day makes me work hard and keeps me away from negative influences that would have dragged me back into problems." CG

Advantages and Disadvantages

Self-employment can be an excellent option for many people.

It is particularly suitable for people who like to be independent, for whom traditional job models do not always fit or for those who have struggled to gain employment due to their criminal records.

It is possible to earn a greater income when you work for yourself because you keep more of the profit which would otherwise have gone to your employer or to shareholders, and also because the tax regime favours self-employed people over employees.

Self-employment really means **owning your own job** and is typically characterised by being a sole-trader (e.g. John Smith t/as Abacus Archaeology), this is different from forming and/or **operating a company** as a director and owning shares in that company (e.g. Abacus Archaeology Ltd).

The cheapest and lowest risk option is to start small as a sole-trader. Once you are up and running, earning a good income and growing, then it is worth paying for an accountant's professional advice to discuss the advantages and disadvantages of morphing into a limited company (this is called incorporating).

The period in-between being a sole-trader and a company is usually called **owning your own business** and may be characterised by employing other people, taking on extra premises, signing long-term contracts but still offering personal guarantees.

Being self-employed takes far greater discipline, self-reliance and initiative than showing up for work every day, following instructions given by someone else and receiving a salary in return.

There is also no safety net; generally, if you are self-employed and you go on holiday, you do not receive holiday pay. If you are sick, you do not earn any money because there is usually no sick pay. When you own your own business then things change because if it is well run, the business may continue serving its customers and generating profit even if you are temporarily absent.

NB: Ex-offenders who are on licence are required to inform their Probation Officer and ask for approval before undertaking paid or unpaid work. Legitimate self-employment is proven to reduce re-offending, so it is likely that you will be offered support, signposting and practical help. You must also ensure full compliance with any additional court orders such as Crime Prevention Orders, Company Director's Disqualification Orders or bans from working in certain industries.

Business owners are the opportunity seekers, pioneers and innovators.

"Many people <u>see</u> opportunities, but it is the entrepreneurs who <u>seize</u> those opportunities." PM

Many people get anxious at the thought of creating a formal business plan.

A business plan is a very helpful tool however because it is the best way to clarify your thoughts and generate ideas, it will also be requested by other people and organisations that you intend to work with.

There are common structures for formal business plans, and these will usually be needed to secure business loans or attract joint-venture partners. There are many templates online or you can ask the organisation requesting a business plan to provide their preferred framework.

For most people it is a good exercise to create your own framework and view your **business plan** as simply you **planning your business**. Pick up a pen or pencil and start writing, move everything out of your head and onto paper. Include all of your thoughts, ideas and potential scenarios, and put these under headers that work for you. There is a tremendous value in an exercise like this. You may want to include advantages and disadvantages or conduct a *'SWOT'* analysis. This is a memory aid that stands for Strengths, Weaknesses, Opportunities and Threats and which helps you to consider both internal and external factors affecting a business.

Business owners know that **failing to plan** is **planning to fail**!

After everything you have been through, you owe it to yourself to plan well and give yourself the best chance of success. Consider the following **informal** example of a business plan after a free-thinking session.

<u>My Business Plan</u> - by Tom H

Background:

After gaining a wide range of skills in prison I am keen to work full time for an employer and then eventually be my own boss; working for myself.

Skills and Abilities:

I attach my CV which reflects many vocational skills and professional abilities which I gained during my time in prison. I have used my time to consistently improve myself. I gained certification in MS Office Suite as well as a Level 2 Award in Business Enterprise, including Financial Management.

Opportunity:

My dream is to own and operate a regular and secure market stall specialising in the sale of ladies' handbags, purses, gloves, scarves and related items purchased new from established wholesalers in the West Midlands.

<u>Location:</u>

'Fresh town' permanent market, eventually expanding online and to second town.

<u>Market Research:</u>

I have visited 'Fresh town' permanent market on 3 occasions and had lengthy conversations with existing and successful market traders. I learned a lot about the gaps available for market traders, the customer type and the range of opportunities for successful retail sales.

I carried out extensive online research, made telephone calls and face to face visits to established wholesalers who have confirmed that they will be willing and able to supply me with the range of stock I would require for resale. My research has identified a core product range of around 30 items which have an average of 60% profit margin.

<u>Timescale:</u>

I am planning to live in an affordable house share which will enable me to build up savings. I would like to start my business within 12 months by saving £560 pcm, but I am flexible. If I do not save up enough money in time, then I will continue working as a full-time employee until I have enough money.

My CV has been professionally drafted and my Personal Disclosure Statement is honest. Agencies and potential employers have already expressed their interest in interviewing me. I hold a Construction Skills Certification Scheme (CSCS) card which is valid until September 2023 and is a pathway to immediate employment on sites. During my initial time working, I will save all of my spare money after paying rent and other necessary expenses.

I will not begin the self-employment until I have sufficient financial resources to ensure personal stability and viability of the business.

<u>Alternative route to start up:</u>

As an alternative, I will consider the following plan:

Stage 1 - Continuing my full-time employment and beginning my part time self-employment on weekends only.

Stage 2 - Going part-time with employer (this is not unusual for construction work) whilst doing 3-4 days' self-employment.

Stage 3 - Full time self-employment.

This alternative route to start up is my least preferred, but it will provide me with a stable pathway into my market trading business.

Capital required:

Before starting self-employment, I will have savings equivalent to 8 weeks of running costs as follows:

Purchase of initial stock		£2,000
Purchase of small van (with warranty) from reputable car dealer		£2,500
Cover sheets, clips, cart to wheel the stock to market and sundries		£400
Site rent 6 days x £20 each day = £120 pw	8 weeks x £120pw	£960
Market Traders' Public Liability Insurance	2 months x £11pcm	£22
Fuel and vehicle maintenance contribution	8 weeks x £60 pw	£480
Class 2 National Insurance Contributions	8 weeks x £3 pw	£24
Van Insurance and road tax	2 months x £160pcm	£320
Total "Getting Started Money" Required		£6,706

Finances:

I expect to sell/turnover around **£160** per day equalling **£960 pw** when full-time at an average **60%** profit margin this equals **£600 pw** gross profit.

From this I will pay my expenses of **£140 pw** giving me an initial net profit of **£460 pw**. This is **£23,920 pa**

Being self-employed means that Income Tax is due on profits, not on income.

I can legitimately use some of this £23,920 (pre-tax money) to pay for expenses associated with the business, such as my mobile phone, clothes which I buy just for work and a percentage of my personal rent and bills (because I will be storing some of my stock at home and doing business paperwork from home). There is a list of allowable expenses located on HMRC website.

> I have a personal tax allowance of **£12,500 pa** and I will have to pay **20%** tax on the income/ take home pay that I earn above this.

> I have a personal National Insurance allowance of **£8,632 pa** and I will also have to pay **9%** Class 4 NI contributions on the profit over this.

> If I have profit of **£23,920 pa** and don't use any of it for allowable expenses, then I would pay **£2,284 pa** tax and **£1,376 pa** Class 4 NI.

I would take home **£20,260 pa** equal to **£1688 pcm** and **£389 pw**. This is comparable to my income as an employed person and I have the freedom to be my own boss, work as much as I like and grow the business to any level.

<u>Legal Framework:</u>

I will be self-employed as a sole trader and will register with HMRC within 3 months of starting in compliance with the rules.

Initially I will complete my own tax return online but once my business is more complex and I am full-time, I will probably pay a local accountant to help me with my paperwork.

I will be honest and fair to my customers and will make sure that I follow consumer protection laws (such as refunding faulty goods).

I will pay for public liability insurance from the Market Traders' Federation and be aware of health and safety risks when loading and unloading as well as around my stall, so that I am not responsible for any accidents.

<u>SWOT Analysis:</u>

Strengths:

Low overheads, Low stock holding, Good profit margins.

I am good with people and can encourage customers to buy.

Customers can physically hold the stock and feel the quality.

Weaknesses:

Weather is outside of my control and it affects footfall and sales.

Seasonal variations in turnover e.g. Christmas and Mother's Day.

Opportunities:

Expand the range of items.

Open up a second site if and when first site is successful.

Sell or franchise sites when they are proven to be successful.

Develop an online presence and promote it with business cards given to customers face to face.

More department stores and high street shops closing leaves a growing void for small retailers like myself.

The possibility of negotiating sale or return on some stock to reduce the risk of items not selling and reducing capital needed.

Meet other people who are leaving prison and invest my profits into their small business ideas for a share of their profits.

Early negotiations show the chance of sub-letting space on my stall to members of a local craft club which makes and sells hand-made greetings cards and knitwear.

Once I have proof of the most popular and fastest selling items I will benefit from economies of scale and have greater financial resources to buy these in bulk from international wholesalers, gaining a larger profit margin.

Threats:

Possible theft of stock.

Competition from cheap online retailers.

Damage or degradation of stock by weather (cold, sun or damp).

Vehicle breakdowns would affect whether I can open for business.

Being careful not to buy fake or poor-quality stock that could get me in trouble or lose me money

Personal Notes:

I am determined to change, particularly because I am very aware that I have wasted such a large part of my life in prison and because I have caused harm and distress to other people. I have not yet achieved a decent life for myself which I would like to do. I am keen eventually to have a healthy relationship and a stable home.

Now is the time for me to follow a legal pathway doing work that I enjoy whilst also making amends, contributing to society and repaying the many people who have put their faith in me and helped and supported me.

In recent years I have developed personal coping strategies and a better understanding of the trauma I endured as a child. I intend to build a productive life and put the past behind me. I have broken all ties with past criminal associates and have formed a support network of family and friends who all live decent positive and law-abiding lives.

Thank you for taking the time to read my business plan, I welcome any feedback, suggestions or questions.

I am not saying whether this example business is a good idea or not, what do you think?

Are there any areas that have been missed out that you think should be included?

The My-Way Code

Learner drivers must study a very important manual called **The Highway Code.**

After passing their test, licensed drivers are expected to display full compliance with The Highway Code.

The Highway Code keeps pedestrians safe, protects the rights of other road users and ensures that we have a sustainable road network

Business ownership mirrors this too. There is a clear and evolved set of laws and structures which keeps customers safe, protects the rights of other business owners and ensures that we have a sustainable economy. Instead of 'The Highway Code', I call this set of laws and structures **'The My-Way Code'**.

Business owners and self-employed people are generally very independently minded they might say "I like to do things my way" and they might not like being told what to do by an employer in a conventional job.

It is important to understand however that we live in an evolved and civilised society in which businesses can thrive and the protections and privileges of living and operating in such a stable environment only come because there is an existing framework of rules and laws.

"The only way to win a game is to play the game and every game has rules." PM

Creative thinkers are always looking for way to improve things, to do things better to be more efficient, to cut corners but we must still work within legal boundaries. I made mistakes, I broke rules. My family and I paid a big heavy price, bigger than most people can imagine. I am still paying a price and facing extra restrictions today.

As ex-offenders we must not be rule breakers, hence **The My-Way code**.

Just like studying The Highway Code to pass your driving test and enjoy decades of motoring, you will need to study **The My-Way code** to enjoy decades of income and independence in business.

There are 5 important considerations to **The My-Way code.**

1) It is different for different businesses.

Car traders, Estate Agents and Travel Agents each have different rules, laws and guidelines than they must follow.

There are general requirements which are common to all businesses, such as keeping records, paying tax and having insurance. In most industries however there are also separate laws and, in some cases, even separate supervisory bodies e.g. The Financial Conduct Authority which supervises financial services businesses.

2) It is very long; there are lots of rules, regulations and laws.

Starting a business is not something that should be done without detailed research and planning.

There are many places that you can go to for advice and guidance.

I particularly recommend joining a membership body and trade association who can point you immediately to appropriate legal guidelines and template legal paperwork and who usually offer advice and guidance to members.

A good starting point for all self-employed people is the local Chamber of Commerce and the internet has made research so easy to do that there is comprehensive and current information made available by reputable organisations.

3) It is constantly changing; we must adapt and stay current.

Some industry sectors, such as recruitment have experienced de-regulation (a relaxation of the legal framework) in recent years, whilst others, such as hiring of consumer goods, have seen increases in the amount of regulations and laws.

As business owners, you are responsible for compliance with the current rules and laws, ignorance of these is not considered a valid excuse or defence.

4) Penalties for non-compliance are severe.

Enforcement is swift by Trading Standards, HMRC, DBIS, Police and other agencies. Investigations result in huge disruption to business and individual lives.

Punishments include asset forfeiture, director's disqualifications, imprisonment, increased reporting obligations, fines, negative publicity and trade restrictions.

Most business offences are called 'strict-liability' that means that it is generally the owner who is responsible even for innocent mistakes and even if they did not know about them, because it is considered that they should have known.

Business owners receive multiple tax benefits and are respected members of society; company directors can even sign passport applications. It is for these reasons that we are expected to hold ourselves to a higher standard of professionalism and responsibility.

5) If you follow all the rules and do things properly then your business is sustainable.

A sustainable and legitimate business is something to be very proud of indeed. You have become self-reliant and maybe you are even offering the opportunity of a job (which is life changing in itself) to other people.

Having a well-run sustainable business means that at well as generating income now, you are also building equity (real value) within the business.

You get paid twice for businesses, once as you are working and generating income and again when you sell the asset you have created.

Marketing and Promoting Your Business

Definition of marketing:

There are many definitions of marketing, some thought up by academics, some evolved by experienced business people and others from the perspective of consumers.

I define marketing as:

The processes by which organisations deliver their messages to an audience.

The messages may be designed to educate or raise awareness, they may be propaganda designed to persuade, for fundraising or to sell a product or service.

In this chapter we are focussing on business marketing in a business context i.e. marketing which is designed to sell a product or service.

Marketing has always been <u>important</u> but a focus on marketing is <u>essential</u> today because customers literally have the world of products and services available at their fingertips.

Customers certainly do have the power to choose, but sometimes this choice is not easy for them to make because they are bombarded with information and messages, so they are literally 'spoilt for choice'.

More than ever customers are looking for leadership and direction that pierces through the general hubbub of marketing messages.

You can build the best website in the world with a fantastic product or opportunity but if you do not market that website or product, very few people will stumble upon it by accident.

This would be like opening a superstore in the middle of a desert with no footfall! A business that is doomed to fail, but before it fails it haemorrhages money and saps the motivation and energy of the owner.

It is marketing that makes the difference because it links people to the product/ service you are selling.

<u>8 Tips for Successful Marketing</u>, Marketing should:

1) **Be tested.**

> Market research should be undertaken for untested concepts, product launches and new ventures to ensure that a marketing campaign will be financially viable.

> Ideally testing can be carried out in limited areas, initially with small budgets. Results should be measured and improved over time.

2) Be repeated often.

Marketing should consistently become more familiar to the audience across a wide range of media and platforms.

A new perfume with a large marketing budget will advertise on buses, TV, radio, national newspapers and social-media and may include face to face promotions and giveaways.

A new takeaway food outlet with a small marketing budget may deliver leaflets in the local area, offer incentives (buy one pizza, get one free), offer rewards for regular customers, have students dressed up as pizza slices standing on street corners and build up an excited following on local social-media pages, all on a small budget.

3) Be relevant to the audience.

The more targeted your audience is based on the product/ service offered, the better response you will get and the more cost effective and productive the marketing messages will be.

4) Accurately reflect the product/service.

Expectation gaps must be avoided or minimised to reinforce the buyer's decision and avoid a buyer regretting their purchase. Under-promising and over-delivering will ensure buyer satisfaction.

The systems for delivering the product/service must be in place before the marketing campaign begins to ensure that demand is met.

5) Focus on the Unique Selling Points (USP's) of the product/service.

Marketing is most successful when it focusses on the USP's and clearly differentiates itself from rival offerings which may appear similar to the audience.

The product/service must be clearly different and in a significant way, to justify people switching brands, breaking a habit or trying something new.

The differences and USP's should be anchored or reinforced to the audience through the use of branding including a name, logo, personality and other identifying features.

6) Reward customers.

Long term customer relationships should be built and loyalty rewarded.

When setting resource budgets, the lifetime value of a customer should be considered rather than just the profit from a single purchase.

7) Encourage recommendations.

Referrals and recommendations should be sought from customers and a system should be in place to capture these and build a referral network.

8) **Appeal to multiple senses** and learning styles.

Marketing should appeal to more than one of the five senses (these are also known as learning styles and processing methods). Each person has a dominant sense which they use to process information, to learn and which help them to make decisions (including purchasing decisions).

ALL successful marketing campaigns will appeal to at least 2 out of 3 of the dominant senses a, b and c.				
a)	Eyesight (Visual)	**Show me**	Stimulate my eyes with colour beauty, interesting sights etc.	**I feel good when I see it**. *"I see what you mean."*
b)	Hearing (Auditory)	**Tell me**	Stimulate my ears with music, jingles, sounds, varied tone of voice etc.	**I like to hear it**. *"I hear what you are saying."*
c)	Touch (Kinaesthetic)	**Let me touch**	Stimulate my touch and feelings by letting me hold and feel textures and unusual objects.	**I like to feel it**. *"I understand what you are saying, I know how you feel."*
The two less dominant senses which should also be considered are d and e				
d)	Smell (Olfactory)	**Let me smell**	Smells can be very evocative and are often associated with happy experiences.	**I like to smell it**. *"Something does not smell right about this!"*
e)	Taste (Gustatory)	**Let me taste**	Taste or the imagined taste should be pleasant, unique and, memorable.	**I like to taste it**. *"that/ he/ she looks tasty!"*

The difference between sales and marketing:

There is an overlap between the two concepts of sales and marketing, (for example where marketing and sales happens almost simultaneously such as *Point of Sale* (POS) marketing sweets at a store checkout) but in practise marketing and selling are two very different things.

I define selling as: ***The process of converting an interest into a completed sale.***

Sales and selling happens after someone has responded to a marketing message. In some businesses this is known as converting leads to deals.

Business owners should give a lot of thought to sales, dedicate time and resources to sales departments and review their processes and results regularly. Do not be afraid to explain the good points (features and benefits) of your product/ service, the easy to follow purchasing and delivery processes and after care guarantees. Selling is a skill that can be developed, and I would encourage you to read books and attend sales courses which will help in this area. **Ultimately, sales come from how well you express your sincere belief and confidence in your product/service.**

The more planning ahead you can do in your business, the more you will:

- Reduce risk
- Maximise profitability
- Identify opportunities
- Act to avoid problems
- Increase likelihood of long-term success

A marketing plan is an important part of your overall business plan and strategy. Your business plan and SWOT analysis will generate lots of ideas and material that can be used in the marketing plan and which will help you to identify areas where marketing will be most effective.

The cheapest form of marketing is to serve existing customers well and to increase the amount they spend. With a new business that does not have existing customers; you may need to offer them incentives before they will switch from their existing supplier or service provider to you. These incentives/discounts may be a hidden part of your marketing budget, even if they show up as income from reduced sales in your accounts.

In many successful businesses 40% of new business comes from recommendations and referrals. Even with a new business, you can offer referral commission or give incentives to introducers and affiliates. This can often be a cheap and low risk form of marketing because you will usually only pay on results and should be a primary marketing channel for all businesses.

The success of marketing campaigns must be measured for effectiveness and to ensure that you are getting value for money. Tracking codes can be added to leaflets, entitling customers to claim a discount and separate website landing pages can be created for each campaign to track visitors.

Some businesses will not have a direct marketing budget but will instead pay fees and effectively outsource their marketing to other companies.

e.g.	Online businesses using EBay and Amazon sales platforms do not need separate marketing budgets because advertising and marketing is included within the fees paid to the platform.
	Many takeaway restaurants no longer advertise themselves but instead pay a percentage of order value and monthly fees to portals such as *'Just Eat'* and *'Hungry House'* who are the marketing and order processing experts.

Tom (whose business plan featured earlier) will not spend much on marketing in addition to his pitch fees because he will rely on regular footfall and advertising carried out by the site operator.

Suggested questions to help you to draw up a marketing plan:

What are the results of my market research?

```

```

Who are my potential customers?

```

```

What is my marketing budget?

```

```

What are the Unique Selling Points (USP's) of my product/ service?

```

```

What marketing are my competitors doing regularly and consistently?

```


```

How will interest in the marketing message be converted into sales?

```

```

How much new business can be handled before customer satisfaction levels drop?

```

```

Are our existing customers happy?

```

```

What could I do to increase income and profitability from existing customers?

```


```

Who can I include in my referral and affiliate network of people and organisations?

```


```

How can I incentivise people and organisations to promote and recommend me?

```


```

Now list the Advantages and Disadvantages of ALL the potential marketing strategies that are within your budget:

Marketing Strategy	Frequency of Campaigns	Expected Cost	Advantages	Disadvantages	How could I test this?	How can I measure the effectiveness?

287

Co-Operative Negotiation - Leaving the Door Open

Negotiation is an important skill in business.

Many people unfortunately approach negotiation competitively as a battle of wills.

This can lead to feelings of confrontation, people defending themselves and getting entrenched in their positions (in response to an attack) and to less deals being done.

In reality, deals are not done, deals are agreed.

Co-operative negotiation is more successful than competitive negotiation.

6 Tips for Successful Co-operative Negotiation:

1) **Consider the needs and wishes of the other party.**

Ask in advance what the other party's ideal or preferred outcome is and really listen to the answer.

This has two benefits, firstly it wins support from the other person because they know that you are considering their wishes and secondly it gives you a benchmark (a figure, or terms) at which as deal can be agreed.

2) **Work with the other party to design a solution.**

Aim to arrive at a destination which works for both of you. Ask information gathering questions e.g. "What do you think?", "What are you hoping to achieve?", "What about if we…", "What is the lowest price you could accept?"

3) **Add value.**

Everyone should be better off in some way for having interacted with you.

No matter what happens in a negotiation, seek to add value to the situation.

Leave the other person is a better position than they would have been without your involvement. They will respond better to follow ups, be more likely to come back to you later and will recommend you to other people if you do this.

4) **Take the PRESSURE off the PRICE.**

Consider more than one thing to negotiate about (multiple negotiation points).

This allows each party to give concessions without losing face and without any offer or suggestion being a final "take it or leave it".

What considerations are important to the other party? Some may be more important than price. Is timescale important? Is volume of sales? Sale or return? Payment terms? Joint Marketing? Regularity of transactions or repeat business?

What else could come into the negotiation as a concession and help to finalise terms and 'seal the deal'?

5) Take the focus off the individual (take the PRESSURE off the PERSON)

Mention third parties and explain external circumstances and drivers of decisions.

e.g. "Unfortunately, we have to be guided by our professional advisors."

"My sales team have told me it has to be delivered by Wednesday."

"It is not me being difficult; my investors will not allow me to go that high."

"I would like to agree to your new terms, but it will not work for my partner."

"I really want to offer more but the credit crunch has meant that our sales volume has fallen whilst our costs have increased by around 8%."

6) Leave the door open

End on an open and positive note so that even if a deal is not done, follow ups can be undertaken, the other party also often comes back to reopen the negotiation or to accept the deal.

Co-operative Negotiation:		
A	**Results in agreed deals making it all the way to completion**	Second thoughts, buyer's remorse and people changing their mind become rare. The outcome is the other party's idea as much as it was yours; you have their "buy in". In this manner people rarely pull out of deals or change their mind.
B	**Is sustainable long-term**	Leads to successful relationships with customers and suppliers, recommendations and a referral network.

Diplomacy has a big part to play in negotiation. You will become a better negotiator if you:

- Work with the other party,
- Take the pressure off the price,
- Take the pressure off the person and
- Sit alongside them (mentally, emotionally and physically if possible)

This means that you will **complete more deals**, whatever type of deals they are (whether sales or purchases, contracts or partnerships or any other type of deal). Any transactions or deals done must, of course, meet your own criteria and be profitable long term.

Co-operative negotiation ensures that deals are the best possible outcome for both parties. Taking all circumstances into account, your solution is genuinely the best-fit.

This is often called **WIN/ WIN**

"The self-employment chapter of your book gave me the motivation and structure to plan my business. Writing things out really impressed probation and they have been 100% behind my project because they know I am doing it professionally." HN

"As an ex-offender myself and running my own company for the past 8 years, I have faced struggles as a result of having a conviction. I'm aware though that offenders with less skills, experience and those at the lower end of the academic or social ladder face a huge stigma. My company has proof that it does work and since opening, we've had roughly around 500 ex-offenders on our books throughout the years and lost a mere 2% of them back to reoffending, again proving that people do want to work."

Krista Brown, Recruitment Director - the SES GROUP

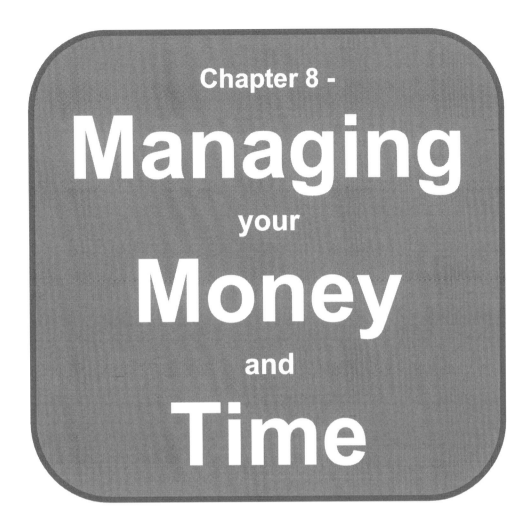

Chapter 8 -
Managing
your
Money
and
Time

"As soon as I took control of my finances and learnt to control my money instead of money controlling me, my anxiety disappeared." NH

Money and **Time** are the two most essential resources that you have.

They are linked together - you can trade one for the other.

As people who are emerging from a personal apocalypse, it is very important for us to understand that good money management (budgeting) and good time management (being organised) are essential if we are to avoid chaotic events and circumstances in future.

Managing Money - Being in Control

Managing your money takes a lot of self-discipline and a determined effort.

Most of us rebel against such levels of control but they are essential if we want to move beyond **'financial fire-fighting'**.

I completely understand how difficult it can be to manage money.

I was brought up in an environment of lack, poverty and second-hand clothes.

I was determined to provide well for my children and give them the abundance that I never had and so I became very successful in business. This led to me being free and easy with money, so much so that I lost control over it. I disrespected it and treated it as 'easy-come, easy-go'. This type of chaos is the opposite of being organised.

Financial laziness is the opposite of self-discipline and it leads to major life problems - in my case, bankruptcy and imprisonment. Ridiculously, I had allowed myself to still be fire-fighting when I had budgets of millions per year, just like I was fire-fighting when I was earning a few hundred pounds a month.

Eventually, after playing at being a big shot for many years, I remembered something that my wise uncle had told me many times, when I was a young boy.

Every time that I saw my uncle Fisel he used to take my hand and say

"Philip, you are a clever boy and I am going to tell you something you must always remember. Listen carefully; yes, you're clever, you will understand. IF you earn £1 and you spend 90p, you will always be happy. IF you earn £1 and you spend £1.10 you will always be miserable. You're a clever boy remember this."

He would then press a coin into my hand to reinforce the message.

Fisel had survived Auschwitz concentration camp and knew what it was like to go without.

He first came to the UK as a refugee aged 17, with just the clothes on his back. He worked for a market trader, then shared a stall with a trader. He progressed further to having his own market stall and eventually he had his own factory, employing almost 100 people and helping them to provide for their families.

Fisel knew about going without, waiting and controlling cash-flow.

Money management is an area where discipline really matters, the discipline to delay purchases, to walk around a supermarket with a calculator (nowadays this is a lot less embarrassing than it used to be because phones have calculators on them!) and to set a budget and stick to it.

Always spend **less** than you **earn**.

If your **upkeep** exceeds your **income,**
then your **outgoings** will be your **downfall**.

Do not overcommit yourself - **next** month's
commitments should be for **less** than **this** month's income.

Planning Overcomes Worry (POW!) because it eliminates fear of the unknown and even if we discover a problem is coming, by knowing about it in advance we can take steps to fix it or make it smaller.

There is nothing that says you should not try to earn more money, of course you should try to legally increase your income and always reach towards your potential.

Give your best efforts to an employer or to your own business. Get the best job you can aspire to at any given time, request pay rises if you believe that you merit them and if self-employed do all you can to legally, ethically and sustainably increase profits.

"I'm open about my past: I broke the law, many times, but I was punished, and I have changed my ways. I've fully left crime behind now, because I wanted to change my life and have got something else to focus on. Staying out of trouble also involves staying away from people I once knew and places I used to hang around."

Derek Jones, founder 'email-a-prisoner' and Director of Social Enterprise SALT academy helping ex-offenders to transform their ideas into businesses.

Planning Cash-flow - 'The Toothbrush Method'

Many individuals worry about bills and many businesses get into financial trouble because they lose control of their cash-flow.

Cash-flow simply means the money in (income) and money out (expenses/ outgoings) of a household or business.

Many of us programme ourselves and our families with sayings like "I can't afford it" or "I don't have the money". This is called using negative self-talk and having a defeatist outlook. It closes our minds to creative ideas and is disempowering (victim mentality).

It is more helpful and more empowering to say, "I am currently working on how I can earn more money", "not just yet" or "we are temporarily under-resourced". Even better if we say "yes, we will definitely be able to achieve that one day - **I will set it as a goal."**

These aspirations and things that we want are within everyone's reach; otherwise they wouldn't be widely available.

Saying "I can't afford it" to yourself is not entirely truthful because you are missing out the key word 'YET'.

You just are not able to pay for it or commit to it **yet**. If you turn this into a goal or a reward however then you could gain just what you need to keep motivated and focussed on the positive and more successful path you have now chosen.

"It is possible to maintain our financial health in the same amount of time it takes to care for your dental health. Our financial health can improve in the same way that our oral hygiene, our wellbeing and confidence improve, by carrying out a simple process for a few minutes each day. Therefore, I call daily cash-flow management and planning - The Toothbrush Method." PM

Yes, it takes just a few minutes each day to monitor and predict your cash-flow.

Sometimes predicting is an estimate - this means a best guess (based on all the information, this is what you think is most likely to happen).

When you are estimating unknown income and expenses it is best to be cautious and plan for the worst-case scenario. This means that estimated expenses should be high estimates and estimated income should be low estimates.

A cashflow forecast is just like a bank statement, but one in which you are predicting the future instead of reading the past.

Consider the chart below. It may be a spread sheet on your computer or phone; it may be entries in a pocket diary or hand drawn on graph paper.

My Predicted INCOME and OUTGOINGS

Predicted Date	Description	Money IN	Money OUT	Money Left (Closing Balance)
16/05/2020	Starting balance			£1200
17/05/2020	**Income 1**	£387		£1587
18/05/2020	Expenses 1		£220	£1367
22/06/2020	**Income 2**	£263		£1630
22/06/2020	Rent		£1500	£130
23/06/2020	**Income 3**	£676		£806
29/06/2020	Expenses 2		£55	£721

We only need to include those dates which show a payment going in or out.

Where I have written income 1, income 2, expenses 1 and expenses 2 etc., you should insert the income or expenses that are relevant to you

e.g.

> **Income 1** may mean **wages** to you,
>
> **Income 2** may mean **tax credits** and
>
> **Expenses 1** may mean **car insurance.**

If we look at this example forecast, we can see that there should be enough money to pay all the bills UNLESS the **rent** is paid before **Income 2** is received on 22/6/2019.

We can now foresee a risk that there may not actually be enough money to make the rent payment and because we can see the risk, we can take steps to plan ahead and avoid a problem.

> In this case we could take either of two avoiding actions.
>
> > 1) We could contact 'Expenses 1' and arrange to pay them on 23/6 instead of the 18/6 (and confirming that there were no consequences in doing so).
> >
> > 2) We could contact 'Income 2' and request the payment a day early if possible.
>
> Either one would ensure that the rent can be paid on time.

This is a bit like driving on a motorway. Looking far enough ahead allows you to take avoiding action if there is a problem.

If you do not look very far ahead, you can't swerve or break in time and you could crash; you certainly have fewer options available to you.

The Toothbrush method is a simple 5 step process:

UPDATE:

1) Update the forecast each day with the closing balance and if you gain more accurate figures on income and outgoings.

INCOME - ask yourself the following questions:

2) How can I increase the money in?

3) Am I able to bring the money in sooner?

4) Am I able to I increase how often the money comes in?

EXPENSES:

5) How can I reduce the money going out?

These 5 steps increase income during any given time period and result in a growth of savings, more security and more peace of mind.

You can practise by using the example template on the next page.

It only takes 28 days to make a habit - A habit of financial planning is a very worthwhile one to cultivate.

"My bad money management was where I went wrong before; I never planned anything and lived to impress everyone else. That pushed me to commit crime. I ended up hurting myself and my family and none of those people I had tried so hard to impress were there for me after I went to prison. I now have less money, I earn less money that I used to 'make' but it is regular, and I manage it better. I always have money now, for day to day essentials and a little bit for emergencies." RS

My Own Predicted INCOME and OUTGOINGS

Predicted Date	Description	Money IN	Money OUT	Money Left (Closing Balance)

"After following this system, I feel more optimistic about my future." TB

Managing Time - Being Organised and Efficient

As people who are emerging from a personal apocalypse, it is very important for us to understand that good time management is essential if we are to avoid chaotic events and circumstances in future.

Managing your time takes a lot of self-discipline and a determined effort. Most of us rebel against such levels of control but they are essential if we want to move beyond being **overwhelmed** and **disorganised**.

I completely understand how difficult it can be to develop the habit of managing your time but I also know that there are two things that really help me to manage my time:

1) **A diary**   <u>and</u>   2) **A 'to-do' list**

1) Your Diary:

All successful people keep a diary or a calendar. Nowadays almost all phones have diaries so that you can plan your days, weeks and months.

Personally, I have kept a pocket diary for 25 years. I always have my pocket diary and a pen everywhere I go. This way I am able to plan ahead, never miss appointments and make the most of opportunities.

2) Your to-do List:

This is also a habit that is widely used by successful people.

Writing tasks down helps you to remember everything and to plan your own time, it also makes you very efficient - you literally achieve a lot more.

Keep your to-do list in your diary during the day and next to your bed at night so that you can plan the next day and write down anything else that you think of to do.

The simple daily and ad-hoc use of a to-do list has been proven to reduce anxiety and stress because Planning Overcomes Worry (POW!).

You can even allocate an estimated amount of time each job will take to do and number them in order of priority. Play around with it and use whatever works for you.

You can use the template ideas on the next page if you like a structure; however, you really just need a pen and paper.

"Since the pen and paper were invented, no one can legitimately use the excuse '*I forgot*'." PM

These success habits take a bit of self-discipline to follow every day; once you have been doing them regularly for a month then the habit becomes instinctive.

You will be proud of the new, organised, version of yourself and you will find that you are achieving a lot more with the same amount of time.

Example to-do Lists

TO DO	TICK
Telephone John Woodward about the job	✓
Update CV with new qualifications	
Finish grant application pack	
Polish shoes	✓
Get new battery for watch	
Renew car insurance	
Check tyre pressures	✓
LESS IMPORTANT ONLY WHEN ENOUGH TIME...	
Book place on next workshop	
Buy Christmas decorations and wrapping paper	
List 3 Beatles records for sale on EBay	

TO DO	Estimated time needed	Order of Priority
Telephone John Woodward about job	15 mins	1
Update CV with new qualifications	15 mins	7
Finish grant application pack	25 mins	6
Polish shoes	10 mins	4
Get new battery for watch	1hr incl parking	3
Check tyre pressures	20 mins	2
Make birthday card for mum	2hrs	5
Renew car insurance before month end	15 mins	8

Avoiding the Pitfalls of Procrastination

Procrastination means avoiding or delaying doing something that you should or must do.

We all do this sometimes; it is usually when we are faced with tasks that are uncomfortable for us or that are unfamiliar to us.

Sometimes we make excuses that other things are more important, and we suddenly must do DIY that we have been delaying or we allow ourselves to get distracted by something less important but that uses up the time.

Have you ever said things like "oh dear, I don't have time now", "I'm too tired now", "I'll do it tomorrow"?

We hope that these tasks (that we know we must do) will somehow get forgotten about, become unnecessary or be done by fairies.

The fact however is that we are just delaying our own progress and success.

Putting something off that you know you should do or that you will have to face up to doing at some point, is the enemy of success - and that is procrastination in a nutshell:

- ➢ It turns excitement into boredom.
- ➢ It turns self-confidence into self-doubt.
- ➢ It turns knowledge into stagnation and irrelevance.
- ➢ It turns dreams and goals into fantasy **and regret**, 'if only'.
- ➢ It turns fun and new ideas into mundane and negative reminders of failure.

Procrastination must be defeated today.

"As soon as I stopped putting things off, I stopped postponing my own results. I realised that I had become my own worst enemy. I adopted the Nike slogan and started to just do it. Within 3 months I progressed to a new job, within 2 more months I became temporary supervisor. Just do it!" HE

I have identified 10 Pitfalls of Procrastination which you must avoid and 10 corresponding ways to push forwards.

When you know that there could be a pitfall or pothole ahead, then you know what to look out for.

An individual may experience one or more of the pitfalls at any given time; they will not all apply to you at the same time but I am sure you will recognise some of them!

1) Procrastinators may be perfectionists.

They feel a need to increase their skill or knowledge before attempting or doing something.

They are not sure how it is going to turn out and they do not want to do something that is not perfect. These people think that everything they do has got to be the best.

You can overcome this by understanding that any worthwhile project **WILL NEVER BE PERFECT** and that it will always be evolving.

A start is all that is needed.

Just like building a website, start with a few pages and gradually grow it and add to it. Do not give in to perfectionism and let it freeze you in your tracks.

Just make a good start NOW!

2) Procrastinators are waiting for inspiration or head space.

Overcome this by just sitting down and start writing or typing, write down pros and cons if you are delaying a decision.

Stop all other distractions, turn the TV off, close all other internet tabs and just start getting your thoughts out.

Carry a pad and pen everywhere, so you can make notes, empty your head throughout the day. Keep your note pad by your bed at night so that you can write down ideas delivered from your subconscious as it problem solves during your sleep.

Writing things down helps to clear your head and create perspective.

Start writing your thoughts down and carry a pad and pen around.

3) Procrastinators are reluctant to ask for the help they need.

Some people put things off because they are not sure **what to do** and need to ask for help but are embarrassed or unsure about asking.

If you are stuck or not sure what to do, ask for help.

Do not let pride get in the way, ask for help.

Save time, energy and stress ASK FOR HELP.

4) Procrastinators are lazy, too comfortable or not motivated enough to do what is necessary.

Being comfortable will not serve you, avoid complacency or being too proud.

Choose a couple of big dreams and goals; really try, try as if you mean it. You can do so much more than you think.

Break out of you comfort zone. Get used to being uncomfortable in pursuit of your goals, laugh a bit, embarrass yourself a bit.

Find something that really moves you and gets you excited, follow your heart and embrace the things that you love to do, not just what other people expect you to do.

If your sofa is getting worn out, your TV remote batteries are running low and you're feeling unmotivated then **get a new dream and set some new goals towards it.**

5) Procrastinators have no sense of urgency.

"I'll do it tomorrow", "I'll get around to it", becomes the type of things they say regularly, almost like their default response.

Winners overcome this by setting themselves targets and deadlines.

None of us know how long we have or what's around the corner. If you put off doing things, life can slap you with a great big monstrous priority and you lose the chance to do it at all.

If there is something that you must do, you want to do, or you want the result, then either

Set aside a time slot to do it in your diary or **do it now.**

If you won't do either of these two things, you are just kidding yourself- that is never going to happen really.

"Someone said to me: 'If you want to change some things in your life, you need to change some things in your life.' It sounds obvious but this was the reminder that I needed to take personal responsibility for my own journey and the direction that I want the rest of my life to take." LR

6) **Procrastinators are afraid and particularly fearful** of the next steps.

They often think that if they complete this task it will result in more things to do and more being expected of them.

Once you have achieved something, what comes next?

Fear of the unknown is one of the biggest fears.

Will more be expected of me? Will it be uncomfortable? Will I lose control?

What if this happens? What if that happens?

Overcome these fears by doing three things:

i) Increasing your knowledge.

Accurate information eliminates fear.

Learn more about what will happen next so that nothing will be left to chance or unknown.

Research and learn more about the thing that you are worrying about.

Facing the facts head on is the opposite of our natural instincts to bury our head in the hand or retreat into our cosy comfort zone (Snail shell syndrome!)

ii) Treat each task or stage separately.

Box them off. When you start worrying about the next steps, deliberately isolate each step and work on just one step at a time.

Remind yourself that Rome was not built in a day, stairs are climbed one step at a time, and you can cross each bridge as you come to it.

iii) Beat fear with positive self-talk.

Any time your imagination goes into overdrive with questions of "what if this happen? oh dear they will need this? Will I be expected to do? hit back with positive self-talk.

Just tell yourself **"I'll Handle It"**, **"I'll Handle It"**, **"I'll Handle It"** in response. (With gratitude to Susan Jeffers, Author, *'Feel the Fear and Do It Anyway'*)

Sometimes I even say something forceful to myself like *"shut up! You're not meant to doubt yourself, you're meant to be your own biggest cheerleader."*

"I used to be full of self-doubt. The more I put things off and avoided taking positive steps, the guiltier I was feeling and the more I saw myself as a failure. It was important to me to stop making excuses. It was the excuses that had kept me stuck where I was." DP

7) Procrastinators don't have enough time for themselves.

They begrudge doing anything else.

They feel pulled in a lot of different directions and out of control.

The key to this is to **switch off sometimes.**

I found an illustration of this in a waterfall in my garden pond.

Sometimes I walk out there and notice that the waterfall has become a set of tiny dribbles, trickling down, instead of a free-flowing feature. This trickle is the result of the big pump being clogged with rotting leaves and sediment. The solution is not as complicated I originally thought. I used to put a wading suit on, get into the freezing water and unclog the pump by hand.

In fact, all I do now is switch it off for five minutes.

I turn the pump off at the socket, leave it for a short while and flick it back on again. Bubbles float up, the sediment and leaves float away, the air pocket unclogs the pump and the waterfall BURSTS INTO LIFE.

If you are not being as productive as you could be, switch off sometimes.

If you think you have a massive task ahead of you, switch off sometimes.

If you feel clogged up with the rubbish that life has thrown at you, switch off sometimes

Switch off and then see your own personal life's waterfall burst into life.

You can burst into life again, meeting your potential to be productive, attractive, appealing and energised.

Switch off sometimes. You deserve it.

"Learn from the past but do not dwell too much on your regrets or past mistakes. Be strong enough of mind to keep focussed on the future and on positive goals. Get yourself a job or start a new enterprise like I did, even if it is not ideal it is certainly better than crime and imprisonment and you will at least have a chance of a good life." SA

8) Procrastinators blame ill health or physical limitations.

A lot of people going through life suffer and are victims of ill health or tragic circumstances but being a victim does not mean you have to stay a victim.

There are so many examples of inspiring people who have suffered or still endure health challenges.

If you are a victim, look for inspiring examples and copy them to **create a victory.**

There are people who have overcome everything that you have suffered and more. They use their anger, pain and problems as motivation to spur them on to achieve and to help and inspire other people.

You can too. **Change from being a Victim to a Victor**

9) Procrastinators over promise.

They told someone they would do something "on the spur of the moment" and later they wish they hadn't committed to it.

They go through life saying YES to people and becoming both overwhelmed and overcommitted. The solution to this is to **learn to say NO.**

Develop a few key phrases which will help, such as:

- "I am currently working on some pressing matters."
- "Sorry I have a previous commitment so won't be able to make it."
- "I won't commit to that because I am very focused at the moment on..."
- "I would love to help but my time is at a premium at the moment, so I won't commit to that right now".

Learn to say NO to those demands made on your time which are not relevant to your goals.

10) Procrastinators have poor or non-existent time management.

The newest demand is always their priority; they get pulled from pillar to post, without achieving much.

The solution to this is to **treat your time as currency** and track it, just like you budget your money or have a cashflow forecast you could have a time-flow forecast; certainly, a diary or calendar will make a huge difference.

Keep a simple diary and develop the habit of planning your time. Where is your own **TO DO list**, right now? (See pages 298 - 299). This is one of the simplest productivity tools that all high achievers use. With this they can plan their time, prioritise, delegate from and focus.

Decide on a simple way of managing your time and use it.

Try your best to stop making excuses. It is up to us to take responsibility for our lives. It is not solely your employer, your spouse, your environments or the governments fault. It is disempowering to blame anyone else for lack of achievement or lack of opportunity. There are opportunities all around.

Look in the mirror and take responsibility. If nothing else be honest with yourself and say, "I don't want it badly enough to overcome my fears, to defeat my self-doubts, to try a new approach, to embrace the new successful me, I don't want it badly enough to break out of my comfort zone!"

Winners in live accept full responsibility for where they are now and for where they are going to be 3, 6 or 12 months from now. **START RIGHT NOW!**

10 Pitfalls of Procrastination	**10 Action Steps to Take**
Expecting perfection.	Just make a good start NOW!
Waiting for inspiration or head space.	Start writing your thoughts down and carry a pad and pen around.
Reluctant to ask for help when it is needed.	Ask for help NOW!
Lazy, comfortable or not motivated enough.	Get a new dream and set some new goals towards it.
No sense of urgency.	Set aside a time slot to do it in your diary or do it now.
Afraid of the next steps.	Increase your knowledge. Deal with each stage separately. Beat fear with positive self-talk.
Don't have enough personal time.	Switch off Sometimes.
Blames ill health or physical limitations.	Change from being a Victim to a Victor.
Over promises.	Practise saying NO to extra demands on your time.
Poor or non-existent time management.	Decide on a simple way of managing your time and stick to it.

Chapter 9 -
Grants for Education, Training and Employment

"We read about the appalling situations in many prisons; drugs, violence and not enough staff so people are left locked up with no fresh air. Then of course after release prisoners have to build a new life. There are two main issues, the development (or redevelopment) of personal relationships and finding work. We who live in the UK are a community, we have got to respect each other, forgive each other and support each other."

The Rt. Hon. Lord Wilson, Patron of the Hardman Trust and Justice of the Supreme Court of the United Kingdom

Applying for Grants

When leaving prison, most people have very little financial resources.

The single discharge grant of £46 does not and cannot last until the first pay check or benefit claim comes in. It is apparent in these circumstances that help is needed to get through those first challenging few weeks and months.

I strongly recommend that you seek help at the earliest possible opportunity from family and friends, resettlement departments and charities.

Money management is one of the seven pathways of resettlement identified by the Ministry of Justice as essential to reduce reoffending and all resettlement prisons are expected to provide help in this area. Some establishments provide the opportunity for prisoners in the last twelve months of their sentence to work full-time at pre-approved companies prior to release (with a 40% deduction from net earnings going to victim support charities). Unfortunately, most prisoners do not get these resettlement privileges and are released from closed conditions with little or no preparation prior to release.

Even if you cannot get to an open prison however, you can still begin writing letters to employers, agencies, charities, councils and DWP prior to your actual release.

A copy of 'The Hardman Directory' is available in each prison library. This is a fantastic resource which lists the main charities helping prisoners and ex-offenders.

Grants and support are available for a wide range of purposes including education, training courses, clothing, tools and mentoring and others give helpful information, advice and guidance. You are not on your own; there are a lot of committed people and organisations who want to help.

Most charities that make awards ask for a personal statement to support each application for funding. This will need to be posted as a letter or pasted into an online form. This is where your Personal Disclosure Statement (chapter 3) serves a second purpose.

"I followed the instructions and with a few small changes my Personal Disclosure Statement became a personal statement with which I could apply to charities. I received funding to attend a ten-day Personal Track Safety course and gained a nationally recognised Railway Infrastructure qualification - NVQ Level 3 Diploma in Engineering and Technology. This will make a huge difference to my employment. My future is clear and more secure thanks to this template and instructions" BE

You have already done the work once and now your Personal Disclosure Statement (PDS), with a few slight changes to the first and last paragraphs, can make an excellent Personal Grant Statement (PGS). The changes we need to make are explained below.

'Grant Builder' - Creating a Personal Statement for Grant Applications

Following these 10 steps will lead to the creation of a sincere, professional and effective Personal Grant Statement (PGS) to support applications which you make to charities.

IMPORTANT: Before following these instructions, you will need to have completed 'Disclosure Builder' on pages 86 - 112.

The first time you follow this 10-step process it should take around 10 - 15 minutes. Each new PGS should be addressed to the charity and these amendments will usually take less than 5 - 10 minutes each time. Of course, any time that you invest in creating your PGS is time well spent!

Examples of successful PGS are included on pages 315 - 317.

Step 1, Contact Details	Type your personal details in the top right corner. **If you are currently in prison** - then use your prison number, prison address and no telephone number or email address. **If you are at home, or shortly returning home** - then use your home address, home telephone number and an email address. There are many easy and free email services such as Outlook and Gmail. Ensure that your email address is clear and professional so that it makes a good impression such as firstname.lastname@serviceprovider.com.	*Name* *Address* *Postcode* *Telephone* *Email* *1st January 2020*

Step 2, Charity Details	On the left-hand side and slightly lower than your address, insert the charity name and address e.g.
	
	    Example C.H.A.R.I.T.Y.
	    Example Address
	    Example Town
	    Example Postcode	

Step 3, Subject & Greeting	On the left-hand side begin the letter with the following text: *Re: Personal statement in support of my application.* *To whom it may concern* *Dear Sir/ Madam,*	

		Begin your letter with the following sentence:
Step 4, Introduction and what you are applying for	**When complete the sentence will look similar to these examples**	*I am applying to _____ (insert name of charity) for financial assistance because _____ (insert what you need the money for and the benefit you will gain).*
		I have applied to Example charity for funding because gaining a HGV1 licence will ensure that I am employed after my release from prison.
		I have applied to Example charity for funding because completing a Gas Safe course will increase my chances of employment now that I am released from prison.
		I have applied to Example charity for funding because completing the 5 week 'GET TO GAS' course will mean my criminal record will be less of a barrier to employment.
		I have applied to Example charity for funding because gaining my driving licence will make a substantial difference to my employment; something which has been hard for me since I left prison.
		I have applied to Example charity for financial assistance because I have been advised that attending a 5 Day Forward Tipping Dumper Truck course with example training leads to permanent employment.
		I have applied to Example charity for funding to enable me to study the Level 1 course "Introduction to Sport and Fitness" (E117) with the Open University which will help me to begin a career I am very interested in.
		I have applied for funding to enable me to study "IET Wiring Regulations (Electa course)". In this letter I would like to explain why I have chosen this course and confirm that I will be entirely committed to its fulfilment.
		I have applied to example trust for financial assistance because gaining a driving licence will greatly increase my chances of employment and also help me to be a more involved father to my young son and daughter.
		I have applied to Example charity for funding because I believe that attending a ten-day Personal Track Safety course with ARC Rail Training will greatly increase my chances of employment upon release from prison.
		I have applied to Example charity for a <u>*Watercolour Pack*</u> *because art has been proven to be therapeutic for me. I also believe that I have a talent in this area and may be able to build a career, or even work part-time as an artist.*

"My personal statement allowed me to express how helpful getting a grant would be in managing my mental health challenges; this led to my grant application being successful. Thank you." RE

		Write a sentence or paragraph about your motivation, work ethic and track record of gaining qualifications or completing projects.
Step 5, Your commitment and motivation	**Examples of motivation**	*I am hardworking and determined to get a full-time job and turn my life around.*
		I am excited at the thought of qualifying as a railway engineer and have a high degree of motivation.
		The PTS qualification leads to long term secure employment. There are several employers recruiting graduates directly from the course.
		I would like to confirm that I will be entirely committed to completing this course and I would become qualified immediately prior to my release.
		I have the skills, ability and motivation to qualify as a railway engineer and this would be a good career because it will give me stability and security.
		I am highly motivated as you will discover from my story below. I am a hardworking person and I never make excuses but always follow through on tasks to completion.
		I know that I have the ability and determination to be a lorry driver and that this would be a good career for me because I will always have work and will be able to work overtime on top of full-time hours.
		I have lots of experience of driving dumper trucks earlier in my career, but I have no current licence. Not having a licence is a barrier to employment and removing this barrier opens many employers to me.
		There is a lot of employment available to people who have gained the PTS qualification. I do have a friend who is a manager within a railway company; I have been assured of a job with his firm once I am qualified.
		I have gained a Forklift truck licence and Construction Skills Certification Scheme (CSCS) card so that I can go straight onto site to work. I have an excellent work ethic and I am also a keen and enthusiastic student.
		I am qualified in Street-works Road Maintenance, Excavation and Reinstatement and I will shortly be gaining my Construction Skills Certification Scheme (CSCS) card so that I can go straight onto site to work.
		I have a lot of previous work experience and I am particularly hoping to gain a placement working with young people at risk of criminal activity. Being able to drive is an essential requirement of my future employment.

311

Step 5, Your commitment and motivation (continued)	**Further examples of motivation**	*I have previous experience of driving a forklift truck in the Army, but I have never been licensed to do it outside of the army. I have the ability to become a forklift truck driver in a commercial setting but just need a formal qualification.*
		*I have worked hard throughout my time in prison and **I attach my CV** so you can see that as well as gaining other work qualifications (such as CSCS card), I have also studied to gain numeracy and literacy qualifications, making up for the education I missed when I was younger.*
		I have already gained a qualification in track renewals but have yet to gain the Sentinel card and the further modules which I would gain from the Personal Track Safety Course. I have qualified in the use of small plant tools including Rail Drill, Strimmer, Generator, Chainsaw, Cobra TT, Brush Cutter and Impact Wrench.
		I have gained a number of associated qualifications which will support me in this career pathway including: Nuco training Level 3 Award in First Aid at Work (RQF) Vehicle Banksman Certificate of Completed Safety Training, Valid Construction Skills Certification Scheme (CSCS) card and Location and Avoidance of Underground Apparatus using Cable Avoidance Tool (CAT) and Genny.
		I sent my CV to many potential employers and was invited to attend an interview with Everyone Active (EA), who own multiple sports centres which went brilliantly. I was offered employment as a lifeguard. I am qualified in Fitness and Physical Activity and this lifeguard role comes with extra training, which builds on my qualifications. I have worked hard to build a relationship with this potential employer who has gone out of their way to help and support me. She was moved by my story and believes in me. My disclosure letter was honest and detailed, and she cares enough to give me a brilliant opportunity, an opportunity that could change my life. Travel to this work placement will take 2 hours each way by bus and train. If I gain my driving licence through your support with the cost of lessons and I buy a vehicle from my early wages, the journey time will more than halve, leaving me a lot more time available for my Open University studies. I am on my third year of a BA (Hons) in Sports Fitness and Management, which is my gateway to additional progress in my career.

"I am so pleased that a charity agreed to pay for my training. My career had stagnated, and I was left behind but with this I can bring my CV up to date and I already have a job offer conditional on completing the course." AY

Step 6, Relevance to rehabilitation and resettlement	Link the request to your rehabilitation and resettlement	
	Write a paragraph similar to these examples	*There are many employers in this field and a national shortage of suitably qualified workers.*
		I have contacted a number of potential employers and several have expressed an interest in employing me once I gain a full driving licence.
		I have a formal offer of employment, conditional on me gaining this qualification and I enclose the confirmation letter with my application.
		I have been a professional courier driver before; I have enjoyed the work and know that I would be able to build a career in this industry.
		I have shown a great deal of positivity, persistence and determination to secure this opportunity; it is my guarantee of never coming back to prison.
		There is a huge amount of work available for qualified excavator operators and in this industry my criminal record wouldn't be a barrier to employment.
		I have informal offers of employment which will require me to drive and also maintaining my family ties will be made possible once I am able to drive.
		Employment will stop me reoffending. I know that if I am permanently employed then I will have neither the reason, nor the desire, to commit crime. Having a job on release will give me a focus and a legitimate income.
		Paying for lessons would be out of my reach without support from you. I am hard working and in good health. Employment and staying free of drugs and (which I am determined to do) will help me never to reoffend.
		Gaining my Gas Safe qualification will give me access to a wide range of career opportunities. There is currently a national shortage of gas safe engineers and in this industry, I would be unhindered by my criminal record. I am hardworking and in good health.
		I have contacted a number of potential employers and have been greatly encouraged by the replies. All have assured me that that I will be able to gain long term secure employment with the PTS qualification. In this industry my criminal record will be less of a barrier to employment.

"I followed 'Grant Builder' and I just received combined funding from Thomas Wall Trust and St Giles Trust which enables me to complete my Construction Plant Competence Scheme (CPCS) A58 360° Excavator training. This costs £1560 altogether and there was no way I could have gained this licence on my own. I am grateful to the charities and also to Phil for the guidance on creating the personal statement. Excavator operators are in huge demand and I will always have work in future." JG

Step 7 Disclosure	Copy your text from *Disclosure Builder* stages 4 - 13 (pages 86 - 112) for the main body of your letter.
Step 8 Feedback	Insert a sentence similar to the following: *If I am accepted for an award, I will provide feedback to you throughout the process and in the future as I progress towards the positive goals I have now set. Thank you for your kind consideration of my application.*
Step 9 Sign-off	Insert the following: *Yours faithfully,* *John Smith BA (Hons)* (Your own full name and any qualification letters)
Step 10 Signature	Sign in-between: Yours faithfully, *Sign Here* Your name

Congratulations on working through this process!

Your Personal grant statement should now be comparable to the examples on the following pages.

"For me, it wasn't just the gift of money to pay for a provisional driving licence, theory test and driving lessons. It is the understanding that there are some kind and generous people in society who care about me. They believed in me and they certainly don't think that I am worthless after all. Doing my driving lessons on ROTL has also given me something constructive to look forward to and helped me to cope with these last few months of my prison sentence better" NN

Example PGS 1

The Belief Fund
Community House
MK91 1AO

Charles Change
Hope Prison
Any town,
AB1 2CD

12th September 2019

Re: Personal Statement in support of my application for a grant.

Dear Sir/ Madam,

I have applied to the belief fund for financial assistance because I have been advised by my former employer that attending a £522 'Vector-works' Computer Aided Design course will be a real pathway into secure employment. I would be unable to fund this myself without your support. I am a qualified and experienced interior designer and before my imprisonment I was highly recommended for plans and three-dimensional drawings. If I become skilled and qualified in vector works, I will be able to re-enter work without being adversely affected by my time out of the industry.

I have a track record of dedicating myself to my studies having achieved a B.A. Hons Degree, Interior Design-London College of Communication. I have a personal enthusiasm for graphic design particularly within interior spaces. I have seen the powerful effects that changing an interior space has on the mood and productivity of the occupants.

I would like to share some background about myself and how I came to prison for possession with intent to supply Class A drugs. I had looked up to some drug dealers who were doing well materially, and I got involved in their dealing to provide for myself and my young family whilst I was studying. After a while I became greedy and I didn't have the strength of will to stop what appeared to be easy money and which appeared to be victimless. Predictably I got caught and arrested. The shock of being arrested and charged was like awakening after a bad dream. I actually needed it to stop this criminal path I was on. I demonstrated that I accepted responsibility by pleading guilty and I was genuinely remorseful. Having completed a victim awareness programme, I know that my so-called victimless crime, drug-dealing, is not a victimless crime at all. In fact, it hurts the users, it hurts society and it hurt my family so much that we separated. I do regret my crimes and I have learnt many lessons, I still have much to give back to the employer who gives me an opportunity to work for them.

I intend to build a productive life and put the past behind me. I will be released in August 2020 to my home area of Bognor Regis, Sussex. In the meantime, because of my excellent conduct whilst in prison, I reside in open prison conditions. I intend to contribute to the community as a decent and law-abiding citizen again. Thank you for your kind consideration.

Yours faithfully,

Charlie Change

Charles Change

Example PGS 2

Art Smith
12 The Willows
Fresh End
Sea Town
5th October 2019

Prison Art Project Manager
Example charity
Example Street
Dumfries
Scotland
SC1 20T

Ref: Letter in support of application form for an art pack.

Dear Sir/ Madam,

I have applied to *Example charity* for a watercolour pack because art has been proven to be very therapeutic for me.

I also believe that I have a talent in this area and that I may eventually be able to build a career, or even work part-time as an artist.

I would like to take this opportunity to tell you about myself and how I ended up hurting someone. My dad was a violent and cruel man and he treated my mum and I terribly. When I was 9 years old, they were going to separate and they asked me who I wanted to live with, I feared my dad's reaction and so I stayed with my dad.

Unfortunately, the next four years were characterised by abuse and neglect often resulting in me having to stay in the garden all night or being left alone with nothing for dinner but biscuits. I didn't see my mum for four years and felt unwanted. My mum did eventually come back for me and I lived with her and my step-dad who was like a proper father to me.

My childhood did affect me a lot, the violence and isolation caused me to have some mental health challenges including anxiety and agoraphobia. I thought that I had overcome these when I began to live a normal life working as an apprentice bricklayer and in other job roles. Work has always been a good focus for me and helped me to stay level headed.

I was managing well and beginning to live a normal life when my step-dad unexpectedly passed away. This bought back all those feelings of loss and confusion and my mental health worsened.

I was prescribed anti-psychotic medication, but I was not advised by my doctor to avoid alcohol. I should have known this, but I was only 19 years old and didn't realise the potentially catastrophic effects of drinking whilst on such medication.

I was hardly aware of what happened that night, but I had gone to a pub and when I walked into the beer garden, I threw my pint glass. It hit a man and hurt him badly. Afterwards, I went home and passed out. Within a day or two there were appeals on social media to find the man who had thrown the glass.

When I saw these appeals, I knew that I had to do the right thing and hand myself in. I telephoned the police and surrendered myself to the police station. I was so very sorry for what I did. I was granted bail and I felt so very low that before my trial, I did try to take my own life.

Despite my defence providing medical reports showing that I was not in a fit mental state I still pleaded guilty in court and accepted full responsibility.

When I came to prison, I decided to use my experiences to help others. A large percentage of the prison population have mental health challenges, many studies put the figure at around 1/3 of the prison population. With this in mind, I worked hard to study, and I gained an NHS qualification in Mental Health Awareness. I learnt about anxiety, depression, eating disorders, schizophrenia, bi-polar and personality disorders. I then provided information, advice and guidance and a large amount of support to sufferers as part of a pastoral care team.

I have completed other personal development courses and achieved vocational qualifications. I am still on my continuous journey of self-improvement and learning to leave the past in the past. I carry a lot of shame and sadness for how I hurt my victim and I intend to live a much better life contributing to society and making up for what I did wrong.

Thank you for your kind consideration of this request.

Yours faithfully,

Art J Smith

Art Smith

"By following this guide to creating my personal grant statement, I have just been awarded the money to study the vector-works design software package. I can now have the confidence to get the work I originally wanted as a designer." JM

"Ex-offenders need help; a leg up to get back into society. If you release them with a few quid in their pocket and no prospects, what do you expect? I'm not condoning it, but that's the vicious cycle these guys are in. They need business leaders to recognise that, intervene and give them another chance in life." Gary Rosewell, Proprietor, Total Ship Services

Chapter 10 -
Closing Thoughts

Providing jobs for ex-prisoners does more to reduce crime than providing the same jobs for non-offenders. (Source: Crime and Unemployment; D. Dickinson, University of Cambridge)

"Compassion is not something that is earned by the recipient; it is something that is freely given by the giver. Humanity is not earned; it is something that all human beings must be shown, lest we lose our own humanity. C.H.A.R.I.T.Y. could stand for <u>C</u>ompassion and <u>H</u>umanity for <u>A</u>ll, <u>R</u>egardless of <u>I</u>mprisonment or <u>T</u>rouble <u>Y</u>esterday." PM

It beggar's belief that, as part of funding cuts, an important resettlement service, *'National Careers Service'* was completely closed in prisons in early 2018.

Unemployment is a root cause of many personal problems and negatively impacts on so many other aspects of their life.

Unemployed ex-offenders are 1.5 times more likely to be problematic drug users than employed ex-offenders.	**The reoffending rate is more than twice as high for offenders without employment after release compared to those with employment.**

(Source: MOJ Impact of employment on re-offending Propensity Matching)

Employment brings numerous benefits to prisoners and society, it provides:

- Stability, structure and routine.
- Dramatic reductions in problematic drug use.
- Improvement to self-esteem and a sense of purpose.
- Demonstrable reductions in reoffending and the creation of victims.
- Legitimate and regular income which allows people to budget and plan.
- Crime free support network and a feeling of acceptance and belonging.
- For employers, a sizeable workforce of hardworking and appreciative people.

"Having a job normalises people and their lives and this is exactly what we want to happen to ex-offenders so that they can become productive and fulfilled members of society who want to, and do, follow rules and remain crime free." PM

Companies which make the decision to employ ex-offenders, report without exception, that it was a good decision for both the employer and employee.

Under current systems and processes, prison and the stigma of a criminal record, statistically result in people who want to work (and who are in the habit of work) being unable to access the labour market.

25% of people are unemployed when admitted to prison	**HOWEVER** **85% of people are unemployed 12 months after release**	**AND** **50% remain unemployed 24 months after release**

(Source: MOJ 2013 - 2019 compilation figures)

These shocking statistics are despite that fact that
81% of prisoners look for employment upon release.
(Source: 'Prisoners' Work & Vocational Training' by Frances H Simon)

'UPON RELEASE' should ring alarm bells because the timing of starting employment matters almost as much as the act of gaining employment.

Most people are released from prison with a single grant of just £46 and a travel pass, and they must wait for benefit claims or for a first month's salary.

Only 6% of people leaving prison receive support to find competitive work. (Source: Centre for Mental Health, From Prison to Work report 2018)

People should begin work at the earliest possible opportunity, either before release or shortly after it, both for financial reasons and also to keep people engaged in purposeful activity. The more seamless we can make this employment transition; the more successful people will be upon release and the more we will reduce reoffending.

"It would be beneficial if employers and prisons worked together to create pathways and opportunities for future employment. There is a large population that have few opportunities open to them, but they want to work and with some guidance they could be a value to society. If training providers, employers and prisons all communicated then everyone would benefit. Without input from companies the likelihood of people reoffending will increase as more people face exclusion from the labour market. We need joined up thinking and working relationships with employers." TD, former prisoner with 18 years' experience in prison

I now urge all Prison Governors to:

> 1) Increase the availability and the instances of temporary release (ROTL) for interviews, training placements and full-time work prior to release. *(Update: This is now in progress - July 2019).*

> 2) Help those prisoners who are preparing for release to also prepare for employment. This means providing employability courses, interview coaching and practical help to create CVs and Personal Disclosure Statements.

> 3) Build relationships with employers to increase the number of academies and training opportunities in prison. Prisons provide numerous skills and qualifications but those links and any clear routes to employment usually stop at the prison gates.

These initiatives would be at <u>nil net cost</u> because prisons deduct a 40% levy from wages paid to serving prisoners who are employed by external companies.

Additionally, I would urge the Government to:

1) Provide incentives to employers who employ ex-offenders, through favourable tax relief or waiver of employer national insurance contributions.

2) Amend the Rehabilitation of Offenders Act, so that all convictions become spent when all orders are completed and when the licence period is spent.

3) Require probation to actively support ex-offenders into employment by forging links with local employers and agencies and to advocate on behalf of the people in their 'care'/ under their supervision.

4) Place responsibility for enforcement of 'right to be forgotten' requests within the remit of the Information commissioner. In this way, Google and historic news sites should not continue to be a huge barrier to employment for people whose crimes were committed many decades earlier, who have completed their licence and who are deemed to no longer present a risk.

These initiatives would also be at <u>nil net cost</u> because employed ex-offenders become financial contributors through taxation, rather than being dependant on benefits. They will be able to contribute to the economy rather than be a drain on it.

It costs an average of £37,000pa to keep someone in prison.	**The national cost of re-offending is currently £16 Billion a year.**

(Source: MOJ June 2019)

By any calculation, £16,000,000,000 is many times the cost of rehabilitating and supporting people to stop them wanting to (or thinking they need to), reoffend.

Allowing people in prison to begin to rebuild their lives having learnt from their crimes, or to begin to build a crime-free life for the first time, will save society many multiples of what it would cost.

Quotes, Memory-aids and Acronyms

"Phil Martin has a unique way of explaining things and when he talks, people listen, you can hear a pin drop." HMP Custodial Manager

Quotes and Sound-Bites

It is my intention that these quotations are clear and concise and that they ease understanding.

They may be republished and shared, subject to you attributing them to:

'Phil Martin, Author - 'How to get a great job when you have a criminal record'.

I hope you have enjoyed this book and found it insightful, thank you for buying it; I hope you found it interesting enough to warrant buying further books in the series!

The meaning of life is to create meaning in your life.
Forgiveness and reconciliation are possible in an enlightened society.
The most progressive attitude to have is to treat every day as a school day.
It is possible to turn Devastation and Despair into Optimism and Opportunity.
You cannot RESTORE rational thought, until you REMOVE emotional distress.
Your CV is probably the most important personal document that you will ever create.
Leave any feelings of shame or anger in the past; these will not help you in the future.
As ex-offenders, we can either: **be** the statistics or **beat** the statistics and build a better life.
The biggest distance you will ever have to travel is to turn around and face a different direction.
The concept of Rehabilitative Culture can only work if we believe that everyone's life is of value.
Rehabilitation and reconciliation must replace retribution, if we are going to reduce reoffending.
We can either: **see** the opportunity or **seize** the opportunity to help people to change for the better.
Remind yourself of this simple acronym POW! - which stands for **P**lanning **O**vercomes **W**orry.
I believe that helping people to change for the better is one of the most worthwhile things you can ever do.
Revenge and Retribution are not justice; Remorse, Responsibility, Rehabilitation and Reconciliation are justice.
Whether we like those people in prison or not is not relevant to whether we should help them, not relevant at all.
Rehabilitation is a process that only happens when it is supported by people, organisations and communities and by society as a whole.
A deficiency in skills with people is responsible, long-term, for more social isolation, depression and poverty than any external circumstances will ever be.

The ultimate goal of Rehabilitative Culture is for people to be personally improved by the prison experience, to be better citizens when they leave.
Our country should feel desperately ashamed at how we still spit people out unwanted and virtually unsupported after giving their all in military service.
The purpose of prison should be intuitively aimed at release day - a day when a successfully rehabilitated citizen is returned to an accepting community.
Rehabilitative Culture is not complicated; it simply needs to support all of the 7 pathways of resettlement and point towards them in every way possible.
Significantly more help must be given to support the gradual reintegration of people released from prison, particularly those who have served long sentences.
It is those people who have lived experience of the Criminal Justice System who know the most effective ways to rehabilitate criminals and resettle ex-offenders.
Surely prison should be a last resort? Imprisonment is palliative; it merely manages and masks the symptoms of crime, whereas rehabilitation provides the cure.
Our prison system in this country is only doing one thing and that thing is making people worse. Prison is terrible, it really does not help people, BUT IT COULD.
Having a job is a massive risk reducer. Unemployment is a proven trigger that increases the likelihood of relapse for both problematic drug use and also crime.
The judgmental days full of hatred for criminals and their families must be relegated to the past if we are to end the cycles of **A**nger, **B**itterness, **C**rime and **D**estruction.
The Justice System needs very long term thinking but frustratingly, few people of influence think or care, more than one electoral cycle or one cabinet reshuffle ahead.
If all the 5 R's of change - Remorse, Reasons, Responsibility, Rehabilitation and Reconciliation, are adopted by an individual, then change can be as permanent as if it was set in concrete.
Most people in prison want to change but they need help and support to do it. Those who are chained by habit cannot usually break those chains on their own; people need help and support to change.
In order to reduce the likelihood of re-offending, our prisons need to be places of healing, not places where people are traumatised and released with poorer mental health or new mental illness.
Nowadays, with the help of modern technology, virtually all criminals will get caught, without question. It is just a matter of time. Not if, but when. *Forensic Footprints* and *Digital DNA* are everywhere.
I define a Rehabilitative Culture as one which encourages and supports positive change and personal growth at every opportunity, and which empowers people to enjoy law-abiding, productive and fulfilling lives.
Rehabilitation manifests in reduced reoffending rates and the creation of fewer victims. If we are committed to rehabilitation, then we need to capture detailed information. We cannot improve what we do not measure.

Having a job normalises people and their lives. Normalisation is exactly what we want to happen to ex-offenders so that they can become productive and fulfilled members of society who want to, and do, follow rules and remain crime free.

ABC - Attitude, Behaviour, Consequences. Attitudes and Behaviour create Consequences. Those same Consequences then re-affect Attitude and Behaviour. The cycle spirals for better or worse until or unless, we consciously change our habitual ways of thinking and behaving.

It is a fallacy that our prisons house the very worst people in society. In fact, our prisons are full of Damaged, Disadvantaged and Disillusioned people - some of the most vulnerable in society. These 'D's are kept alongside a small minority of the worst people we hear so much about.

In order for them not to contribute to a worsening re-offending rate, modern prisons must become centres for rehabilitation and positive change. Prisons should heal people and help them to gain pride and self-worth, to feel that they can contribute and thrive, unique and valuable as they are.

Prison is a temporary home for all but the 75 prisoners serving natural life terms; the other 82,600 will all one day become eligible for release. The simple question is: *Do we want these people to be more or less likely to re-offend; more or less likely to create victims of crime, after their release?*

"Don't let it change you" **is not** good advice. Life's experiences and lessons are meant to change you, we are meant to be learning and growing all the time. You must let the storms of life change you. Just bear in mind that like a pebble in the sea, those same storms can either GRIND YOU DOWN or POLISH YOU UP.

Traumatic events in our lives can act like a ball and chain, keeping us stuck and holding us back, long after the events themselves have finished. Difficult life experiences leave many of us with low self-esteem, little confidence, guilt and fear. BUT no matter what has happened in your past, you can have a fulfilling future.

Compassion is not something that is earned by the recipient; it is something that is freely given by the giver. Humanity is not earned; it is something that all human beings must be shown, lest we lose our own humanity. C.H.A.R.I.T.Y. could stand for Compassion and Humanity for All, Regardless of Imprisonment or Trouble Yesterday.

Few people acknowledge that prison destroys a person's life. If we do not help, support and empower them to build a new positive crime-free life on solid foundations, then they will inevitably be released into chaos, confusion and crime. We need to stop abandoning people on release day with no hope and nothing else to lose.

It is possible to maintain our financial health in the same amount of time it takes to care for your dental health. Our financial health can improve in the same way that our oral hygiene, our wellbeing and confidence improve, by carrying out a simple process for a few minutes each day. Therefore, I call daily cash-flow management and planning - **The Toothbrush Method.**

Daily Diplomacy™; literally developing good skills with people does not mean that you need to change who you are as a person. You just need to become consciously aware of the dynamics of human interactions, to learn a few simple shortcuts and strategies, and make a sincere effort with other people. This is like pouring oil on the gears and cogs of life, making everything run easier and more smoothly.

I am convinced that we could do a far better job than we do at present, of raising children in the care system to feel that they have an identity, that they can contribute to society and that they are valued. It is essential that we put steps in place to reduce the institutionalisation and abdication of responsibility that children in care experience, so that as young adults they do not develop the subconscious yearning to return to an institutional life i.e. prison.

I believe that housing should be treated as an essential utility - I would ask why people in our country are protected from having their water supply disconnected (they cannot legally be left without running water) yet they can have their housing disconnected and be left without a roof over their heads? Perhaps this is an oversimplification but why the difference in policies? What help is running water with no home? Surely a modest home and protection from the elements is a basic human right - as essential a utility as water?

Many members of our society determinately hang on the outdated assumption that all prisoners are evil, wicked and cruel, a sub-species of humanity that is beyond any hope of reformation. They believe that the people in prison deserve neither compassion nor support and at best should be shunned or met with disinterest. Before grouping all prisoners together however we should consider that the majority of people in our prisons are not there for crimes against a person (including violence, sexual harm and robbery) Source: House of Commons, Prison Population July 2019. When we look deeper into the circumstances and the minority of those perpetrators who have committed crimes against a person, most would still not merit the label 'evil'.

We have now entered an era where someone can make a mistake, break the law and be punished. Then pay the price that those who are most qualified to decide (the judges), have said they must pay. Despite having served their time however, they and their family still suffer for their crime for decades because the internet never forgets. You may ask, "Aren't you curious, wouldn't you like to know about someone?" and I agree; that is why we have DBS checks, so that <u>when it is absolutely necessary to know, we will know</u>. When it is not absolutely necessary, we should not know. We should not have the opportunity to pre-judge someone based on their past. Whatever happened to someone paying their debt to society? There must be a time by which one sided media reports are archived and third-party keyboard warriors are silenced, so that people can at least have a chance to build a life and contribute to society.

Memory Aids and Acronyms

6 Steps to take before attending a job interview
(From: How to Get a Great Job When You Have a Criminal Record)

P.R.O.P.E.R.

Plan	Research	Organise	Prepare	Enquire	Rehearse

The 5 Primary ELEMENTS of EMPLOYABILITY
(From: How to Get a Great Job When You Have a Criminal Record)

Q.U.E.S.T.

Qualifications	Understanding	Experience	Specialist Skills	Transferable Skills

The Purpose of Prison
(From: If Criminals Can Change Then So Should Society)

S.C.R.A.P.P.E.D.

Safety	Change	Remand	Assistance	Punishment	Profit	Example	Deterrent

The New Purpose of Prison / Essential Elements of Ex-Offending
(From: If Criminals Can Change Then So Should Society)

A.T.R.E.H.A.B.

Addiction	Thinking	Relationships	Employment	Health	Accommodation	Budgeting

The People in Prison
(From: The People in Prison and Their Potential)

D.A.M.A.G.E.D.

Desperation	Addiction	Mental illness	Accident	Greed	Evil	Disillusioned

10 areas of Disillusionment Predicting Prison
(From: The People in Prison and Their Potential)

T.H.E.N.P.O.L.I.C.E.

Trauma	Homelessness	Education	Nothing (to lose)	Parenting
Opportunity	Law	Inequality	Care	Enlisted

The Vital Role of Faith and Pastoral Care in Prison
(From: The People in Prison and Their Potential)

F.A.I.T.H.C.A.R.E.

Fellowship	Acceptance	Inspiration	Teaching	Help
Community	Accountability	Rehabilitation	Empathy	

6 Primary Drivers for Personal Development in Prison   I.M. P.A.S.T. I.T

(From: The People in Prison and Their Potential)

Intervention	Mentors	Pain	Age
Self-Image	Time	Incentives	Training

The 7 Primary Transferable Skills

(From: How to Get a Great Job When You Have a Criminal Record)

IT skills	Functional skills	Work ethic	Organisational skills
Skills with people (interpersonal skills)		Problem solving skills	Mind-set management

The A B C D staircase of job progression

(From: How to Get a Great Job
When You Have a Criminal Record)

Dream Job

Career Job

Better Job

Any Job

NB: This ABCD is widely used and was not originated by the author

The 5 R's of Change

R1	Remorse	I am sorry for what I did, and I do regret my crime(s).
R2	Reasons	I understand the background circumstances and my personal buttons/ triggers well enough that I can explain to others.
R3	Responsibility	I admit that it is my fault and I am not passing the blame.
R4	Rehabilitation	I will not do it again; I have learnt lessons and changed.
R5	Reconciliation	I want to make up for what I did wrong and contribute.

20 ways that people change for the better in prison

(From: The People in Prison and Their Potential)

1. Tolerance	2. Future goals	3. Personal fitness	4. Caring for others
5. Appreciation of family	6. Personal development		7. Overcoming addictions
8. Personal responsibility	9. Emotional intelligence		10. Counselling and therapy
11. Contribution and community		12. Functional skills education	
13. Higher/ further education		14. Leadership and mentoring	
15. Charity awareness and fundraising		16. Work ethic, skills and experience	
17. Work (vocational) qualifications		18. Understanding wider impact of crime	
19. Understanding criminal urges and triggers		20. Sharing lessons learnt to discourage crime	

The ABC of Creating a Rehabilitative Culture

(From: If Criminals Can Change Then So Should Society)

A	**Allocate** time, money and resources.
B	**Believe** that change is possible.
C	**Care** and show compassion, allow yourself to feel empathy.
D	**Decide** "I am here to change lives".
E	**Examples** to follow.
F	**Find** their motivation.
G	**Give** people opportunities to grow and develop.
H	**Help** prisoners and practically support them.
I	**Individualise** your approaches.
J	**Journey** with prisoners.
K	**Knowledge** is important and should be shared with others.
L	**Look** for good, praise and encourage.
M	**Make** the effort. RC is hard work and a difficult process.
N	**Never** give up on anyone.
O	**Organise.**
P	**Pathways** to resettlement are ready to be followed.
Q	**Question** everything.
R	**Relationships** are to be valued.
S	**Sustainably** implement each new policy.
T	**Test** prisoners.
U	**Underutilised** is the prison population.
V	**Victims** should be involved.
W	**Windows** of opportunity are what we have.
X	**X-Offenders.** Okay it should be spelt ex-offenders, but the point is the same!
Y	**You** have the power.
Z	**Zero** deaths in custody, zero self-harming and zero re-offending are the only acceptable figures; anything else needs investigating and understanding.

Today I have a CHOICE. My choice is to be...

C.H.O.I.C.E.

(From: 'Your Positive Life After Prison (or any other apocalypse)

Confident	Happy	Optimistic	Inspiring	Caring	Enthusiastic

GLOSSARY
Taking you from JUSTICE to JOB

"This glossary was very helpful to me. There is not enough information available for people going through criminal trials and their families, no one really explains much, and have to try to find our way in the dark." *CO*

<u>Important Reminder</u>	The author has used his best endeavours as a layperson to ensure that all information is correct and current in the UK at the time of printing. Laws, rules and processes may be different in Scotland. This book is for general guidance only, the content should not be relied upon in isolation and nothing within the book constitutes legal, financial or medical advice. Personal advice should be sought from qualified third parties. No liability is accepted at law for the outcome of any decisions made whilst relying on the content of this book.

This helpful guide simply explains the processes, terminology and legal language that people experience from when they first enter the justice system to when they gain employment after release. If you would like any terminology or processes added to this glossary or if you have any resettlement related questions, please contact the author.

Aggravating Factor	**Something that worsens**	Aggravating factors are considerations that increase the severity of a crime and the sentence given. Examples include continuing to commit crime whilst on **bail**, abuse of a position of trust, substantial and deliberate pre-planning, exploitation of vulnerable victims, intimidation of witnesses etc. These are the opposite of **mitigating** factors.
AL	**Application Letter**	This letter introduces your **CV** and your Personal **Disclosure** Statement. AL is also known as an introduction or covering letter.
Appeal	**Application to reconsider a sentence or overturn a conviction**	An appeal can be made by any **convicted** person who feels they have grounds for the conviction to be overturned or for the sentence to be reduced. The **prosecution** can also appeal sentence lengths under the 'unduly lenient scheme'. The first stage of an appeal goes to a single judge, it can be funded by legal aid (for eligible appellants) and there is no risk of a **loss of time order**. If the single judge feels that the appeal has: a) <u>Merit</u> - the appeal can be renewed to a panel of three judges, legal aid would continue and there is no risk of a **loss of time order**. b) <u>No merit</u> - the appeal can still be renewed but legal aid stops and there is a risk of loss of time. This risk increases substantially if a warning box is ticked on the single judge's decision notice. In these cases, the loss of time order could be for the entire amount of time served from when the appeal is first refused, up to when the renewed appeal is heard. If the box is not ticked then there is still a risk of loss of time, but it is a lesser risk and usually a smaller loss of time of 28-56 days. In summary, there is no risk of extra time with the first stage of an appeal but renewing an appeal after refusal by the single judge, carries a real risk of extra time in prison.

Bail	A type of licence	Bail allows people who have been accused of crimes (and who present as low risk of harm to the public) to continue to reside at their homes in the following circumstances: • Whilst the crime is being investigated. • Between **charging** and **conviction.** • Between conviction and **sentencing.** and occasionally: • Between **sentencing** and imprisonment. • Whilst an **appeal** is waiting to be heard.
Burden of Proof and Standard of Proof	Who is responsible for meeting the standard of proof that must be met before an accused person can be convicted	The burden of proof means who is responsible for proving something. In a criminal trial the burden of proof falls to the **Prosecution** to prove guilt; theoretically, it does not fall to the **Defence** to prove innocence. The standard (level of proof) is different for criminal and civil trials: Criminal trials must meet a standard of proof known as 'beyond all reasonable doubt'; technically, the jury must be 99% sure before they can convict. Civil trials must meet a much lower standard of proof known as 'balance of probabilities'. The judge only needs to be more sure than not, meaning 51% sure before they can rule in favour of one party.
Categorisation	Risk level and accommodating individuals appropriately	The categories in the UK prison estate range from higher security categories AA (Maximum Security), A and B, and C cat and the lowest security D cat (resettlement prisons) - known as open conditions.
CCRC	Criminal Cases Review Commission	The Criminal Cases Review Commission investigates possible miscarriages of justice they are the last-ditch body for **appeals** against conviction and /or sentence. The CCRC will only investigate cases where an appeal has failed and where there is new evidence or argument that has not previously been seen or heard by the court, or by the court of appeal. The CCRC refer a very small percentage of cases for appeal but if they do then the applicant is not at risk of any extra time being added to their sentence **(loss of time order)**. Unlike the normal appeal process, when the CCRC are successful in overturning a conviction, compensation can be claimed by the wrongly imprisoned person. The equivalent body in Scotland is the SCCRC.

Charging	**Formally accused of an offence**	The police have decided that there is enough evidence to refer the case to the **CPS** for a charging decision and the CPS have subsequently given the police permission to formally charge (accuse) a person with the crime. A date will be set for Magistrates Court who will either hear the case or refer the matter to the Crown Court if it is deemed serious.
Circa	**Approximately**	Used in job adverts to mean 'in the region of' e.g. 'Salary circa £24,000 pa' means that the salary will be around £24,000 a year depending on the applicant's skills, experience, qualifications and ability to negotiate.
Concurrent	**At the same time (the opposite of consecutive)**	Frequently when a person is convicted, they will have committed multiple offences or committed the same offence multiple times. If the crime is similar, or if it forms part of the same overall criminality within the same timeframe, then the multiple sentences will usually run concurrently. e.g. someone who committed two crimes with a sentence of 2 years for each crime, concurrently, would receive a 2-year total prison sentence.
Confiscation Order	**An amount of money which a defendant must pay after a POCA Confiscation Hearing**	When a Confiscation Order (See **POCA**) is generated, a defendant generally has 3 months to pay the full amount of the order or to apply to extend based on legitimate reasons e.g. sale of the house not completed yet. Where a defendant deliberately does not pay, a default prison sentence is issued. This prison sentence is usually similar in length to the original prison sentence issued by the criminal court. Even after the serving of a default prison sentence, confiscation orders remain due and enforceable for life; the debt cannot be extinguished until it is paid.
Consecutive	**Following on from (the opposite of concurrent)**	Frequently when a person is convicted, they will have committed multiple offences or committed the same offence multiple times. If the crimes are serious or very different from each other, then the multiple sentences will be usually run consecutively. e.g. someone sentenced to 2 years for each of 2 crimes, consecutively, would receive a 4-year total sentence.

Conviction	An offence has been admitted or proven in court	Conviction is the point at which someone is now guilty of an offence; they may have pleaded guilty but at guilty they were found guilty by a jury or they may have pleaded guilty without a trial.
CPS	Crown Prosecution Service (aka The Crown)	The organisation which conducts most criminal prosecutions in the UK.

The CPS regularly review charging decisions and court proceedings to ensure that the prosecution has a reasonable chance of success and is in the public interest. N.B. this does not mean that the public are interested in it but rather means that a prosecution would be of benefit to society. |
| CRC | Community Rehabilitation Company | Privatised probation monitoring the lowest risk and shortest sentenced prisoners when they begin their supervision in the community.

CRC delivers 'through the gate' services for **MOJ** including delivery of resettlement courses, (such as 'Getting it Right' and 'Thinking Skills Programme') and provide resettlement support such as making referrals to housing charities and councils. Most CRC contracts are ending in 2020 due to poor outcomes. |
| CRL | Childcare Resettlement Leave | A form of **ROTL** where a prisoner is allowed to leave the prison for a set period of time to look after their child or children.

CRL is subject to risk assessments and passing **FLED**. Only for those parents who are the sole carer for a child or vulnerable adult are eligible.

These criteria are very hard to meet because someone else will obviously be looking after the child in the place of a parent, when a parent goes to prison. It is for this reason that CRL is exceptionally rare. |
CSU	Care and Separation Unit	CSU is a recent rebranding of Segregation unit to reflect a move towards compassion and rehabilitation. See **SEG**.
CV - also known as résumé	Curriculum Vitae	A formal document which provides an overview of your personal strengths, qualifications and employment experience.
DBIS	Department for Business, Insolvency and Skills	A department of Government that often undertakes criminal prosecutions for business offences. Sometimes they act on behalf of, or alongside, the Insolvency Service or Trading Standards.
DBS	Disclosure and Barring Service	Records details of criminal convictions and related intelligence and provides access to approved organisations for DBS checks.

Defence	**Acting for accused and convicted people**	The defence team are tasked with protecting their client and serving the client's best interests, they do this by: • Advising and supporting their client/ defendant. • Persuading them to plead guilty to benefit from a reduced sentence. • Identifying weaknesses in the prosecution's evidence and casting doubt on their assumptions, assertions and arguments. • In the case of conviction, arguing for a lesser punishment by explaining mitigating factors and relevant historic cases.
Determinate	**Prison sentence with an end date**	Also known as a 'straight sentence'. A determinate sentence has a fixed end date. The prisoner is released at their **ERD** and unless they are recalled, will stay on licence in the community until their **LED**.
Disclosure	**Revealing a criminal conviction**	Disclosure of criminal convictions is usually requested by employers, insurance companies, financial institutions and before travelling to most other countries. Full disclosure includes all unspent convictions, sentence lengths and background circumstances and is usually done on a Personal Disclosure Statement (PDS).
Discretionary	**There is a choice**	A discretionary life sentence means that it was the judge's choice to hand out a life sentence - this is the opposite of **mandatory**.
EDS	**Extended Determinate Sentence**	A prison sentence used where the risk to the public is higher than normal and rehabilitation is unpredictable; almost as a middle ground between **determinate** and **indeterminate.** With EDS the prisoner is not released at the halfway point (as is usually the case) but instead serves 2/3 of the sentence and only then becomes eligible for **parole** (consideration for release). EDS prisoners have extended supervision, under **licence** in the community which are set at the time of sentencing, typically being 1 or 2 years after the full sentence end.
ERD	**Earliest Release Date**	The date when 50% of a standard custodial sentence has been served. At this point (or the day preceding it, in the case of weekend and bank holiday) the prisoner will be released to serve the remaining time on licence in the community, unless recalled for a breach of licence conditions or charged with a new offence.

FLED	**Facility Licence Eligibility Date**	The date when a prisoner has served 50% of their custodial period or when they have 2 years left to serve, whichever date is the latter. A prisoner becomes eligible to apply for **ROTL** for resettlement purposes (family ties, interviews, work, driving lessons etc.). **SPL** is not dependent on FLED having been passed although these will usually be escorted by prison staff prior to FLED.
HDC	**Home Detention Curfew**	A home monitoring system that allows the lowest risk determinate sentenced prisoners to be released earlier that their **ERD** to an approved address (usually home) and subject to a curfew (usually 7pm-7am). The prisoner can serve up to a maximum of 4.5 months on HDC but in the case of weekend and bank holidays will be released the day after. Under current rules, HDC is only available to those prisoners who are sentenced to less than 4 years imprisonment.
Indeterminate	**Undecided/ not fixed**	A sentence which does not have a fixed end date (**IPP** or life). **Parole** must be granted before an indeterminate sentenced prisoner can be released and they will be subject to a life **licence** (monitoring and accountability).
IPP	**Imprisonment for Public Protection**	A controversial and now abolished type of Indeterminate prison sentence. The sentence came with a minimum tariff and a minimum of ten years' supervision under licence upon release. Despite its abolition, thousands of people are still serving IPP sentences in prison and many years over their tariffs. Recent changes to the **Parole** test have seen more prisoners being released or re-**categorised** to D Category to be "tested in open conditions".
LED	**Licence Expiry Date**	The date when a released prisoner is no longer monitored by probation and is informally considered to have become an "ex-offender".

Licence Conditions	**Licence conditions for the second half of a determinate sentence or for indeterminate sentence prisoners who are granted parole.**	Prisoners are released under licensed supervision by The Probation Service (or CRC for the lowest risk prisoners) in the community. There are three purposes of supervision which are to: 1) Help resettlement. 2) Protect the public. 3) Prevent re-offending. The standard licence conditions (simplified) are: 1. Be of good behaviour. 2. Only carry out pre-approved work. 3. Allow probation to visit as required. 4. Keep in touch with probation as required. 5. Reside permanently at a pre-approved address. 6. Not travel outside of the UK without permission. 7. Not to touch or use fireworks or any objects containing gun powder. Additional licence conditions may be imposed to reduce risk but to be lawful, each condition must be proportionate, reasonable and necessary to achieve the three purposes of supervision. Such additional licence conditions may include, but are not limited to, exclusion zones, curfews, drug testing, non-association with named individuals, courses to complete and additional reporting. Sometimes courts and police impose additional conditions which run for a timescale which is separate from the licence duration (see **SCPO**).
Loss of Time Order	**Penalty for un-merit worthy appeals**	A loss of time order can be made for any **appeal** which is renewed to the panel of three appeal judges after rejection by the first judge and which is deemed to have no merit. A loss of time order can be for the entire amount of time served, from when the appeal is first refused, up to when the renewed appeal is heard, to no longer count towards the sentence. Such a penalty is rare however and is reserved for the most frivolous of appeals. More usually, the loss of time order is in the region of 1 - 2 months.
Mandatory	**No Choice (the opposite of discretionary)**	There is no choice. A mandatory life sentence means that the judge had no choice but to hand out a life sentence.

MAPPA	**Multi Agency Public Protection Arrangement**	MAPPA is the name given to police, prison service and probation (the "responsible authorities") who work together to assess and manage the most serious offenders who pose a high risk of harm to the public. Cooperation is required from other agencies as well including housing, health, social services and education services. All agencies contribute to the creation of a personalised risk management plan for each individual offender. MAPPA offenders are categorised from 1 to 3 with **1 being the highest** and 3 lowest risk. The multi-agency management is then tiered from Level 1 to Level 3 with 1 (reversely) being the lowest and **3 being the highest** level of monitoring and management.
Mitigating Factors (Mitigation)	**Something that lessens**	Mitigating factors are considerations that reduce the severity of a crime and the sentence that will be given. Mitigation covers a wide range of possible circumstances and may include repaying money taken by fraud, references provided by respected people, poor mental/ emotional state, medical aid given to a victim, previous good character etc. These are the opposite of **aggravating** factors.
MOJ	**Ministry of Justice**	The Government department responsible for the management of the court system, prisons, prisoners and ex-offenders.
NVQ	**National Vocational Qualification**	Widely recognised qualifications related to employment and careers e.g. Bricklaying, Catering, Customer Service or Childcare.

OASys	Offender Assessment System	OASys is a substantial and detailed record which is designed to help with sentence planning and manage, and reduce the risk of reoffending.
		OASys contains a wealth of historic, current and future information such as housing, family, education, employment, finances, associates, mental and physical health, lifestyle, drug and alcohol misuse, attitudes, thinking, emotional management, courses completed, background and reasons for offences, and may also include verified and unverified information from court records, police intelligence and other agencies.
		This information is invaluable when identifying 'criminogenic needs' i.e. those areas which are problematic for the offender and which are likely to trigger re-offending, e.g. someone who has: • Problems with their family ties will be able to complete a course on personal and family relationships as part of their sentence plan. • Challenges gaining employment due to a lack of functional skills may be required to attend Maths and English classes. • An identified problem with past criminal associates may have an additional **licence** condition on release banning them from associating with known criminals.
		OASys generates risk scores, as percentage predictors for re-offending and serious harm.
		OASys is respected worldwide but it is only as accurate as the information placed into it by people; much of which is based on opinions rather than evidence and it is for this reason that many question its accuracy and impartiality.
		Prisoners and ex-offenders can get a copy of their OASys by sending a **SAR** to Data Protection Compliance, MOJ, 16 NDC, Burton Road, Branston, Burton Upon Trent, Staffordshire. DE14 3EG
OMU	Offender Management Unit	The OMU is the department within prison which is responsible for sentence planning.
		The majority of prisoners are allocated an Offender Supervisor (OS) within OMU and an Offender Manager (OM) from outside Probation. The OS and OM liaise with offenders, police and prison staff to create and update **OASys** and a sentence plan.

Parole	**The board which considers whether a prisoner should be released or re-categorised**	Parole means consideration for release from prison, under supervision in the community. The Parole board will only consider releasing **indeterminate** sentenced prisoners (around 5% of prison population) when they are satisfied that their risk has been reduced enough that they can be managed in the community. An alternative to release, or precursor to release, is for the prisoner to be re-**categorised** to D- category to be "tested in open conditions".
	"Overall the serious rate of re-offending is less than 1%, which suggests that the Parole board makes the best decisions it can." Dean Kingham, Head of Prison Law and Crime, Swain and Co Solicitors	
POCA	**Proceeds of Crime Act**	Civil proceedings aimed at removing the benefit of criminal conduct. The Act is "deliberately draconian" (with far reaching extreme consequences for criminals, families and associates) apparently to serve as a deterrent rather than punish further. A benefit figure is arrived at by adding conviction amounts to unexplained income over 6 years, civil claims and adjusting the total for inflation. The benefit figure is based on turnover not retained profit, hence why it is almost always substantially more (by many multiples) than the real amount by which the criminal benefitted. Once a benefit figure is established, investigation into assets and past transactions will uncover tainted gifts, sales at undervalue, realisable and hidden assets. A **confiscation order** will be generated for the amount of the realisable assets together with any assets or money deemed to be hidden. POCA trials are based on balance of probabilities (see **Burden of Proof** and **Standard of Proof)**.
Proprietary	**ownership**	Owned by the worker typically self-employment as a sole trader.
Pro Rata	**In the ratio**	Used when advertising part-time jobs to show the equivalent annual salary. A 20hrs per week part-time work salary of £24,000pa pro rata means that the salary you receive will be £12,000 each year (because 20hrs per week is half of the usual 40hrs per week you will receive half of £24,000).

Prosecution	**Acting on behalf of a prosecuting authority (usually CPS) against the accused and convicted**	The prosecution team are primarily focussed on: • Providing enough evidence of a person's guilt and presenting it in a compelling way such that it encourages an accused person to plead guilty. • Proving and/or convincing jury members of an accused person's guilt. • Arguing for the harshest punishment after **conviction**, explaining aggravating factors and relevant historic cases.
RDR	**Resettlement Day Release**	A form of **ROTL** where a prisoner can leave the prison for a set period of time to undertake resettlement activities e.g. to rebuild family ties, attend employment or university. Subject to passing **FLED** and risk assessments, eligibility (not entitlement, nor guaranteed) for RDR for family ties purposes is generally a maximum of 1 RDR every fourteen days. RDR for other purposeful activities e.g. attending employment or driving lessons does not affect the allowance for family ties.
Recidivism	**Re-offending**	Returning to patterns of past behaviour; usually used in the context of "reducing recidivism".
Recall	**Being returned back to prison**	Returning a prisoner, who has been released on **licence,** back to prison. Any person on licence can be recalled by probation for a range of reasons including, but not limited to: • A perceived increase in their risk. • An allegation made by a third party. • They have been **charged** with a new offence. • They are in breach of any **licence conditions.** No court process is required for recall decisions.
Remand	**Imprisonment before trial (the opposite of bail)**	Remand is supposedly reserved for people accused of the most serious crimes, who pose a flight risk or who face overwhelming evidence of guilt of a crime that would definitely result in imprisonment. Many thousands of people are remanded into prison and kept for long periods of time before they have been found guilty of any crime. Many are released from prison after being found not guilty and they receive no compensation, little or no resettlement support and do not even qualify for the £46 discharge grant because they are not considered to have been serving a prison sentence.

Right to be Forgotten	**Legal entitlement to request an end to linking to historic online content**	Under Right to be Forgotten you can request that search engines no longer link to historic articles and web pages which feature you if the content is out of date and/or no long relevant. Many search engines will argue against de-indexing stating that listings are still in the public interest or that subjects are still being discussed.
ROR	**Resettlement Overnight Release**	A form of **ROTL** where a prisoner is allowed to stay overnight at their home, approved premises (hostel) or resettlement address. Subject to passing **FLED** and risk assessments, eligibility (not entitlement, nor guaranteed) is generally 1 ROR every 28 days. First ROR is generally 2 nights/ 3 days. Second ROR is generally 3 nights/ 4 days. Third and subsequent ROR's 4 nights/ 5 days.
ROTL	**Release on Temporary Licence**	Permission to leave the prison temporarily under certain conditions (available after **FLED**). All ROTL is at the Governor's discretion and is subject to police and probation checks. ROTL may be **CRL**, **RDR**, **ROR** or **SPL**.
SAR	**Subject Access Request**	A letter requesting a copy of all personal information held on you under the General Data Protection Regulations (GDPR's). No fee is payable for the provision of this information unless a request is repeated or excessive. Here is an example of the wording to use: Dear Sir/ Madam, I am writing this letter to you as a Subject Access Request. My date of birth is _____ and I enclose evidence of my identification. *Enclose copy of driving licence, birth certificate or passport, (serving prisoners writing to MOJ, will not need id.)* I am the subject and owner of substantial amounts of data that you hold and I formally request ALL such information. In line with the revised GDPRs I understand that the timescale for fulfilment is now one calendar month and that there is no longer a fee to be paid. I believe that this satisfies the requirements of the GDPRs; should you require additional confirmation of my identification however or if you require a template form to be completed, please advise immediately by return. Thank you in advance for your kind attention, Yours faithfully,

SCPO	**Serious Crime Prevention Order**	Designed to prevent or disrupt future crime, these orders are effectively personalised laws which place requirements or restrictions on ex-offenders after release from prison. Restrictions may include only having one mobile phone, one bank account, one vehicle and to provide full details to the police, not to conduct certain types of transactions, not to carry more than £100 in cash, not to access certain websites etc. SCPO's run separately from **licence** conditions and can continue after a licence has finished. Suspected breaches can result in **recall** and proven breaches can result in up to 5 years in prison, based on the low, civil, rather than criminal, **burden of proof**.
SED	**Sentence Expiry Date**	Usually called **LED** (Licence expiry date)
SEG	Segregation Unit aka Care and Separation unit (CSU) or 'The Block.'	Single cells in a higher security part of each prison where each prisoner is subject to intense monitoring and a restricted regime. People are sent to the Seg for many reasons, sometimes for their own protection, for control or behavioural issues or prior to being '**swagged**'. Prisoners who are the hardest to manage, who have been violent, unpredictable or involved in drug supply in the prison can be managed better in segregation where officers are able to wear body protection and follow specialist safety protocols. Generally, prisoners in the Seg get daily access to phone calls, showers and exercise and a limited range of library books. Conduct and the need for segregation is regularly reviewed.
Sentencing	**Deciding on the punishment**	The process that a judge works through to decide the most appropriate level of punishment. There are sentencing guidelines for each offence and for the brackets (levels) of culpability. Previous cases are researched for guidance, known as 'authority' to help with sentencing. Consideration is given to **aggravating factors** put forwards by the prosecution and **mitigating factors** put forwards by the defence, to finally arrive at the sentence. There is a lot of discretion in sentencing and many sentences are successfully **appealed** where they are considered to be "manifestly excessive" (too long) or unduly lenient (too short).

Spent Convictions	**No longer disclosable**	Convictions resulting in prison sentences of 4 years and less become spent after a certain period under The Rehabilitation of Offenders Act unless they overlap with further convictions in which case, they do not become spent until and unless the later ones do. Spent convictions do not need to be disclosed but they may still show on Disclosure and Barring Service (**DBS**) checks. If this is the case, you may prefer to still disclose and explain your side of the story upfront. Original news and commentary may remain accessible online and links to these may still show in search engine listings. The **Right to be Forgotten** can be used to de-index listings unless they are still deemed to be in the public interest.
SPL	**Special Purpose Licence**	A form of **ROTL** which can be applied for at any time during a prison sentence, purposes include attending medical appointments or funerals of close family members.
Suspended Sentence	**Delayed subject to certain conditions**	A prison sentence that is not served unless the convicted person commits another crime during the period of the suspended sentence. If another sentence is ordered, then the new sentence will usually run **consecutively** to the triggered/ activated suspended sentence. Suspended sentences count the same as normal prison sentences for **disclosure** purposes i.e. they have the same rehabilitation period before they become "spent"
Swagged aka Ghosted/ Shipped out	**Suddenly transferred between prisons**	Involuntary transfers to different prisons due to security concerns or overcrowding. These are different to resettlement or re-**categorisation** transfers which are usually nearer to home and for which the prisoner will have some limited input in the decisions. They are also different to pre-planned transfers for progression purposes e.g. to complete courses which are unavailable in the current prison.
Tariff	**Minimum sentence**	The minimum amount of time that **indeterminate** sentenced prisoners must spend in prison before they become eligible for **parole**.

Ex-seed™
Free Help and
Support for YOU
to Gain employment

A New Chapter for Ex-offenders

Ex-seed™

Recruitment Network

A New Chapter for Ex-offenders

Ex-seed™
Recruitment Network

Introduction

Ex-seed™ is an employment agency and recruitment network which is dedicated to placing ex-offenders into well-suited, stable employment and supporting them to enjoy crime-free and fulfilling lives.

Ex-seed™ have two guiding principles:

1. <u>No-one Gets Left Behind</u>. Personal support, individual attention and ongoing mentoring ensure that we understand our applicants from day one and find the best work-fit for them.

2. <u>Matched Effort</u>. We invest substantial efforts in championing our applicants and placing them into suitable employment; we correspondingly expect a similar level of effort and commitment from our applicants.

Ex-seed™ works:

✓ Both inside and outside of prisons.

✓ With people who are still serving a prison sentence.

✓ With those who have paid their debt to society and been released.

✓ With people who have never been to prison but have a criminal record.

✓ Without discrimination and with respect for diversity and equal opportunities.

✓ With approved representatives, recruitment partners and supporters across the UK.

✓ With prison resettlement departments, probation officers, job centres and charities that support people with criminal records.

✓ Completely without charge to applicants and offering them a wide range of pro-bono support services, including help with CVs and Disclosure.

✓ On competitive terms and a reasonable recruitment fee basis with forward thinking employers, across all industry sectors, who believe that people deserve a second chance and who have an interest in gaining loyal and hardworking employees.

People in any of the following four groups, are invited to apply to Ex-seed™:

1. Living in the community and have a criminal record.
2. Living in the community under licence and supervised by probation.
3. In D-Cat, open conditions with less than 24 months before release or parole.
4. In closed prison conditions with less than 12 months before release or parole.

If you send us rough draft versions of your CV and Personal Disclosure Statement, we will type and professionally improve them. If you do not have access to a computer, you can handwrite your documents and we will write back to you with questions or anything that needs clarification.

By working with you, we will create a professional CV and a Personal Disclosure Statement which explains your story in an honest and upfront way and will inspire employers to want to give you a chance.

As soon as you have approved these finished documents, we will get to work finding your ideal job and placing you with an employer who understands and wants to support you.

"Phil, the CV's, Disclosure Statements and Grant Funding letters that you have been producing with ex-servicemen who have been to prison are absolutely FIRST CLASS! Well done."

Trevor Chrich - *Soldiers, Sailors, Airmen and Families Association (SSAFA)*

A New Chapter for Ex-offenders
Ex-seed™
Recruitment Network

Application Form

PAGE 1 of 2
Name:
Date of Birth:
Email address:
Current Address:
Telephone number(s):
Preferred jobs or industries:
Other helpful work-related information not already included in CV:
Relevant health conditions or any other important considerations:

I _____ **(insert name)**

Request that Philip Martin trading as Ex-seed™ (Henceforth 'ES') acts on my behalf in relation to seeking employment.

I consent to ES processing and storing my personal information and contacting me regarding employment and resettlement related matters. I give permission for ES to share my personal information, with individuals and organisations for purposes associated with the employment of ex-offenders. ES may work in partnership with and may assign or sub-contract all or parts of this agreement, to any employment agency they approve, whilst remaining responsible for their obligations under it.

I agree to:

- Inform ES if I become unavailable for work for any reason.
- Inform ES of the outcomes of job interviews with employers they introduce.
- Inform ES immediately if I receive a job offer from any employer (whether introduced by ES or sourced by myself).
- Conduct myself well and represent ES professionally and to the best of my abilities when attending interviews and during the period of any employment.
- Remain fully committed to my rehabilitation and avoid risk factors including, but not limited to, drugs, alcohol, past associates and negative behaviours.

I confirm that:

- I have been given and retain a copy of the ES' policies document which includes Privacy Policy, Equality and Diversity Pledge, Crime-free Policy, Health and Safety Policy, Gangmaster and Vulnerable People Policies and my Right to Cancel.
- The employment information and criminal records disclosure I provided is complete, honest and accurate to the best of my knowledge and recollection.
- I have been made aware that on 24th May 2016, Philip Martin was convicted of offences of fraud and fraudulent trading and that he is, and remains, the subject of a Company Director's Disqualification Order.

I understand that:

- I will not be required to pay any money at any time.
- ES are a *'Profit for Purpose'* business that will receive a fee for their services from any organisation that employs me after their introduction.
- This agreement is not exclusive, I am under no obligation to accept any job that I am offered and at any time I can source my own employment.
- ES are not obliged to find or provide employment and reserve the right, at their sole discretion, to decline applicants and to stop acting for them.
- ES will not begin sourcing employment for me until I have provided them with copies of my *'Right to Work'* documents (proof of National Insurance number and identification); whilst awaiting these, ES may, at their discretion provide guidance and help with my CV and Personal Disclosure Statement.

Signed _____ **, Date** _____

A New Chapter for Ex-offenders
Ex-seed™
Recruitment Network

Letter of Authority

To be completed by <u>serving prisoners</u> and those <u>on licence</u> in the community - **in addition to the application form**.

Serving prisoners to complete	Prison Address:
	Prisoner Number:
	Resettlement Area:
	Release or Parole date:
	Offender Supervisor name:
People released on licence to complete	Current Address:
	Probation Address:
	Offender Manager name:

To whom it may concern

I _____   **(insert name)**

have appointed Ex-seed™ to act on my behalf in relation to seeking employment.

I Hereby authorise HMPPS to release/provide my most recent OASys report, the last 6 months of NOMS comments, as well as personal information and professional opinions specifically relating to me undertaking employment, to Philip Martin trading as Ex-seed™ by email to info@ex-seed.co.uk or post to 5 Crabtree Drive, Northampton. NN3 5DR.

If you have any questions relating to this authority, please do not hesitate to contact me.

Signed _____

Dated _____

"On one hand you could say that we are working to fulfil our corporate social responsibility, but we're also sourcing quality, highly committed people who want to work with us."

Simon Little, Sales and Marketing Director, Powerday Construction

A New Chapter for Ex-offenders
Ex-seed™
Recruitment Network

Application Checklist

	Tick
Enclose rough draft version of **CV**.	
Enclose draft **Personal Disclosure Statement**.	
Two-page **Application Form** completed; it can also be photocopied or downloaded from www.ex-seed.co.uk/apply.html	
Letter of Authority completed (only required for serving prisoners and those on licence in the community).	
Enclose copy of **'right to work'** documents: a) National Insurance number - <u>evidence</u> e.g. one copy of P60, P45 or HMRC letter. (A letter confirming your NI Number can be ordered free from HMRC by telephone, post or internet). **AND** b) Identification - <u>evidence</u> e.g. one copy of passport, long birth certificate, biometric ID card or certificate of naturalisation. *If you need to wait for replacement copies of your documents to arrive then you can send the form without them and we will begin work on your CV and Disclosure. When you have sent the 'right to work' documents we will begin helping you into employment.*	
Send everything to Philip Martin t/as Ex-seed™, email to info@ex-seed.co.uk or post to Ex-seed™ 5 Crabtree Drive, Northampton. NN3 5DR	

"My work is the centre of my crime free life; I have been able to build everything else around it. Working legally makes both me proud of myself and my family proud of me." FP

A New Chapter for Ex-offenders
Ex-seed™
Recruitment Network

Our Policies

Please Note: Where 'ES' is used throughout this document it refers to Philip Martin trading as Ex-seed™. ES can be contacted by email info@ex-seed.co.uk or post 5 Crabtree Drive, Northampton. NN3 5DR

Right to Cancel - You are free to cancel your agreement at any time without prejudice and without objection by putting your request to cancel in writing by email or post to ES. If you cancel this agreement, then we will no longer contact you or act for you. After cancellation, we continue to liaise with employers to secure fees due for introductions resulting in employment.

Equality and Diversity Pledge - ES is committed to inclusive recruitment and upholding the nine protected characteristics of the Equalities Act. (Namely: Age, Disability, Gender, Marriage and Civil Partnership, Pregnancy and Maternity, Race, Religion, Sexual Orientation and Gender Reassignment). ES will not work with anyone who practises unfair or unlawful discrimination. ES believes in equal employment opportunities based on objective business-related criteria. ES treats work-seekers, clients and all others without prejudice or discrimination and with dignity and respect.

Crime-free Policy - ES are anti-crime FULL STOP. Please do not attempt to speak to us about any criminal plans or ideas; we will not become co-defendants in any alleged conspiracy! Crime hurts people, families, communities and society and we exist to help people leave criminal activity in the past.

Health and Safety Policy - ES is committed to strict adherence to all health and safety protocols and conducts risk assessments before beginning any work, on a monthly basis and after each significant change in the working environment. No representatives of ES are authorised to begin work until a risk assessment has been carried out. Work-seekers will only be introduced to employers once health and safety information has been provided, risks have been explained and after they have been suitably trained and qualified to mitigate any risks.

No Fees Policy - ES do not charge work-seekers for introductions to employers, for ancillary services offered (e.g. help with CVs and Disclosure) or for reimbursement of expenses, however incurred. ES are absolutely fee-free to work-seekers.

Vulnerable People Policy - ES do not supply work-seekers to work with, care for or attend a vulnerable person. *'Vulnerable person'* means any person or persons who by reason of age, infirmity, illness, disability or any other circumstance is in need of care or attention and includes any and all persons under the age of eighteen.

Gangmaster Policy - ES do not supply work-seekers to the UK fresh produce sector which includes agriculture, horticulture, shellfish gathering and any associated processing and packaging.

Privacy Policy and Data Protection Information - ES is registered with the Information Commissioner's Officer under registration number ZA557947.

ES collects, processes and stores personal data for a range of purposes associated with the recruitment and resettlement of ex-offenders. Subject to your consent (which will form the lawful basis for processing your data), ES will process your personal data, which is likely to include sensitive information, including, but not limited to, employment history, criminal convictions, release date and area, for commercial purposes associated with helping you to gain employment, to aid resettlement, for industry research and to improve processes. Any information, comments or quotes provided to ES for any purpose may be used for research, training, marketing and literary publication, subject to all identifying information being removed.

ES will safeguard your personal data and will only disclose it where it is lawful to do so, or with your consent. Subject to your consent (which will form the lawful basis for sharing your data), ES may share your personal data with individuals and organisations for a range of purposes associated with the recruitment and resettlement of ex-offenders. You may withdraw consent from data sharing by sending a written request to ES.

Your personal information will not be retained for any longer than is necessary to ensure that it does not become inaccurate, out of date or irrelevant. Data will generally be retained for 6 years after our last communication. You can ask at any time for your data to be deleted, for no further contact and for data processing to stop, by sending a written request to ES. After you have withdrawn consent, ES will only retain data which may be necessary for compliance with our legal obligations.

You can access your personal information by making a written subject access request to ES.

If you consider that your information has been handled incorrectly you can obtain independent advice about data protection from the Information Commissioner's Office, Wycliffe House, Water Lane, Wilmslow. SK9 5AF Tel: 0303 123 1113 www.ico.org.uk

Books by the Author

"With the right resources and the right motivation, it is not that difficult to help most prisoners to prepare for release and to live crime free lives after release. People need somewhere to live (home), something constructive to do (job), something to eat and wear (basic needs met), health care and a support network of crime free family and/or friends."

CK, HMP Senior Officer - 22 years' service

The author has produced the **Prison Pathways** series of books with the sincere desire to reduce re-offending and improve outcomes for society.

How to get a
GREAT JOB
when you have a
CRIMINAL RECORD

Phil Martin

A clear pathway into employment or self-employment including all the templates you need to get results

An easy-to-follow and proven system which helps ex-offenders secure meaningful employment that provides structure and stability in their lives.

120,000 words, 360 pages generously printed in an easy to use A4 workbook.

£14.97   ISBN: 9781 696 100 205

e-book also available via Amazon

"This book will be a huge asset to those that are taking that very difficult step to move away from a life of crime, which becomes an addictive and powerful vortex."
Tariq Usmani MBE

"It is no exaggeration to call this book a masterpiece. Phil Martin's step by step guide should be in every prison library and every job centre. If the MOJ gave a copy of this book to everyone leaving prison the costs saved by preventing reoffending would be significant."
Trevor Chrich, SSAFA

Benefit from the author's experience of employing ex-offenders and of establishing and running a careers department for serving prisoners. In this invaluable book you will discover:

- Full guidance on improving employability.
- The legal framework for disclosure and employment.
- How to prepare for interviews and then interview well.
- How to maintain employment and manage your money.
- How to be self-employed or operate your own business, legally and profitably.
- How to use the 'CV Builder' system to easily create a clear and professional CV.
- Using 'Grant Builder' to secure grants for education, training and employment.
- How to use 'Application Builder' to successfully apply for jobs on and off-line.
- How to use the 'Disclosure Builder' system to turn a negative criminal record into a positive Personal Disclosure Statement that inspires.
- More than 500 easy to use templates (including the skills and experience gained from 100 prison jobs and 200 conventional jobs) to copy and amend to suit.

Includes free support for people in prison to draft their employment documents and an invitation to register with **Ex-seed**™ the specialist recruitment network for ex-offenders.

Preface by the Rt. Hon. Lord Wilson,
Justice of the Supreme Court of the United Kingdom

An uplifting book which reveals the potential of prison to help people change for the better.

90,000 words, 240 pages

£9.97   ISBN: 9781 696 356 886

e-book also available via Amazon

"The most well-articulated, easiest to understand and best presented argument for prison reform in my lifetime" RL

"The book that stopped me resigning from the prison service. I was reminded why I originally chose this career - to help that one person, to change one life each day." MF

Following on from "If Criminals Can Change Then So Should Society", this book includes 200 further real-life accounts from people who broke the law and the lessons they learned. This captivating book also includes:

- Discussion of the types of people who come to prison.
- The root causes of the majority of crimes and the lessons for society.
- How to support institutionalised people and really achieve rehabilitation.
- Explanation of how the justice system works and the terminology within it.
- The devastating effects of closed prison conditions and how people can recover.
- Insights into the life changing work of Pastoral Care and Faith Provision in Prison.
- A detailed study of how people change for the better in at least 20 different ways in prison and how the system and society could capitalise on this knowledge.

"By 2019 I had become so fed up with warehousing people - locking them up and only moving them around so that they don't hurt each other (or themselves). Working in a resettlement prison in open conditions is my dream job because now I can actually make a difference and help people to turn their lives around."

HMP Governor 28 years' experience

Your Positive Life After Prison (or any other apocalypse)

Phil Martin

How to Create and Maintain a Fulfilling New Chapter in Your Life Story

A light hearted and easy to follow book, containing strategies which help people who are emerging from personal crises, to live happy and productive lives.

Includes the author's personal story as well as numerous inspiring accounts of people who have built lives of meaning and purpose after imprisonment.

Have you ever felt like your life was over? Even in our darkest times we can be reminded that there is still a purpose to our life and that one snapshot in time does not reflect an entire life.

Not everyone in society believes in revenge and karma, many instead believe in forgiveness and redemption. Labels do not need to define you. There is more to you than your mistakes and you still have more to give.

Your life has a value and I can prove it - if you were climbing, hit bad weather and got lost, millions would be spent on search teams, dogs and helicopters trying to rescue you. They wouldn't say "don't bother looking for him/ her, they went to prison!" If you were donating blood, they wouldn't reject you exclaiming "we don't want this criminal blood!" Bringing this home, is the true story of a life-sentenced prisoner who recently, whilst in open conditions and a year from parole, received a heart transplant. This proves that society feels that your life has value and meaning - the ultimate gift, the gift of a heart.

But we all have that chance of a new life, a new chapter in our lives, with the past firmly in the past we can move forwards with positivity and hope, a new feeling of gratitude and appreciation for each day and wanting to make a contribution.

Your life still has value and purpose and this book will help you find yours.

"It was great to meet you Phil, what you are doing is truly inspiring!" HMP Governor

"Phil Martin is very inspiring and caring about people and wants to help make positive changes in people's lives." Serving Prisoner

"The talk you delivered on faith provision and pastoral care in prisons was the highlight of this regional event." Prison Chaplaincy Development Manager

"When Phil delivered his talk called 'Your New Chapter' he was like a breath of fresh air to the residents and staff in attendance." HMP Regional Education Manager

"Phil Martin has a unique way of explaining things and when he talks, people listen, you can hear a pin drop." HMP Custodial Manager

"Your workshop called 'Your Problem Solving Action Plan' was excellently written Phil, you kept all the men engaged and involved and filled them with confidence and positivity. Well done a good day was had by everyone!" Prison College Tutor

"Phil Martin delivered two talks about Rehab Culture, change and self-worth at our annual award ceremony at HMP Stafford. He was truly inspiring to the residents, the staff and honoured guests. Well done Phil - you smashed it!" HMP Governor

"I was in prison, stuck with no release date. Phil was a company director at the time, he spoke at my parole hearing and helped me to get out of prison straight into a full-time job; I have been out for 14 years since then and have not reoffended."
MJ, a former prisoner

"Mr Martin gave an outstanding motivational speech to a packed auditorium at HMP Stocken. He was asked at the last minute and multiple groups joined the session along with numerous members of staff. He did not bat an eye-lid and inspired us all."
HMP College Manager

"Thank you very much for participating in the interview for Prison Service Journal. It was a great experience to hear you talking with such insight and sensitivity. I believe that it will be well received when published and will help to promote rehabilitative cultures." HMP Governor

"You have played an important role in supporting the work of HMP Springhill towards Enabling Environment Accreditation, building the culture required to sustain this and demonstrating our shared commitment. The assessment day was a really inspiring session to be involved in. I offer you my personal thanks for your contribution."
HMP Governor

"I really love the guide to creating a rehabilitative culture you've created. This is brilliantly and imaginatively presented, using the alphabet, with entries from A to Z and in your usual accessible style. I have distributed this to the National Rehabilitative Culture Team to be used as a resource for staff induction. I am so grateful to you for your work on this document and really appreciate your generosity with your talents."
HMP Governor

"Philip Martin spoke at HMP Brixton about rehabilitation. The event was attended by representatives from 5 London jails including Governors and Operational Staff. His presentation was excellent and his content inspirational; he spoke about his experiences of rehabilitative culture and how staff can have had a big impact on the people in their care. He also produced quality hand-outs for all of the attendees to take away. Overall the day was a big success." HMP Custodial Manager

About the Author

Phil Martin is a family orientated businessman and the founder of Ex-seed™ - the recruitment network dedicated to placing ex-offenders into employment.

Phil is a widely consulted authority on the rehabilitation of prisoners and resettlement of ex-offenders.

'The ABC of Creating a Rehabilitative Culture' (from his book entitled *'If Criminals Can Change Then So Should Society'*) has now been repurposed by HMPPS Rehabilitative Culture Team to form part of a national training programme for prison officers.

In May 2019 Phil met with then Justice Secretary, David Gauke, to discuss the employment of serving and released prisoners, rehabilitation within prisons and effective resettlement after release; particularly focussing on ways to reduce reoffending and create fewer victims of crime.

He is a memorable public speaker and is frequently invited to talk at rehabilitative culture conferences, third sector events and award ceremonies. He has changed lives and inspired audiences at a diverse range of prisons including HMP's Brixton, Coldingley, Lincoln, Springhill, Stafford, Stocken and Woodhill.

Phil is also in demand at business conferences and workshops where he speaks about strategy, mind-set, motivation and change. He has shared insights at several hundred property investment events, networking groups and self-improvement seminars. He offers business consultancy and personal mentoring, by referral only, to a small number of clients each year, both individually and in group training settings.

Phil is known for simplifying complicated subjects, sharing practical tips, for inspiring people to break through comfort zones and create turning points in their lives.

In 2025, by merging his earlier expertise in the property sector with his lived experience of the needs of ex-offenders, Phil intends to begin purpose-building and nationally providing supported housing and temporary homes for ex-offenders and homeless people.

Phil is a devoted family man with a wife, their five daughters and two grandsons.

Feedback, comments and questions are welcomed. These can be submitted by email to info@philmartin.co.uk or post to Philip Martin t/as Ex-seed™ 5 Crabtree Dive, Northampton NN3 5DR.

"This book is excellent; I wish I had got hold of it earlier." AS
"This book helped me to explain where I had gone wrong." RT
"This book has given me the belief that I can now get a job." LI
"I have never had a CV before and this handbook made it easy for me." RB
"This book and the CV I have created gave me the confidence to find work." MK
"I would recommend this book to everyone with a record; it was helpful to me." JT
"A brilliant map to show the way into work for people like me who messed up." CW
"My confidence has got a massive boost! This book has helped me a great deal." VP
"This book has helped me to turn my life around and gain full time employment." LD
"This book has made me realise that I am more qualified than I thought and has given me more confidence in applying for future jobs." CG
"Creating my CV and other documents helped me to engage my mind and reminded me of all I had actually achieved. Now I have prospects for the future." SN
"After a major mess-up in my life, I have got a full-time job which pays a good wage, by following these clear instructions. If I can do it, so can you!" CP
"This information is really helping me to get back to work; after being stuck for so long, I now have a CV that I am proud of and much more of a chance of employment." RA
"I had got CV guides from the library before and they helped a little, but this guide helped a lot! It took me step by step through the process and that is what I needed. It even had the right words I could use to express myself in the best way. Brilliant!" KS
"I followed your system and applied to charities for grant funding to attend a ten-day Personal Track Safety course. I was fully funded; I completed the course, gained the qualification and now have a job offer. I cannot thank you enough." GP
"Working through the process of creating a CV in this book was interesting because I had previously dismissed many things like prison jobs, but now I realise the importance of including these experiences and skills. This book was very helpful!" JF
"Looking at the CV which I created by following this guide, I can see in one place all the things I have actually achieved. Writing my experiences and my abilities down has been a good exercise. Looking at my finished CV, I would want to hire me!" SC
"Having previously worked in HR, I know that this invaluable blueprint has been prepared by someone who is proficient in creating CVs and handling disclosure. Following the templates was a great idea and it helped me to gain a respectable job." ML
"When a family member gave the book to me, I thought "oh no - it's too hard!" I could not see myself working through it. I started FOR THEM but I kept going FOR ME. Now I am proud of my documents and ready to put them out. I feel more confident that in the future I can get work that I actually want to do." RA
"This book is not only easy to follow but it gives a huge sense of hope for the future; it instils the accurate belief in ex-offenders that they can move past their earlier mistakes and build a brighter future for themselves and their families. So proud of you Phil, this is an exceptional achievement." Mrs Wendy Martin (wife of the Author)

Printed in Great Britain
by Amazon